Daisy Pedals

SUSAN MUSGROVE

Daisy Pedals

FOREST HOUSE PRESS

Cover design by Kelly Wagner, ReDesign Creative Studio, O'Fallon, Missouri.
Layout by Shelly Houston of Rising Graphics + Printing, Evergreen, Colorado.
Cover photo by Clarke Cohu, ©1989.

ISBN-13: 978-0-9843084-1-5

To order more copies of this book, contact:
Forest House Press
547 Castlewood Drive, Evergreen CO 80439
www.foresthousepress.com

To Daisy, who dictated while I typed

The story you are about to read is true.

Only the personalities of the bicycles may have been invented.

Chapter 1

ALTHOUGH I GOT A bit of a rough start, it only makes sense to begin at the beginning. A blue Specialized Rockhopper, part of a litter of mountain bikes born on the same day, my first vivid memory was being pulled from a box by a human who stood me all wobbly next to my brothers and sisters and a dozen unrelated bikes. "Does anyone know where we are?" I asked the group in general.

"A bicycle store in the Colorado mountains," a young Trek replied, red as an apple. "You're lucky that you're a mountain bike like me," he added after looking me over. "We're much stronger than skinny road bikes, and we're always bought by athletes who let us chase deer in the Colorado mountains and rabbits in the Utah desert. Our poor city cousins have to play in traffic and smog." I got pretty excited then, and every time someone came into the store, I tried to look perky and strong, ready for adventure.

Finally, a young man planning a trip to Utah that weekend chose the red Trek. As they left the store together, obviously thrilled with each other, I imagined my friend wheeling through rocks and crags, lickety split, and couldn't wait for my turn to be purchased by someone young and fun and wonderful.

The very next day, a middle-aged woman asked the owner to recommend a mountain bike. "I haven't bicycled in thirty years," she explained, "so I don't want to spend very much."

"You'll love mountain biking," the owner assured her, "but if you buy a cheap bike, you'll regret it. I have just the one for you." Uh-oh, I thought, scrunching behind my littermates. If I can just tuck my pedals flat to my sides, maybe I can disappear behind this post. As I peeked to make sure that no one could see me, the owner pulled me from my hiding place. "This is a terrific bike," he said to the woman, "and just the right size for you." I took my punishment, standing meekly for inspection.

"It's very nice," she agreed, "but what if I've forgotten how to cycle?"

The storeowner smiled. "You haven't," he said. "Let me explain the shifting mechanism, and then you can try it out."

"My last bike was a one-speed with foot brakes," continued the woman, gingerly touching me with one finger, "in elementary school." I panicked—this was even worse than I thought. "Come on, friend," she said to me, "let's see if we can stay upright." It was the first time that any human had talked directly to me, and I was so surprised that I didn't topple her off as I'd planned. In fact, as we tottered around town together, she seemed very nice—although certainly not the owner I was looking for. I felt sorry for her and hoped that she'd find a nice cruiser for trips to the grocery store, obviously the limit of her abilities. "What a wonderful bike," she exclaimed when we returned to the shop. "I'll take it."

I was crushed. As the shopkeeper filled out my paperwork, I tried unsuccessfully to fling parts all over the floor in protest, but nobody paid any attention. Beyond sad, I hugged my littermates and friends in my imagination, then rolled slowly out the door, sniffling, mentally wiping away tears with my handlebars. We went only three blocks, to a restaurant, where my new owner hitched me to a post and disappeared. All alone, slumped against the post, I cried in earnest, wondering if I'd ever be able to make something of the biggest disappointment of my new life.

After awhile, the woman came outside with two couples, all laughing. Pulling myself together, I stood straight, doing my best to look brave and shiny. "Great bike, Susan," said one of the men. "Rockhoppers are terrific."

"Gorgeous blue," noted one of the women. "Let's get our own bikes and ride up to Redstone."

"That's twenty miles uphill," Susan protested, but her friends just laughed.

At least I get to meet more bicycles, I said to cheer myself up. And sure enough, a few minutes later, I was surrounded by four other bikes. I was the shiniest, so I preened just a bit and swished my rear end. Two of the bicycles were road bikes, tall and skinny like fashion models. "Gee, you have long legs," I said to one.

"I'll race you, fatso," he replied, sneering.

Off we went, single file, up a narrow highway next to the river. The scenery was beautiful, but I didn't like being on pavement—it felt weird to my off-road tires and I worried that a car might hit me from behind. "Hurry up, shorty," one of the road bikes called back, and I forgot about everything but catching up. After all, I was young and strong and state-of-the-art—and had eighteen speeds to their ten.

"My knees are killing me," Susan complained after half an hour. "And my rear is in agony!" Why won't she shift into a lower gear, I wondered, panting to keep up as we struggled uphill and finally crossed the river to Redstone. Out of five bikes, I came in fourth, actually beating one of the road bikes. "I'd rather die than pedal back to town," Susan announced as we stopped outside a cafe.

"But it's all downhill," one of the men pointed out.

"I don't care. I'd still have to put my seat on that seat! Let's get a beer and call for reinforcements." Without even thinking to get the bicycles a drink of water—after all, we'd done all the work—our riders flocked inside the restaurant, deserting us.

"Not bad for a baby," one of the mountain bikes congratulated me.

"Thanks," I answered, slightly mollified.

"Humph," muttered the road bike I'd beaten.

Soon, someone arrived in a pickup and all five of us were loaded in back. Part way back to town, Susan extricated me from the tangle. "Here's your new home, friend," she said, walking me up a steep hill and tucking me into a big garage next to a green sports car that introduced himself as Zeezer.

"What's your name?" he asked.

"I don't know," I answered, disappointed that my new owner hadn't bothered to give me one.

"Don't worry, little one," Zeezer chuckled. "This woman names everything!"

The next morning, Susan came into the garage, but instead of getting me, she got into Zeezer and drove away, leaving me alone with the snow shovels and tools. She didn't come home until dark, and never said a word to me. The next day was the same, and the next.

I wondered what my brothers and sisters were doing and if they'd been bought by someone nice. They're probably all chasing deer in the forest by now, I thought sadly, then scrunched into the corner, wishing that I could tuck my nose under my back wheel. Won't Susan ever ride me again?

Several weeks later, the garage door opened and in came Susan with a man I'd never seen before. "There's my new Rockhopper," she said, pointing me out. I gave a shake, fore to aft, to fluff up, and stood proudly, neck arched, for inspection.

"Nice," he said. "You'll love this bike."

"Maybe," Susan replied doubtfully, "but my knees and rear hate it. I'm ready to try again, though, if you'll give me a lesson in shifting."

Loading me with another bike onto the back of Zeezer, they drove to a dirt road near the top of a mountain pass. This is more like it, I decided, wondering how I'd fare with the other mountain bike, a sleek and expensive model that looked very experienced and cool. "Hello," I greeted him shyly, but he ignored me. His owner definitely looked like a jock also, and within seconds, they left us far behind on the steep trail. I was mortified.

For some reason—I guess she thought that making me harder to pedal gave her more leverage—Susan kept shifting up instead of down. Between us, we barely rolled forward, and the steeper the road got, the worse she made it. The other bike was long gone by the time Susan stopped to rest, arms draped over my handlebars, panting.

Her friend finally came back. "Shift down when it gets steep," he instructed casually.

"How? What's down?" Susan asked.

Off he went without explaining. Finally, we all got to the end of the road and stopped for a picnic. "I thought you were supposed to be able to ride straight up the side of a mountain on one of these bikes," Susan growled, peeling an orange.

"You can," the man assured her.

"*You* can," she grumbled.

Downhill was much more fun for all of us, although things got a little scary when we got going too fast and Susan was afraid to brake hard in the loose dirt. "I don't know, friend," she said as she rolled me into the garage later. "I may not have it in me anymore."

The next day, not even Zeezer got to go anywhere. Late in the afternoon, Susan hobbled past the garage, hopping on one leg, supported by her bike friend. "Thanks for taking me to the doctor," she said to him.

"Hopefully, draining that knee and the shot of cortisone did the trick," he replied, carefully helping her up the stairs toward the house.

She sighed. "Maybe three knee surgeries and bicycling don't mix after all. All that money wasted."

From then on, I stayed in the garage by myself, talking to Zeezer at night, sleeping during the day. I gathered dust, and spider webs, then started making friends with the bugs. My feet got soft but I cried only when Zeezer wasn't home to hear me. "Susan, where are you? Did I do something bad?"

Chapter 2

I STAYED IN THE GARAGE for over a year. In spite of what Zeezer said, I still didn't have a name and still spent my lonely days sleeping, or fantasizing about all the places I could have gone if someone else had bought me. Anyone else. I didn't care any more about chasing deer or rabbits—just being outside once in awhile would be enough. Please, Susan, just ride me to the stupid grocery store!

All summer I huddled alone in the corner, waiting, then sadly watched the leaves turn yellow through the little garage window. Every day, Susan would get Zeezer and they would go off together, ignoring me. Then the snow fell, and the garage turned bitterly cold. Susan never came to get me, or even talked to me. Spring came, then summer again, then fall. Would I really spend the rest of my life here, alone and unused and unloved? I couldn't stand to think about it.

Then one winter day Susan came inside the garage with a man that Zeezer said was her new husband. Behind him was a blue mountain bike, a brand new Trek. My heart started to beat a little faster; I held my breath, wagging my rear end ever so cautiously. Was Susan coming toward me? Yes, she was! Oh, joy of joys, she was decked out in bicycle shoes, long winter riding pants and a Gore Tex jacket, no less. My tail end thumped hard against the garage wall. Had she gotten new knees?

"I still think you're crazy, Clarke," she was saying, "but I'm willing to give it a try. Even though I'm as fit as a slice of white bread, I'll do anything to live in Europe for a year, even bicycle!" My heart leapt with excitement—a year in Europe, wherever that was, must be infinitely better than weekends in Utah! Wow!

After Susan washed off my face with a damp cloth, Clarke rolled me out onto the snow and pumped up my feet. Ah, sunshine! Fresh air! It didn't matter how cold it was—I was out and Zeezer was in. Stretching my cramped muscles, I shook, flinging cobwebs and dust into the bright air. Goodness, the snow was cold on my bare tires! "Hi!" I said to Clarke's Trek, excited. Before he could answer, Susan and Clarke jumped aboard us and we headed toward the highway.

From then on, every morning we hurried uphill to Redstone in the icy cold, then while the Trek and I waited outside a little cafe, hopping up and down to keep our tires from freezing to the snow, our riders warmed up with hot coffee; then we raced home downhill, freezing our frames. I didn't mind—anything was better than staying in the garage, and I loved listening to Susan and Clarke discuss their plans as we hurried along in the icy air. "Let's spend a month training in the desert before we leave for Europe," he suggested.

"Good idea," Susan replied. "I need to make sure that my old knees can hold up." Yes they can, yes they can, I cheered her on, and Clarke agreed. If only I could tell my littermates about my good fortune! I thought of all the times I'd wanted to trade places with them—now I wouldn't trade places with anyone!

The Trek and I tucked together on the back of a yellow VW van while Susan and Clarke drove to the Arizona desert. The morning after we arrived, we left the van to fend for itself and started down a dirt road that deteriorated into rocks and sand. Yuck. And hills. More yuck. I couldn't believe how out of shape I was after a year in the garage. Poor Susan could hardly manage, but Clarke and his bike were doing great, riding circles around us, trying to encourage Susan but making us both feel worse. Every time we hit deep sand, Susan pitched over to the side and jammed her knee. Ouch. I did my best, but it was really hard—we covered twenty-five miles before Clarke let us stop.

Two days later, Susan fastened two packs to my rear. Whoa! Who said anything about packs? Hey, I'm not a mule! I tried to buck them off, then tried to buck Susan off, but everybody was too attached. Up ahead, Clarke and his bicycle sailed away, with heavier packs, and I decided that if they could do it, so could we. Panting and puffing, I did the best I could and so did Susan.

Then she put on two more packs, this time on my front, and added a duffel bag in back. I felt like a fat bus. "Hurry up, Susie," Clarke called from up ahead. Susan and I growled together.

That night, leaned together next to the van, the Trek and I discussed our progress. He was an okay bike, I guess, but getting a bit snooty about how much stronger he was. I was sure that I was the better bike, even though I was out of shape and maybe a bit heavy, but figured that it was a guy thing and let him brag. "Where are we going first?" he asked after claiming that he'd hardly broken a sweat all day.

"I'm not sure," I answered, flat on my frame with aching muscles. "Spain or Portugal, I think. What I'm wondering is how we're going to get across that big ocean!" I'd peeked over Susan's shoulder one day while she and Clarke were studying a map.

"We'll fly."

"Dream on, child," I said, yawning. "We're bicycles, not birds."

"I'm serious," the Trek insisted. "I heard them plan it—they'll put us in boxes and we'll fly over the ocean." Although I tried, I wasn't able to imagine two brown boxes floating high overhead but was too tired to worry about it so decided to leave it at that. The Trek was just an infant—how would *he* know?

As Susan cinched on my heavy packs a few days later, Clarke suggested that we cross the border into Mexico. "We didn't bring our passports," she objected.

"We need to see what it's like to bicycle in a foreign country," Clarke insisted, so off we went, packed to the hilt, heading south. I was a little scared—what if some bigwig bicycle wanted to see my credentials and we all ended up in a Mexican jail?

For two days, we pedaled through the hot sun without seeing a town. Susan said that if we didn't reach civilization by the second afternoon, we'd have to turn back, with or without food and water, or else miss our flight to Germany. I hurried as fast as I could, feeling like a pregnant cow. Susan was breathing hard, sweating, struggling to keep up. Finally, we found a little adobe house in the middle of nowhere and asked a dusty man how far to Puerto Peñasco, the nearest town. "What does '*doce millas*' mean?" Clarke asked after the man answered.

"Twelve miles," Susan and I said together. How did I know that? "We've already ridden over thirty miles today," she groaned. "I don't know if I can pedal that much farther."

But she did, and as we struggled down the highway toward the setting sun, I finally got my name. "I think I'll name my bike Daisy," Susan announced, "for Oopsy Daisy or Lazy Daisy, depending on the circumstances." She called up to Clarke. "Your bike should be Ferdinand, because with my laptop on his back, he looks like a bull."

"I think I'll go with Fred," Clarke responded, then complained again about Susan's insistence on bringing along a computer to keep an accurate account of their trip.

In Puerto Peñasco, the owners of a crowded RV campground let us squeeze into a little corner next to a light pole. While our riders showered and ate dinner, Fred and I rested on the gravel, exhausted. "Are you ready for Europe?" I asked him.

"Are you?"

Both of us fell asleep before either of us could answer.

Chapter 3

H EY, BILLY!" I HEARD the muffled drawl of a voice outside my box. "These two bikes from Denver weren't supposed to terminate here in Dallas—you should have put them on this morning's flight to Frankfurt."

"Sorry, boss," Billy replied. "I reckon I'll get them on tomorrow's flight."

After what I'd already been through, lugging Susan 400 miles through Arizona and Mexico and then having my body dismantled so that I'd fit in a flat box again—Fred had been right—being left behind while our riders escaped to a foreign country didn't really surprise me. "Are you okay, Fred?" I whispered, concerned that he'd be frightened, all boxed up in a strange place by mistake. After all, Fred was only four months old.

"I can't breathe," he complained in a muffled voice, "and I'm getting squished on both sides."

"Get some sleep," I suggested. "We have a big day tomorrow." Nudging some of the clothes that had been packed around my frame into a pillow, I closed my eyes and rearranged my parts into a more comfortable position, all wedged in. One of my pedals, which Clarke had removed so that I could fit in my box, poked my side and I struggled to scrunch away from it.

After hours of listening to the noisy drone of airplane engines the next day, I heard Susan's voice outside my cardboard prison. "Okay, you two," she said to Fred and me. "I don't care if you *are* dismantled—you're not getting out of these boxes until you're on the train to Paris. No more getting left behind!!"

Embarrassed that they wouldn't let us roll by ourselves to the train station, Fred and I made ourselves as heavy as possible while Susan and Clarke dragged us down the escalator and stuffed us inside a tram. Finally, at the station in downtown Frankfurt, Clarke put us back together while Susan went to see about shipping us to Paris, where the plan was to turn south toward Spain or Portugal.

Goodness, it felt wonderful to be out of that box! Fred and I stretched and yawned and shook, making sure that everything fit. Clarke, I thought, my left pedal is a little loose; would you tighten it, please? He must have heard me because he did.

Susan came around the corner. "The baggage agent doesn't speak English," she explained, "but he does speak Spanish. What I think he told me was that we'll have to pay extra for the bikes once we cross the French border." She and Clarke walked us to the baggage area, where we were whisked away by a German agent.

Soon, Fred and I were crowded together in a grubby boxcar. "These Germans sure don't care about their tourists," I grumbled. "We don't even have a window!"

The train stopped several times, waking us from a light sleep. Then someone yanked me away from Fred. "These bikes will have to go off here," a burly man said in German. "Their freight has been paid only to the border. Hans, put them in the baggage room," he ordered his companion.

"Wake up, Fred!" I screeched. "We're being kidnapped!" Although we wrestled with the Germans, and I know I jabbed at least one with a pedal, the humans were too strong for us and we ended up in a corner of a dark storage room in a train station on the border between Germany and France. What would become of us now?

"I couldn't understand a word of what those men were saying," Fred said after he calmed down.

"They were speaking German."

"You understood them?"

"Now that you mention it, yes," I answered, surprised.

"How?"

"I don't know, Fred, I just could. Go back to sleep. Susan and Clarke will be frantic."

Hours later, Susan ran toward us across the baggage room, throwing her arms around my handlebars. "Here they are, Clarke!" she screeched. "If you two only knew what we've been through to find you," she said to me, breathless.

"No trains run from this station to Madrid," Clarke explained late that afternoon as we gathered in the Paris train station, together in the same place at last. "You've been to Paris before, Susie—do you know where Gare D'Austerlitz is?"

She sighed. "On the other side of the city, of course."

Clarke eyed Fred and me and all of our baggage. "We obviously won't fit in a taxi. I guess we'll have to bicycle across Paris."

"In rush hour?" Susan wailed. But what choice did we have?

Susan packed the bike panniers with clothes and camping gear as Clarke hastily pumped up our feet, checking to make sure that they and our brakes were securely fastened, then helped load us up like fat mules again.

We stood at the top of the train station steps. Fred's eyes were as big as dinner plates as he watched the French automobiles speed down the street in the dusky light of early evening. "Daisy?" he whispered. "Can we do this?"

"I hope so," I said, thumping down the stairs one at a time and wondering what had happened to Fred's cockiness.

"Wait for me," he called, flinging himself down in a rush to catch up.

Because the streets were too crowded, we headed off down the sidewalk, our tires a bit soft, breathing hard, all four of us with wide eyes. The sidewalks were too crowded also, so we plunked down into the street and were almost sideswiped by a Peugeot. Cars zipped everywhere, honking, taking up more than the whole street; the curbs were jammed with parked cars, many double-parked, and we lurched in and out of the mass confusion like drunk elephants. "My first time in Paris," Clarke called back at a traffic light, "and all I can think about is whether someone will open a car door into my face."

As the light faded from the sky, we lurched and pitched through the city, tossed on a sea of cars. "There it is, off to the left, across that plaza," Susan called out finally.

My wheels wobbly with relief, we were soon standing in front of yet another baggage agent, who fastened a ticket to Irún, Spain, around my neck and rolled me into a waiting train. It took me no time at all to fall sound asleep next to Fred.

In the morning, Susan and Clarke were standing by the train when Fred and I were unloaded, then they checked us onto a late afternoon baggage train to Madrid and themselves onto an express that would leave earlier in the day.

Fred and I were in Madrid forever before Susan and Clarke came to get us. After Clarke scurried off to buy tickets to Valencia, where they had decided to start our official bicycle journey, Susan grumbled about why they hadn't met our train as planned. "We had to get off the express train—it's too complicated to explain why—then carried two hundred pounds of luggage two miles into town because they wouldn't let us sleep in the station. Then I sprained my ankle this morning lugging it back in the rain. So be nice, Daisy. I'm not in a very good mood." Who was? After being kidnapped by the Germans and almost sacrificed to the street gods of Paris, Fred and I weren't very delightful company either.

Outside our Valencia-bound boxcar an hour later, the wind screeched and whistled, louder and louder. Crash! "What was that?" Fred jumped.

"I think a tree just hit the train," I replied, glad to be inside a heavy boxcar instead of outside on our own. "Great weather for bicycling—maybe we'll be blown to China next."

Fred snapped at my front tire and braced himself between two boxes as the train rocked back and forth in the storm. "Shut up, Daisy," he growled.

We arrived intact in Valencia about eight o'clock the next morning, the wind still shrieking as we pulled under the train station roof. Finally dressed for bicycling, Susan and Clarke pulled us off the baggage car. Frustrated and tired, the four of us soon stood on the top step of the station, surveying the tail of a hurricane.

Chapter 4

IT WAS SUNDAY MORNING, a week since we'd left America. Packed to the gills, Fred and I stood quietly, overwhelmed, at the top of the train station steps. Now it was up to us, no matter what. The weather was terrible—palm trees were shredded to leafy green strings and rainwater flooded over the curbs. "Now what?" I asked Fred, nervous, as we surveyed bricks and broken glass in the deserted street. For once, I thought, I'd be grateful for my safe and lonely garage in Colorado.

"C'mon, Daisy girl," Susan encouraged me. "Let's see if you can get down all these stairs with your packs." I bumped down the steps, one by one, while Clarke and Fred clippity-clopped down much faster and waited at the bottom.

We started off, single file, and were instantly soaked. The wind pushed at my panniers and I leaned into it, pushing back as hard as I could, squinting against the rain. As I crossed a narrow bridge behind Fred, a gust of wind pushed me off balance; flailing, I fell into the road in front of an oncoming car, scraping my frame and Susan's knees as we tucked up like turtles while the honking driver swerved around us.

Dead animals were all over the highway, like Frisbees with furry feet. "I can't stand this," Susan called up to Clarke. "I can't just pedal past these animals."

"Surely you don't plan to bury them!" He stopped, amazed, as she stared sadly at a squashed black cat.

"Of course not, but couldn't we take their spirits with us some way? I'm sure they'd rather be with us than flat on the highway."

Clarke chuckled. "Anyone who can talk to bicycles as if they're alive can certainly find a way to reincarnate dead animals." Excuse me, sir, I *am* alive, I said under my breath, making a mental note to trip him sometime, then felt a tiny jolt as the spirit of the flat cat climbed up on my handlebars and settled itself in the middle, tail waving.

"More kitty litter!" Clarke shouted a few minutes later.

"C'mon, hon," Susan called out gently, and its little soul scrambled up next to the other dead cat's, suddenly full and fluffy and ready to see the world.

As we slogged south down the coastal highway, the weather deteriorated from worse to worst and by mid-afternoon we decided to stop at a campground rather than drown. As the wind howled and the black sky disintegrated into waterfalls of cold rain, Clarke lashed Fred and me to a tree to hold us down while Susan scrambled their bags inside the tent to hold it down; then they both disappeared inside the tent while Fred and I huddled together outside for fifteen hours, exhausted and miserable, pounded by the worst storm on the Costa Blanca in a hundred years.

It was still raining in the morning. Not a bit rested, we squished out of the campground to the road, twisting in and out of broken tree limbs and fallen highway signs as we waded south along the coast. Soon my handlebars were crowded with the spirits of cats and dogs and rodents that had drowned the night before. "I'll call this the spirit ark," Susan decided.

Hour after hour we slogged through the rain and wind. None of us talked. At dusk, Susan and Clarke hurriedly put up their tent near a fence in a deserted campground. Two wet kittens scrambled inside for shelter while Fred and I wrapped our cold handlebars around a tree to keep us from blowing away. "How long can this last?" Fred wailed.

"Probably forever," I answered bleakly.

In the middle of the night, as the wind grew even stronger, if that were possible, Clarke tumbled outside the tent and ran off into the blackness while Susan and the tent tried not to turn into tumbleweeds and Fred and I clung for dear life to our tree. Finally, Clarke returned. "Follow me!" he screamed, and all of us, including one of the kittens, crowded together inside a cement shower building. Our owners and the cat stretched out single file on the dirty floor in front of the toilets while Fred and I leaned against a wall, handlebars sore from digging into the tree and each other.

Morning dawned overcast and windy. "I don't think I can go any farther," I whispered as Susan and I peered dismally outside at the sky.

"I can," Fred replied. "It smells in here."

After battling headwinds almost strong enough to stop us in our tracks all day, we sneaked into an orange grove for the night. "Will tomorrow be better?" Fred asked in a weary voice, stretched out under a gnarled old tree, gooey with mud.

"I don't know, Freddy. Go to sleep."

The next day, we traded wind and rain for hills as we moved inland away from the storm. Up and up we went, through hairpin turns like stairsteps, steaming, barely moving toward the top. "I'll take the Mexican desert," groaned Fred. "Flat is good."

I couldn't answer. The sun fried my back and the still air steamed with humidity. Including our riders, I carried 200 pounds on my back and Fred hauled at least fifty pounds more. For five hours, we strained up the pass, rolling one foot in front of the other, an inch at a time, in our lowest gears. "I can't believe that yesterday we were cold," I moaned.

Mid-afternoon, we rolled over the top of the pass, cheering, then raced down the other side—for about two minutes. Then the road turned uphill again. I whimpered.

"Let's stop here for the night," Susan suggested, maybe hearing me.

"We have no food," Clarke reminded her. So what? Fred and I never got to eat anyway. "Besides," Clarke continued, "there's no place to put up our tent unless you want to lie on a forty-five-degree angle." Hey, we're happy to sleep standing up, Clarke! Several miles farther on—or up, I should say—we found a town with a market, and after eleven hours on the road, a flat place big enough for a small tent. Fred and I were asleep before it was built.

Blue skies and bright sun greeted us the next morning, and the road was downhill to the coast, to Benidorm, where Susan and Clarke decided on a campground so that they could shower and do laundry. I was delighted, anxious to wash the dirt and sweat off myself, but Susan wouldn't let me into the showers. Grumbling, I slept as far from the tent as I could.

After battling our way to Alicante the next morning through bumper-to-bumper traffic, we took a train to Seville in order to get Susan's finicky computer serviced. Outside the city afterwards, at a family picnic area, Fred and I stood watch while Susan and Clarke put up their tent in the dark.

Around midnight, I heard a noise. "Fred! Wake up!" I jostled his front tire. "We're being attacked!" As motorcycle headlights flashed through the trees, Fred and I pulled ourselves into thin lines behind a big elm and watched several young men dismount only fifty feet from Susan and Clarke's tent.

"What'll we do?" Fred whispered. "Shall I bite them?"

"Don't be stupid," I hissed. "You don't have teeth."

"My gears do," Fred huffed. Soon, however, a crackling campfire and laughter assured us that this was a party instead of a burglary ring, so we stayed out of sight, alert but unneeded, until the men and their girlfriends roared off into the lightening sky just before dawn.

Five hours by bicycle outside of Seville—half an hour by car—we stopped at an old hacienda to ask permission to camp, our riders unwilling to hide in deserted orange groves and unable to afford campgrounds every night. After the housekeeper explained in Spanish that the owner of the house would be home shortly, Fred turned to me. "Did you understand what she said?"

"Yes," I answered, perplexed. Where had I learned foreign languages?

When the owner returned, he gave us permission to camp. Because we didn't need to hurry in the morning to avoid discovery in someone's orange grove, Fred and I were allowed to sleep late while Susan and Clarke washed clothes at the well, and then tied t-shirts and underwear to our packs and handlebars before pedaling off into the sunshine.

I had an accident late that afternoon. After turning into a rutted gravel road to a dilapidated farm to ask permission to camp, we discovered that no one was home except turkeys, dogs, cats, chickens and junk cars. On the way back to the highway, I tripped in a patch of deep gravel and Susan and her dead animal spirits flew over my head in a tumble of fur and feathers. We both sat on the ground inspecting our scratches as the farm turkeys and dogs came to investigate and Fred and Clarke stood together on the highway, laughing. Hurriedly, Susan and I sorted her spirit ark from the farmer's chickens and herded the right family back on my frame. As I carefully picked my way back to the highway, Susan picked feathers out of her hair.

The next day, after sleeping in a construction dump full of rats, we started on a steep grade. "These stupid roads were designed by mountain goats," I complained to Fred, who was proving himself far superior on steep hills as a result of youth, twenty-one speeds to my eighteen, and a stronger rider.

"I'm dying, too," he assured me late in the day. "We've been on twelve percent grades for hours." Finally, Susan dismounted and started pushing me, unable to pedal any farther. I helped as much as I could, but was on my last wheels also. At least Clarke and Fred weren't doing much better.

At dusk, we found a game reserve and settled down behind a big rock. Fred and I stretched out in the soft grass as Clarke unpacked pans and Susan wrote a letter. "Keep your head down, Susie," Clarke said nonchalantly. "A bullet just whistled over my head."

Fred and I ducked but Susan kept on writing. "I'd rather be shot than pedal an inch farther," she declared.

By morning, we were fog bound. Fred led, instantly disappearing into the mist. We rolled along enveloped in thick fog, only a few feet of road and our own tires visible to each of us, the clouds damping all noise to silence. It was creepy.

When the sun finally broke through, we rolled straight into the cloud and were surrounded by sparkling bright mist. "I'm flying!" I called up to Fred, feeling much better.

All morning, we chased the clouds east toward the sea. Slowly, the fog burned off and the road dried, then finally sunshine turned the gray skies to blue as we moved higher and higher to a mountaintop village, then raced down the other side to the valley below in a whoosh. This was more like it!

At the bottom, we looked up, surrounded by towering peaks, then staggered on, up the next mountain, out of the valley, winding slowly up and up, drenched in sweat. Finally, I couldn't carry Susan another foot and tumbled her off with a mental apology, making her walk. She pushed me up the hill a hundred steps, then climbed on again and pedaled, head down, until I tumbled her off again, this time without an apology. You're too heavy, Susan!

At Gaucin, the road finally dipped down, and Fred and I flung ourselves over the edge, screaming and laughing like maniacs. "Yee-haw!" Fred shouted, kicking up his wheels. Then they skidded up under him. "Stop!" he and Clarke screamed.

The road disintegrated in front of us. Hearts pounding, we tiptoed through chopped up asphalt from an unfinished road repair, then started up the third mountain of the day to look for a place to spend the night, twisting up and up to a hillside farm, only to find a locked gate. "Make Clarke quit, Fred," I begged.

"Maybe there's another farm around the corner," Clarke said hopefully. Susan didn't answer.

Thankfully, there was, and that night we slept in a barnyard. I stretched out, head on Susan's clothes pack, exhausted and sore, while Fred snored softly beside me as the sky covered itself in bright stars.

We were near the southern tip of Spain. One more mountain and we would be at the coast again, near the Straight of Gibraltar. Clarke wanted to go to Morocco but Susan didn't, so I didn't either. After a final windy pass, we coasted through village after village toward the sea, checked ferry prices to Morocco, then pulled into the first campground in San Luis de Sabinillas, giving us one last chance to convince Clarke not to send us to Africa. "Going to Morocco is insane, Clarke," Susan said, stripping off my packs. "Haven't you heard about the hustlers, the robberies, the corruption? Everything we own is in plain view!"

"So?" he replied. "Does your life always have to be easy and comfortable?"

"Since when has this trip been easy or comfortable, Clarke?"

I looked at Fred. "Do you want to go?" I asked.

"Maybe Morocco will be flat," he replied.

Chapter 5

I SHIVERED IN THE COLD wind as the old gray ferry banged into Africa. Susan clung to my handlebars, silent, while Clarke leaned forward eagerly, thick brown hair tousled, one hand steadying Fred. The doors of the hold opened up like the maw of a whale and the four of us emerged from the darkness, Fred and Clarke in front, all of us nudged along by cars and trucks reeking of exhaust fumes. As the hold emptied, I was skittery, watching for someone to jump out of the shadows. "Are you scared, Fred?" I asked.

"Nah," he replied, but I didn't believe him.

It was cloudy in Ceuta, the Spanish city on the tip of North Africa; high wind whipped trash through the streets as we looked for the highway to the Moroccan border. By the time we arrived at Customs along with hordes of Moroccans on foot, the sun was low on the horizon. "Welcome to Morocco," a voice boomed from a huge Arab wearing a long brown caftan and gigantic pointy slippers. "I am Hamid, from the Ministry of Tourism," he explained to Clarke. "You come with me." Flipping his huge hand in dismissal toward Susan, he continued, "And you, lady, wait here. Do not take your eyes from your belongings."

As they strode away, Fred and I huddled close to Susan, who put a hand on each of us as we watched the streams of people walk into Morocco. The women wore long robes head to ankle, scarves covering everything but their eyes, and the men wore dark caftans or t-shirts.

The sun had set when Clarke and the Arab returned. "You cannot bicycle into Tetouan at night," Hamid was insisting. "The roads are unsafe. I will escort you in a taxi for two hundred dirhams."

Susan jumped up. "We're not paying twenty-five dollars for a cab," she stated firmly.

"I will see what I can do." Hamid shrugged, then melted into the crowd. Returning, he held up his arms joyously as if bearing a gift. I didn't trust him, not a bit, and felt like rolling over his big clown foot. "I found a good friend who says he will take you to town for one hundred dirhams, as a favor to me."

Before any of us could object, strange hands grabbed Fred and me, pushing us roughly toward the cab, where we were stripped naked and shoved on top of an ancient Mercedes. "Ouch!" Fred complained. "Get your handlebar out of my hip, Daisy."

"If you'll move your chain ring off my neck," I growled as someone threw a rope over us both and the car careened off. Fred and I clung together as the taxi swung this way and that, avoiding oncoming cars by inches. Once, the cab ran another car off the road into the ditch, horn honking, as the other driver furiously shook his fist out the window.

In Tetouan, Fred and I were handed down off the car as our panniers were pulled from the trunk. I hurried over to Susan as Fred crowded close. After Clarke reluctantly paid the driver for the heart-stopping ride to town, he and Susan carried us and our packs up three flights of stairs to a dirty room in a tiny hotel. Hamid came also, carrying only the empty food pack, then plopped down panting on the only chair while Fred and I scurried as far from him as possible to the other side of the rickety metal bed. "I like Americans," Hamid said. "If you wish, I will show you my city."

"I need a shower first," Susan replied. While the trusty transportation team guarded Susan and Clarke's belongings and glared at Hamid, our riders took turns in the bath down the hall and left muddy footprints on the dirty floor when they returned from the drippy shower. Then the three of them left Fred and me to our own devices, locked inside the room; we slept fitfully, sore from being jostled and bounced on the taxi roof.

When the doorknob rattled, I jumped. Susan and Clarke entered alone, very late. "I feel a lot better than I thought I would," Susan said with relief. "The rug market was fun, although they sure do put on the pressure to buy."

"Morocco is just as bizarre as I thought," Clarke replied excitedly. "I love it!"

They left us alone again the next morning. To be honest, I felt safer inside the hotel room than outside, but I worried about Susan. When they got back to our room, however, Clarke was the one worse for wear, his torn shirt revealing a bloody gash where he'd been stuck in the back by a donkey carrying a load of sticks at the food market. "The hustlers drive me nuts," Susan said as she washed Clarke's wound. "I'm ready for the countryside."

"Me, too. But if we hadn't talked to Hamid's cousin last night, I would have chosen the southern route to Fès, through the Rif Mountains. At least now we know to head for the coast, where we'll be safer and the cycling will be easier."

It was noon before we shuttled down the stairs into the street, extricated ourselves from the hustlers, and started off with a hot, humid tailwind. Susan wore a long-sleeved t-shirt and sweatpants. "Why on earth is Susan dressed like that?" Fred asked as we cleared the city limits, already sweating.

"She doesn't want to offend anybody, Fred. Muslim women always cover their arms and legs."

"How do you know?"

"I have no idea."

The scorching wind pushed hard at our backs. "Uh-oh," Clarke said several kilometers outside of town, after checking the map. "We've missed our turn."

"I'm not anxious to go back to Tetouan, especially into a headwind," Susan said and I wholeheartedly agreed. "Surely we can find a secondary road that cuts across to the west."

As it turned out, there were no roads west and the nearest village was sixty-five kilometers south through the Rif Mountains, the place that we'd been told to avoid. I dug in, clambering up the first steep pass, sweat streaming down my frame. Poor Susan in her hot clothes!

Occasionally, I'd notice the gorgeous scenery, but mostly my eyes were on the steep road, concentrating on my task. I didn't see the battered old van until it stopped beside us and four men jumped out, holding plastic bags in their hands, gesturing wildly. "No!" Clarke said adamantly. "We don't want any." The men argued in broken English, then threatened. "Go away!" Clarke yelled. Finally, the men piled back in the van, then drove slowly, keeping pace as we struggled up the hill, frightened. Yelling out the van windows, the men waved their little plastic bags in our faces, then drove off in a shower of dirt.

Tensing as each car sped past on the narrow road, I hurried up the hill. Several times, approaching cars slowed, their occupants hanging out the windows to scream threateningly before speeding off, spraying gravel at our feet. Occasionally, we'd pass a house or two built close to the road, where men ran from the doorways to scream, shaking their fists. "Faster, Daisy, faster!" Fred kept calling back to me. I was going as fast as I could.

Then the children came. Threading down through the roadside rocks, they waved their arms, demanding candy and cigarettes in English and Spanish. When they realized that we didn't have any, they chased us, screaming and spitting and throwing rocks. Up the steep hills, they could easily outrun Fred and me because of our heavy packs and exhausted riders.

Once, a boy grabbed Fred's rear with both hands, trying to pull him over as Clarke pedaled furiously. The child yelled, yanking at poor Fred. "Let go!" screamed Clarke, skittering sideways as a bus approached from behind, honking. The boy finally loosened his grip and tumbled along the roadside as the bus barely squeezed past.

"Are you all right?" I asked Fred.

"No!" he replied hoarsely. "Come on!"

We hurried, all four of us pedaling up the long, steep hills in the stifling heat, too afraid to rest, dreading each bend in the road. Around a long curve, three pretty little girls in red dresses sat in the rocks near a small flock of sheep. Susan waved tentatively, but the girls screamed what were no doubt obscenities, then spit and threw rocks.

After sixty kilometers in four hours, we stopped to rest at the turnoff to Chechaouen. "I'm really scared, Freddy," I said, no longer feeling older and wiser, happy to stay close to his bulk.

"Me, too," he admitted, scanning both sides of the road for approaching humans of whatever size. Suddenly, half a dozen boys climbed up from the river. Two teenagers strode toward us; one pulled a long knife from behind his back. I gasped, slipping with Susan behind Clarke, who straddled Fred, feet on the ground.

"Hold my bike, Susan," Clarke ordered, dismounting. I held my breath while Susan held Fred, who shifted his weight nervously back and forth from one wheel to the other. Clarke walked toward the boys, his eyes never leaving those of the young man clutching the knife. "Just what," he asked in English, "do you intend to do with that knife?"

The boy stared at Clarke for a long moment, then sullenly turned away and motioned his friend to follow him down the hill. We all started breathing again as Susan handed Fred over to Clarke. Please, oh please, Susan, can't we leave Morocco now? A nice hurricane in Spain would be lovely.

As the four of us struggled on foot up the steep road to Chechaouen, our riders too hot and tired and stressed to pedal another inch and their bicycles too hot and tired and stressed to carry them, a group of young boys gathered. Perhaps intimidated by Clarke's bravery, they seemed content just to walk with us, chattering in Arabic and French while Susan and Clarke answered in English and Spanish. What a relief! Then Clarke asked them to help push Fred and me; delighted, they complied and Fred and I appreciated the boost. My head hurt, and every muscle in my frame was a knot. Who put the cement in my panniers?

Buoyed along by an ever-growing group of bike-pushers, I flew up the mountain like a magic carpet, but soon I was going so fast that Susan lost hold of me and called to the boys to slow down. They ignored her, playing with my shifters. Ouch! "Stop!" Susan yelled from behind me on the hill. One boy, laughing wildly, tried to climb aboard, kicking me. I bucked, but was held down by too many boys to get away. Far ahead, Clarke kept a firm hand on Fred, oblivious of me. "Stop!" Susan screamed again. "Get off my bike!" Faster and faster pushed the boys, racing me up the hill toward a cliff. One boy unzipped my frame pack, grabbing Susan's bottle of pills for her knees before I could twist away. Help, Freddy!

A villager walking toward us assessed the situation and yelled something in Arabic that I didn't understand. The boys stopped dead in their tracks, heads down, relinquishing me immediately to Susan as she caught up, her heavy clothes soaked with sweat. "These children were trying to steal your money," the villager admonished her in English. "You should have never allowed this." As if she could have helped it! I bristled, ready to poke him with a spoke even though he'd saved my life, but he walked off briskly and the boys dispersed, grumbling, their pockets lumpy with stones.

Two village men helped push and pull and lift Fred and me up steep streets and several flights of stairs to the center of town. Susan was still shaking but wouldn't take her hand from my handlebars as one of the men explained about the children. "Americans always give them candy and cigarettes," Mohammed shrugged. "If they do not, the children become angry. Ignore them," he instructed.

"That's easier said than done on a bicycle," Susan pointed out.

"Just kick them away." Mohammed looked at her, considering, then turned to Clarke. "You should not bicycle in Morocco, especially with a woman. The roads are too dangerous, too lonely. But you are here, and with your wife," he continued. "I advise you to continue by bus, particularly if you are traveling south to Fès. Never stay in campgrounds and trust no one. I know everyone in my village, yet I do not trust one person. It is the way everyone lives in Morocco," he added after Clarke looked surprised.

Inside our locked second-floor hotel room, Susan and Clarke chained Fred and me to the metal bed frames. "We may laugh about this when we get home, Clarke," Susan said in a shaky voice, "but tonight I'd chain *us* to the bedposts if I could. I hated today! I can't bicycle anymore in Morocco."

"I can't either, Susie," he agreed. Fred, eyes haunted with strain, leaned against the bed to sleep while I wondered how to get us out of Morocco without our being here while I did.

In the morning, Susan and Clarke left Fred and me tethered to the beds, then returned later with two giant bags of groceries. "The only good thing about this country," Susan remarked as she sat on the dirty bed, "is the cost. Fifty cents for seven pounds of vegetables."

Clarke was examining the oranges. "These moldy old things aren't the ones we picked out!" he exclaimed.

"And you're surprised?" Susan sighed. "Let's see if we can get bus tickets back to Tetouan for tomorrow." She and Clarke had apparently decided to return to Spain instead of going on to Fès. Delirious with relief, Fred and I tried to hug.

The next morning, we tiptoed down the stairs into the street, wary of ambush, but everyone in the village seemed to be gathered at the bus station, a large bare lot at the foot of a hill. Every time someone came near me, I skittered, pulling away. "Easy, Daisy," Susan whispered, holding tightly to my handlebars.

Fred jumped when a boy touched him from behind, and when the baggage handler grabbed his frame to hoist him aboard the ratty old bus, Fred whirled around, knocking him aside; then another man snatched me and we were both shoved on top of the bus next to large woven baskets of live chickens and tied down with a heavy net. Through the open window of the bus, Clarke argued with the baggage handler about our fare, then the angry man climbed on top and started untying the net that secured us to the roof; before he could throw us off onto the street, however, the bus started to move and he jumped down, yelling and shaking his fist.

Half an hour later, on the main road, the police stopped our driver, who pulled three of the rooftop chickens out of a basket and relinquished them, squawking, to the proper authorities before racing toward Tetouan at astonishingly fast speeds for the rickety bus. At least Fred and I hadn't been donated to the cause!

At the bus terminal in Tetouan, Fred and I and the rest of the suffocating chickens were unloaded together; then I discovered that our packs had been thrown into someone's vomit. I gagged as Susan hung a smelly pack on my rear, but I wanted out of there as much as she did so behaved myself.

At the little hotel where we'd stayed before, we regrouped for three days. The first morning, we were all afraid to go outside and sat crowded in our tiny room, arguing. Clarke threw a squishy orange at Susan, and Fred and I quarreled over whose fault their argument was and I kicked his rear tire. The second day, Susan and Clarke went for a walk to see if they could avoid the hustlers while Fred and I guarded our room. Then the third night, they went out to dinner and were arguing when they returned. "All you want to do is bicycle, Clarke, day after day, mile after mile. Can't this trip be fun?" Susan asked as they banged into the room.

"Just what do you want to eliminate from the day, Susan? Planning our route? Getting water? Shopping for food? Finding a place to sleep, maybe?" He was getting really sarcastic. "Eating, perhaps? Look, you're the one who had to bring a computer along to keep a journal. I'll gladly ship it home to save you some time!" They climbed into bed, facing opposite walls. Fred and I faced away from each other also, like bookends, taking sides.

In the morning, we woke without speaking; outside, the weather was as cold and gray as our moods. In silence, Susan gathered our gear and we thumped down the stairs to the street in shifts while Clarke got a taxi to take us to the border and tussled with one last hustler who wanted payment for help we didn't need. As the old Mercedes sputtered off with Fred and me strapped to the roof, a trail of Arabic expletives followed like exhaust fumes until we turned the corner to the highway.

Chapter 6

I<small>T WAS RAINING AS</small> we climbed back up the steep pass to Gaucin, but I didn't mind because we were out of Morocco. Draped in cheap fluorescent orange rain gear, Susan and Clarke looked silly, like sloppy orange crows flapping along the highway, and by late afternoon, the flimsy plastic had shredded. At the top of the mountain, they deserted their bicycle buddies, poor us, to drink hot chocolate in a tiny cafe. "Guess what?" I asked, crowding under an eave for shelter, my packs dripping.

"What?" Fred answered, pushing me aside to make more room for himself.

"I couldn't understand Arabic. I understand German and Spanish, but not Arabic. Maybe they just talk too fast." Fred looked at me curiously, then shook, front to back, spraying raindrops and rattling his packs. "Stop it!" I screeched as Susan and Clarke scampered out of the restaurant carrying double fistfuls of heavy pesetas for a telephone call to Susan's sister, our central contact at home.

By the time Susan said, "Hello, we're safe, we're out of Morocco," the phone had swallowed a day's allowance. "I love you," she hollered into the dead connection.

We lost the rain the next day, but not the wind. At two o'clock, after six hours of climbing up tight switchbacks through deserted villages, we stopped for lunch. Susan sat next to me on a stone wall in the pale sunshine, eating yogurt, her tan face windburned from the morning's ride. Suddenly, a huge bumblebee landed with a thud on her arm and wandered up the inside of her sleeve. I jumped away, shrieking, and Fred looked at me curiously. Susan froze, and when the bee finally emerged, she flung herself off the wall. I hid behind her. Startled, the bee flew straight at Clarke, who scooped it up in an empty yogurt cup and threw it off the mountain.

Back on the road, disaster averted, Fred asked, "Why on earth were you afraid of that bee, Daisy? I can imagine a bicycle afraid of a chain saw, maybe, but not of a bee."

"Well, it *sounded* like a chain saw, Fred. Don't make fun of me—it could have bitten your tire, you know."

Clarke chose a 4000-foot pass out of Ronda the next day. The sun was bright and hot and I was already sore from the climb the day before. Mile after mile, we climbed up the pass, resting often. Finally, unable to roll another inch, totally done in, I stopped, sliding Susan and the spirit ark to the ground. Okay, you cats and dogs and hedgehogs and rats, give us a push, will you? Fred continued slowly up the mountain, barely making headway. Equally frazzled, Susan draped her arms over my handlebars in surrender. Together, we breathed sizzling air as the sun burned our backs and blood pounded in our ears. "C'mon, Daisy," she said finally.

In the mountains of Spain, the roads follow the contour of the countryside, stringing tiny mountain villages like beads, beautiful but brutal. Starting and stopping like an ancient conveyor belt, we staggered up the mountain in the blistering sun, miserable.

At the top of the mountain, Fred and Clarke leaned against a low wall, rested and ready, looking smug. Susan and I were neither rested nor ready when we arrived alongside, and while Susan enjoyed the scenery, I stood immobile, head hanging, soaking up the silence, enjoying the relief of not moving.

Now I was ready. "Let's go!" I called to Fred, racing off before he could reply. Hurtling down the pass, I squealed with delight, my pain forgotten, freshly-washed socks and underwear streaming like flags from my packs.

At the bottom, however, the road turned up to another mountaintop. When we saw that the map showed a twelve-plus percent grade, Susan and I balked. Clarke wasn't pleased with us. "We haven't even ridden forty kilometers yet today, Susan," he snapped. "You agreed to fifty."

"I said I'd average fifty, Clarke. When it's this steep, my knees won't last that long. Look, I'm doing my best—I've had three knee surgeries, for Pete's sake." So there, I said to myself, wondering how Fred was able to keep up with Clarke's pace.

"All you do is whine about your precious knees," Clarke continued. That's not at all fair, I thought, giving Fred a shove.

"Hey," he said, pushing me back, "leave me out of this."

That night I lay outside the tent, worrying. I had done my best, but it obviously hadn't been enough for Clarke. Not wanting to get Susan in any more trouble, even though I hurt all over, even *my* knees, I decided to deliver her to Málaga the next day, seventy-five kilometers away, even if it killed me, just to show Fred and Clarke that I could.

Luckily for Susan and me both, it was mostly downhill.

"Let's go back into the mountains," Clarke suggested as we battled heavy traffic and smog up the coast after minimal rest at a noisy Málaga campground. Groaning, I hung a left and started up another pass. Fred sailed ahead of me, showing off, oblivious of the steep grade. By late afternoon, however, he was tired also, cheered only slightly by the Spanish cars that flashed their headlights in salute to our efforts.

That evening, we were able to ask permission to camp in English because the hacienda where we stopped was owned by a family from London who responded to Susan's request with tent space, a double handful of freshly-dug potatoes, local wine, and a picnic table and benches. While our riders drank wine with our hosts, Fred and I relaxed in the lemon grove next to the tent. "Is all of Europe this steep?" I wondered out loud.

"Probably," Fred answered, just to be mean.

But it got even worse. A few days later, in downtown Granada, we found ourselves groaning up the side of a cobblestone cliff toward the largest medieval castle in the world. The street was so steep that if we stopped, we couldn't get started again—thank heaven that the cars and their drivers made way for us, cheering. Finally at the castle—all I saw was a long red wall—Susan and Clarke decided that it was too dangerous to leave Fred and me and their belongings unprotected in the crowds, so we coasted down the other side of the cliff while Fred and I complained about our wasted efforts.

If that weren't enough, the next day we had to climb ninety kilometers, fifty-five miles, after being passed by a flock of shiny Spanish racing bikes that sneered at our dirty frames and heavy panniers. "Tell me, Fred," I gasped after an old man passed us on a clunky black utility bike, "are we having fun yet?"

"Hush, Daisy," he replied, huffing and puffing to catch up with the ancient pair.

We were in olive country, where the roads weren't as steep but the weather was hot and dusty. One night, we stayed outside the courtyard of an old hacienda inhabited only by a friendly dog, and while Fred and I watched clouds crowd the sky, Susan and Clarke ate dinner inside the tent, ignoring us. The sky was dark long before nightfall. "This'll be a doozy," I predicted as huge raindrops pelted my frame.

Fred jumped as lightning struck across the valley, then jumped again at the thunder. We huddled together all night as lightning flashed, thunder crashed, and the rain soaked us through to our bones. Why couldn't we *all* share the tent?

If anything, it was raining harder at dawn, and our riders didn't budge from their shelter. Finally, about two o'clock, Susan burst from the tent. "I can't stand being cooped up in here another minute!" she exclaimed. "At least if we ride, we'll warm up."

They loaded us quickly, covering our panniers with their tattered orange rain gear, then hurried us toward the highway after throwing the last of their bread over the courtyard wall to the whimpering dog.

Fred and I waded down the road shivering, kicking up rooster tails of water all over our backs. Each time a car passed, it sprayed us with a wave of icy water, drenching us, but it didn't matter; it was impossible to get colder or wetter.

Two hours later, we'd all had enough and turned off the highway onto a gravel road toward a hacienda. Soon, however, the gravel disappeared and I found myself in a foot of muddy clay that stuck to my feet, and then to Susan's feet after she got off to push. By the time we got to the house, she was shoving me along like a sled, my wheels locked, her own shoes caked with six inches of goo. The housekeeper directed us back up the hill to the property line and a muddy field.

"Gross," Susan said as she and Clarke laid us in the mud, pitched their tent and took off their shoes before scrambling inside with wet clothes and wet packs.

It was a long night. The rain finally stopped, but Fred and I couldn't get warm, even snuggled together. It started to snow lightly, then changed to freezing rain. "You're slimy," Fred grumbled.

"Well, you smell like a rusty tin can."

The next morning, Susan and Clarke emerged from their tent in wet clothes, grumbling also, then spent an hour scraping the mud off our brakes before rolling us back toward the highway, where they scraped us again and it started to rain. Then it rained harder, and after two hours and a long, steep downhill that froze us all, Clarke called a conference. "Drivers can't even see us," he said as a truck careened past, spraying water over our heads. "Let's find a hotel."

At the next town, Susan and Clarke went inside a cafe for hot coffee and hotel information while Fred and I complained about always being left outside to guard the packs after doing most of the work. "Thirty dollars for a hotel is three days' allowance," Clarke was grousing when they returned twenty minutes later.

"Let's just go on, then, and find a place to camp," Susan replied unhappily.

We ended up after another wet hour at another abandoned hacienda. Fred and I slumped against the wall of the house as Susan and Clarke found partial shelter for their tent under a grape arbor. It was another wet night.

It stopped raining at dawn the next morning. About seven, a grizzly old man brought his pony into the field to graze, then asked Susan and Clarke why they hadn't slept warm and dry inside the deserted house. "Because it doesn't belong to us," Susan tried to reply in Spanish as she hung wet socks on a fence and Clarke tucked their dripping tent into its cover. They were not happy campers, and Fred and I stayed out of their way while they packed. Our moods were no better and all of us argued most of the afternoon.

It took two more rainy days to find an affordable hotel in Albacete that would allow Fred and me inside. Locked together to a jukebox in the restaurant downstairs, we struggled to get comfortable. "Move over," I grumbled.

"I can't," Fred groused back, kicking my left pedal with a muddy tire.

We were headed toward Barcelona on a day with thin sunshine. Clarke turned to wave at some construction workers, then looked at the sky above my head. "Go, Susan!" he screamed.

She kicked me and I lurched forward. But within seconds, the sky turned green, then ripped open, spilling hail. The wind blew it like needles as lightning flashed in my eyes. Boom! Thunder ricocheted from the low hills. Flash! Boom!

Fred, all out, was widening the gap between us. "Over there!" Clarke pointed to a little stone hut by the edge of the road, dismounted running and pulled Fred inside after him. I followed as fast as I could, clearing the doorway as thunder rattled my teeth. Susan and I looked at each other, panting, both covered with goosebumps.

Worried that the hut would be struck by lightning, Clarke paced while Susan tried to warm her frozen bare legs and fingers and Fred and I huddled dripping in the corner, jumping at each flash of lightning outside the doorway, then again at the thunder. "Let's get out of here," Clarke finally said, poking out his head to look up at the black sky. "This stone hut is just as dangerous as being out on the road."

"Fine with me," Susan replied, rolling me outside into two inches of hailstones. "This place seems to be the local outhouse."

Clarke had fashioned a 'U.S.A' sign out of printed brown bags he'd found in a dump, then pinned it to Fred's rear and wondered if Europeans would understand the initials—after all, in Spain the words for America are *'Estados Unidos.'*

We were nearing Barcelona. For once, the weather was mild and we chunked along, enjoying the sunshine, everyone agreeable for a change, even the spirit ark. There apparently had been a disagreement earlier between a skunk and a bunny that both wanted the exact middle spot on Susan's handlebars.

Suddenly, up ahead, I saw something scattered in the road, like skinny stars all over the pavement. They were chicken feet, bloody at the ends. Where were their bodies? "C'mon, hons," Susan said to them as I picked my way through the mess, horrified, "climb on up on the ark."

"Yuck," I said as the feet clambered aboard, wedging themselves like a stack of warped records between the bunny and skunk, right in the middle of my handlebars.

"This might work pretty well," Susan decided. "With a few flat hedgehogs on top of these guys for ballast, I might have a pretty good demilitarized zone."

"What about the chickens whose feet you have?" Clarke wanted to know.

"They can come, too, of course. I'll imagine them tied to the handlebars with strings like a balloon bouquet because obviously they have no feet to hold on with."

"Obviously."

Fred had had health problems off and on for a few days, but at the bottom of a steep pass to a tiny village named Rasquera, he gave out, moaning. Clarke knew right where the problem was. "My bottom bracket is shot," he announced. "We're thirty kilometers from a town of any size, and, damn it, it's Sunday!"

All four of us walked up the mountain. Fred leaned against Clarke, obviously in pain, and I nudged him along, offering encouragement. In Rasquera, Clarke laid Fred in the grass, then began emergency surgery. "What can I do to help?" Susan asked.

"Find a mechanic who's open on Sunday," Clarke snapped sarcastically.

Glad to have a task, however hopeless, and not wanting to watch the operation, Susan and I hurried off to look for signs of life in the sleepy Spanish village. Spotting a goatherd, I approached quietly, trying not to scare his animals while Susan explained Fred's situation in horrible Spanish. The goatherd smiled and gestured toward a cinderblock building down the hill.

We scampered back to Clarke, who didn't believe our good fortune. "Nobody works in Spain on Sunday," he said, but gathering up pieces of Fred's insides in a dirty cloth, rolled him carefully down the hill to discover that the mechanic not only had the tools that Clarke needed to finish the job, but also was willing to drive to a friend's house to get bearings that were the right size.

"How do you feel, Fred?" I asked as he limped up the next hill.

"Not great. Clarke installed my chain ring out of balance."

"Only one more pass to the coast and a bike shop," I assured him, concerned. Although we'd been in Europe seven weeks, I hadn't seen a bike shop yet—admittedly, we'd kept mostly to the tiny ancient villages of Andalucía, but what if we couldn't find a bike doctor in Barcelona?

In Tarragona two days later, however, we found a bicycle store and a new bearing, but the store didn't have the right tools to fix poor Fred, who by now was in agony.

That afternoon, we found ourselves on a terrifying ribbon of road that clung to the face of a tall, gray cliff above the ocean. So narrow that the white lines marking its edge were painted under only occasional guardrails or on the rock wall itself, it was nevertheless crowded with traffic, no place for bicycles—crippled or healthy—on a windy day or any other, I decided after a few seconds.

Holding my breath, frightened, I climbed carefully up and up, rolling my feet in an absolutely straight line along an inch-wide corridor—a tiny jig to the right and I would fall into the sea hundreds of feet below; a small jog to the left would send me into the long line of traffic to be squashed like a bug and added to our own spirit ark. Once, a wide truck forced Fred into a guardrail—Fred staggered, but didn't fall.

Then it started to rain. Each time we rounded a corner, the wind pushed us either toward the edge of the cliff or into the heavy traffic. Three times, I misjudged the wind shift and stumbled, saved by Susan from going all the way over into the cars or off the cliff. Up ahead, Fred limped along, concentrating, sucking in his pedals to be thinner, cursing the tent poles that folded horizontally across his rear.

Eventually, the road widened. As I blew out a long sigh of relief, Fred leaned against a bridge abutment to rest, sweaty around the eyes, leaning away from his injured bottom bracket like a puppy with a thorn in his foot.

Late in the afternoon, our problems went from narrow to wide with a vengeance, as the width of our highway doubled and tripled and quadrupled as it neared Barcelona. Finally, our eight lanes converged with two lanes to the right and we stopped at the junction, trapped, unwilling to cross in front of the speeding cars to get to the right shoulder. Clarke stuck out his arm, motioning at the traffic to yield. Nobody did. Then he started pedaling poor Fred, who squeezed his eyes shut and whimpered, and they pulled into the fast lane while Clarke waved frantically at the cars. Unwilling to be left behind, I leaped in behind them, cringing, imagining what it would feel like to be crushed by a car moving a hundred kilometers an hour. Somehow, we made it to the other side.

It was rush hour, and after several more tussles with Barcelona drivers, the four of us opted for only the briefest of sightseeing before deciding that the better part of valor was to leave the beautiful city to the big guys. Unfortunately, we couldn't find our way out of the crowded city center and wandered this way and that, getting nowhere, until a Spaniard on a racing bike offered his help. "Follow me," he said in Spanish, then zipped off through the heavy traffic before Fred and I could introduce ourselves to his bicycle.

After eight hours of mountain climbing, I could no more zip than Fred could ballet dance with his injuries, but zip we did, over and under and around and through and back and forth, following roads and streets and underpasses and overpasses like tangled thread, turning left from right-hand lanes, swerving in and out of traffic like maniacs, muttering. Finally, the Spaniard stopped on a corner at the edge of the city, smiled broadly and pointed to the road we should take to France, over the Pyrénées. His bike smiled at Fred, mission accomplished, then winked at me as I tidied up Susan's spirit ark, which had been doing its best to hold on for dear life around the edges of my frame.

After ninety kilometers, the day ended behind a smelly factory in the industrial outskirts of Barcelona. As Susan and Clarke put up their tent in the dark, I considered early retirement but didn't know how to get home. Fred plunked down on the ground, checked his wounds briefly, then fell asleep, too tired to consider anything.

In Cardedeu the next morning, the owner of a tobacco shop hauled Clarke around town until he could find the right-sized wrench to fix Fred while Susan and I discussed routes over the Pyrénées with the folks at the tiny bike shop.

Three nights later, Fred whole and hearty again, we were ready to cross into France after 2300 kilometers, 1400 miles, and eight weeks on the road.

Chapter 7

AFTER CROSSING THE PYRÉNÉES on a windy, rainy day—it was no big deal, just another difficult pass—I wondered if I'd understand French, as I had German and Spanish, or if French would be like Arabic, unintelligible.

"More kitty litter!" Clarke announced just over the border. As Susan mentally picked up the first French addition to her ark, two Spanish spirit cats humped up into furry horseshoes, hissing. The little French spirit cat huddled on a side pack, claws clinging to the canvas, terrified.

"I don't think the *gatos* like the *chat*," I said to Fred. "Do you suppose that animals have the same prejudices humans do?"

"I hope not," he replied.

"Stop it, you guys," I admonished the Spanish spirit cats, "or Susan will make you sit on the bloody chicken feet!"

Our first French city was Perpignan, where Susan and Clarke hoped to pick up their first mail from home. After being lost in traffic for two hours in the rain, Fred dumped Clarke in the street after he tried a too-tight turn in a cul-de-sac. Finally, we found the main post office and Clarke went inside for the mail.

Leaning against the gray stone building, Fred and I watched Susan while she watched the French watching us. Susan was dirty and frayed, and Fred and I looked more like old burros than fancy bicycles. Muddy and wet, scratched, packs faded and fat, we tried to be polite, greeting the sophisticated French as they passed, arm-in-arm, detouring around us in wide circles. *"Bonjour, monsieur-madam,"* Susan and I would say as Fred nodded politely. Occasionally, someone would smile and give us a thumbs-up, but mostly they just looked at us, amazed. We *were* pretty amazing, I decided.

Clarke came out of the post office empty-handed. Susan was crushed. "Let's come back tomorrow," he suggested.

But when there were no letters the next day, Susan's eyes filled with tears. I sniffed back tears, too—I hadn't expected to hear from anyone, of course, but I knew from my year in the garage what it felt like to be lonely. "Let's ride into the mountains for a few days, Susie," Clarke suggested, "then come back for the mail." She nodded, pulling on her dirty bicycle gloves, then slowly pulled me away from the wall.

"Poor Susan," Fred said, nudging her gently.

Just outside of Perpignan, we were caught by a northwesterly wind that blew so hard that it took four hours to travel only twenty-three kilometers. Every truck that passed sent us skittering, first from blocking the wind we'd been leaning into and then from sucking us back into its slipstream. Inevitably, there was another vehicle behind each truck. "Yipes," I said, twisting away from a car that I'd swerved into when I overcorrected. "Watch it, buster," I yelled after it.

We finally found a little village, and at the town fountain, five old Frenchmen deep in lively conversation. The markets were still closed for mid-day siesta, so Susan and Clarke invited themselves to a language lesson. Because Clarke had listened to a few French tapes years ago, he was in charge of communication. Susan, who'd been in charge of Spanish, discovered that one old man had lived in Spain for a time. *"Pomelo,"* she said in Spanish.

"Pamplemousse," he translated into French. Sure enough, I knew that he'd said the word for grapefruit, and by the time the market opened, Susan and Clarke knew the French names for all of the fruits and vegetables they usually bought. As they trotted into the market, Fred and I stayed at the fountain, where I chatted with the old men in my imagination because they couldn't seem to hear my perfect French.

Dawn offered a clear and dry day, and Susan and Clarke decided to see the Chateau de Quéribus, an eleventh-century mountaintop fortress. By noon, we'd climbed 2000 feet, then the last kilometer up to the castle was a seventeen-percent grade. How come these two never want to visit the beach, I grumbled, leaning forward into the hill to keep from tipping backwards down the mountain. Finally, they dismounted and pushed us, straining also; inch by inch we rolled up the incline.

At the top, Fred and I flung ourselves on the ground, panting, while Susan and Clarke ate a picnic lunch and hiked around the castle. As they packed us afterwards, a Dutch couple mounted the stairs to the ruins. "I'll bet that steep hill cost you both a chain," the man paused to say, looking at Fred and me admiringly.

"Actually, no," Clarke said. "We have eighteen and twenty-one speeds— our bikes are made for this stuff."

"No matter how many speeds you have," the Dutchman responded, shaking his head, "you still have to pedal. Bravo!" How about *our* efforts, I thought. How come no one worries about those of us who do all the *real* work?

Going down the mountain was worse than coming up. It took about four seconds to get out of control on the steep dirt road. Digging in my wheels just caused my tires to slide and I almost couldn't roll fast enough to keep up with myself. Scrambling down the mountain with our own little rockslide, I was certain that any oncoming car would push me off the cliff. Brake harder, Susan, brake! Brake!

Ahead, Fred scrabbled and tripped, hind wheel up under him, out of control also. At the bottom, amazed to be in one piece, we stood together, breathing hard, horrified. It occurred to me then that we could really be killed on this trip, and I coveted my safe garage at home with the snow shovels and bugs.

Late in the day, Susan spotted a small stream. "Time for a bath," she announced, unpacking us in a grassy clearing. The four of us jumped into the cold stream, kicking and splashing, glad to be alive after our heart-stopping fall from the castle. Fred and I had a water fight while our riders washed t-shirts and socks, then spread ourselves on the grass to dry in the sun as Susan strung underwear in the bushes.

At sunset, we pedaled to a nearby village market without packs—it felt weird to be naked, and I weaved back and forth across the road, insubstantial, as Fred raced after me, laughing, nudging me faster and faster.

Back at the tent, clean and relaxed, we watched the moon come up. "You smell good," Fred said softly.

"So do you, for a change," I replied, smiling. We slept nuzzled together.

Susan and Clarke bought a five-liter jug of rosé for less than five dollars at a wine cooperative. Happily for me, the extra weight was loaded on Fred. At lunch, however, our riders made a big dent in the wine supply, and on a tiny road near Vingrau, sang stupid songs and made chicken noises all the way down a small pass, half looped, legs held out straight on each side of us. Fred and I shook our heads in disgust and stomped down the mountain, tempted to dump them both by the roadside.

On our way back into Perpignan—where there was still no mail—we picked up an interesting addition to our spirit ark. A white, floppy dog lay dead on the highway, fur ruffling in the wind. "C'mon, hon," Susan said as usual. As the moppety dog climbed up on my frame, I felt more than just his spirit—he felt warm and whole as he tucked his head under Susan's chin.

"Can you balance there?" I asked, imagining his trying to keep all four feet on my narrow top tube.

"Sure," he actually answered. "I can do anything or be anything. I can run next to you and never need to rest, or sit up here and keep Susan warm. It doesn't matter to me, only to your mother."

"My mother?" I asked, then realized that of course she was, and had been since adopting me at the bike store in Colorado.

The fluffy dog continued. "My name is Nagle—that's Susan's nickname for all animals." How would he know that? Odd, yet I'm absolutely certain that Susan, oops, my mother, heard my whole conversation with the dead dog.

As we rolled along the tiny roads of France, Fred and I were entranced by the countryside and its flowers, by the beautiful voices of its people, by the thick stone walls of its ancient houses. The wind didn't let up, however, and the language barrier was proving difficult for my mother and Clarke. They also couldn't seem to find places to ask for shelter at night after having been told that it's illegal to camp wild in France, even in someone's fields with permission. Things were getting pretty tense between them.

"Look at that church. Over there." Susan pointed to a gothic point that towered over the tiled rooftops in a tiny village. Clarke didn't respond. At the far edge of town, they stopped for lunch. Susan tried again. "Let's go see it," she suggested.

"I'm game," said Fred.

"Me, too," I agreed.

Ignoring all three of us, Clarke zipped up his plastic yogurt spoon into Fred's side pack. Finally, he turned. "It's downhill," he pointed out. "You'll just have to ride back up afterwards." I waited, confused. All we ever did was go down and up, up and down. Why not this time, to see the pretty church?

"I don't mind," Susan replied, but when Clarke didn't respond, she sighed, then pedaled off. A few kilometers up the road, we could hear the bells of the little church, clear and bright. "I was willing to ride back up that hill, Clarke," Susan announced, sounding more than peeved. "Why couldn't we go see the church?"

"So what do you want from me, Susan?" Clarke asked sarcastically.

"Nothing," she snarled. "This is obviously your own private trip."

It was our day to lead and Susan and I continued in silence, having chosen our route in the morning. At Lignan, however, Clarke directed us to turn east instead of north. I turned east, cringing, sensing a human storm brewing on my back. "Which way?" Clarke asked innocently at the next intersection.

"I don't even know where we're going, now that you've changed the route," Susan snapped, then furiously pedaled me up the next hill and the next while Clarke and Fred dawdled along, taking photographs. One of Susan's duties on the trip was to record in her daily log the place and number of each picture. "What number is this one?" she asked grimly as Clarke stopped again to photograph a tiny cemetery tucked between two ancient houses in Corneilhan.

"Don't get so excited," he answered, taking his time.

"Do you have to dictate every move I make, Clarke?"

The tension was unbearable, and I kicked at Fred with a pedal, just missing his back tire. "Hey!" he said, scooting out of reach. "Don't act like Susan."

"You beast!" I hissed. "It's Clarke that's awful."

All the way out of town, we snitted back and forth, stopping only long enough to greet three women who pushed baby carriages along the side of the road. *"Bonjour,"* we all said brightly, then bared our collective teeth again as soon as we'd rounded a corner.

"That last photo was number three on this roll," Clarke announced finally.

"Great. I suppose you want me to stop this instant to unpack my notebook and write it down," Susan replied.

He didn't answer. Instead, he and Fred raced up ahead, then whirled around to face us. Clarke picked up a rock and threw it into a field. "Do you have any idea what it's like to put up with you, Susan?" he yelled viciously.

Fred growled as we approached. "Or to put up with you, Clarke?" Susan shouted. Clarke and Fred galloped away, kicking dirt in our faces.

Susan laid me down in the grass and sat on the edge of the roadside, elbows on her knees. "Let them go," she said. A gentle spring breeze cooled our faces and late afternoon sunshine caressed the fields in gold. "They're long gone by now," she decided finally. "C'mon, Daisy girl."

We rolled up the road alone, in peace and at our own pace. Then we spotted Clarke and Fred looking like a roadblock. Cursing, Susan pedaled furiously to where they stood together. "You've been whining all day, Susan," Clarke started in.

"And you've been a dictator!" Clarke rammed Fred into me, twice, and I fell into the ditch. "Hey!" Susan exploded. "Don't you touch my bike!" she screamed, lunging for Clarke. They wrestled back and forth across the deserted road while Fred and I growled nose to nose in the ditch. My front tire hurt.

As Susan yanked herself out of Clarke's grip, her sunglasses fell broken to the ground. "I won't live with anybody who treats me like this," she announced, backing away.

"If you want to even up the score, go ahead." Clarke shoved his thumb into his chest.

Fred and I stopped snarling, amazed, as Susan charged across the road like an enraged mother protecting her young, slamming her fist into Clarke's ribs. "Ouch," flinched Fred.

"Ouch," I agreed.

"Ouch," howled Clarke, stepping backwards, wide-eyed. "I think you broke one of my ribs."

"Good!"

Fred and I looked at each other, afraid to move, as our riders stood across from each other on the road, feet apart, glaring.

Clarke broke the standoff. "I request twenty-four hours of silence."

"Fine," Susan agreed. Pulling me from the ditch, she adjusted my crooked packs none too gently. "After you help me fix this flat." No wonder my tire hurt—Fred had pushed me onto a thorn, the brat.

"Sorry," Fred whispered as Clarke yanked open a side pack to pull out the tire repair kit.

Everybody finally apologized, and although Clarke said that his chest was sore for a couple of weeks, we all forgave each other and got back to enjoying France and the French.

One day, after picking our way through a leftover flood in Montpelier, we stopped for lunch inside a bus shelter to avoid the strong winds that had stuck to us in this country like glue. As we pulled across the under-construction highway, the food pannier came unfastened from my front rack and the metal hook caught in my axle. My foot's caught, Susan, I called to her, unable to move out of the way of the cars.

"Stop, Clarke!" she yelled. Clarke and Fred turned to see our bicycle island in a car river; shoving Fred up against a road grader with a pained grunt, Clarke grabbed me out of the way of the traffic, then straightened out the pack hook with a pair of pliers. Thanks, Clarke, I said, spinning my foot to make sure it still worked.

As we crossed a narrow isthmus, the wind almost tore us to shreds. Although Fred managed to stay upright, I fell down twice; all of us were frustrated and frightened as we fought hour after hour to keep moving. "Enough," Susan finally announced.

"We can't stay here," Clarke pointed out, defeated also. "The ground's too soggy from the rain." We turned inland at sunset on a narrow road, looking for shelter from the wind. All we found were vineyards. Finally, a stone wall poked up from the surrounding countryside and we hurried toward it, fighting the howling wind. "It's a chateau, Susie," Clarke moaned. "The owner of a castle would never allow a dirty tent on his precious property."

"Why not?" she asked. "He certainly has plenty of space."

Clarke hesitated. "My French isn't good enough," he admitted finally.

"The guy's just a human being, for heaven's sake." Yanking on the long bell pull at the door, she stood back as a stately old gentleman emerged and looked curiously at his dirty visitors.

I shook, to fluff up, then nudged Fred in the ribs. "Stand up straight!" I ordered.

"Bonjour, monsieur," Susan began hesitantly because Clarke didn't say anything. *"Nous sommes Américains,"* she continued, blowing her whole French vocabulary in one sentence. Turning to Clarke, she hissed, "How do I tell him that I don't speak French?"

"I don't speak American," the man interrupted with a smile, "but I do speak English."

Susan smiled back. "It sounds to me like you speak British," she said, then asked if we could camp on the grounds for one night.

"It is forbidden to camp in France, you know," the man explained, "especially at historical monuments like this. This chateau has been in my family since the tenth century, and I must follow very strict rules in order for the government to allow me to live here." As we slumped in disappointment, the man looked from one of us to the other. "Perhaps if it is only for one night," he smiled, "the authorities may not mind too much. French laws are made not to be respected, eh?"

Ushering us to a gorgeous rose garden next to a stone wall just perfect for a windbreak, he turned to us. "Will this be sufficient?" As Fred and I sprawled in the grass after a leisurely tour of the grounds, the man returned with a basket of fresh eggs for breakfast.

"So rich folks wouldn't want us, eh, Clarke?" Susan teased after he left.

"Oh, hush," Clarke answered good-naturedly.

Chapter 8

A FTER A SCORCHING MORNING of climbing switchbacks piled onto each other like blocks, Susan panted, "I've got to cool off! Does a river cross this road anywhere, Clarke?"

"Just once, about ten kilometers from here."

"Fine. I'm taking a bath." Hooray, I thought, I want one, too!

But when we finally reached the swimming hole, it was in plain view of the highway without even a bush to hide behind. Of course, I wouldn't consider bathing out in the open, but Susan hesitated only a moment, then stripped. Oh, no, Mom, you wouldn't! But she did. "Turn your back, Fred," I shrieked as she happily lathered her legs, then rinsed in the clear stream. Bending over, the sun drying her rear end, she had just started on her hair when a little truck rattled along the highway toward us.

"Oh, dear," she said, turning her back as the truck passed with a honk and a wave.

"You just mooned your first Frenchman," Clarke laughed.

"*C'est la vie*," she said, grimacing, her face red.

Clarke had asked the Perpignan post office to forward any mail to St. Flour, a town part way to Paris. As we approached the city, Susan made me gallop and then run, then Fred and I raced the last ten kilometers and thundered into town like the Pony Express, reigning up at the first traffic light.

Shading my eyes from the hot sun, I looked for signs to the post office and discovered that the city appeared to be built in two parts. The new part, where we were, spread out from the base of a steep cliff; the old part was crouched on top of the cliff like a hat on a straight face. "We'd better hope that the post office is down here," I said to Fred, who was craning his neck to look up at the old village.

"I'm not going up there," he assured me.

But it wasn't and we did. Lured by the thought of news from home, Susan insisted that we climb up the side of the cliff. Already tired from the sprint into town, Fred and I inched our way to the top in the blistering sun squeezed between bumper-to-bumper traffic and the precipice. How could Susan's knees hold up? How could mine? "There'd better be mail up here," Susan gasped, wiping sweat from her face with the back of her bicycle glove.

"Come on," Clarke encouraged tiredly. "It's almost five o'clock."

In front of the post office, Susan took a long drink from her water bottle, then poured the rest over her head and slumped to the curb, rubbing her knees, to wait with the transportation team while Clarke retrieved our mail from the clutches of the French postal system.

Minutes later, she stared at Clarke's empty hands as he emerged from the big building. Sitting on the curb next to her, he held her gently as Fred and I crowded close to add our comfort. Poor Mom! She'd written so many letters home over the last eleven weeks—didn't anyone miss her? "Do you want to call your sister?" Clarke asked sympathetically.

"Yes!" she responded, jumping up, leaving only the floppy spirit dog Nagle and the ark to look after Fred and me. When they returned, she was smiling a little. "At least my sister mailed an envelope," she was saying. "She said it had lots of letters for us!"

"I'll see if I can arrange to have it forwarded to Calais." Clarke went inside the post office a third time, and Fred and I sat with Susan. I knew that she'd been looking forward to reading dozens of letters from her friends and family tonight at dinner. Now, she'd have just us—Clarke and Fred and me, along with Nagle and the rest of the spirit ark—and I hoped that we'd be enough.

The next day, we added flora to the fauna of the ark—trees, hundreds of them that lay stacked next to the highway. "C'mon, trees," I whispered to our fallen friends, "sneak up on Fred. He'll never notice." Stiffly, the tree spirits settled sideways across Fred's computer pack, no doubt preferring travel to the sawmill. As far as I was concerned, it was about time that Fred helped out with the spirit ark, and I made a mental note to start giving him the overflow rodents and reptiles.

Because the weather was clear that evening and we'd found a thick forest to sleep in, Susan and Clarke pulled only what they'd need for cooking off our backs, making life easier for them but not for Fred and me. I didn't like trying to sleep standing up, still loaded, and complained about it until Fred kicked my chain ring. "Stop, Daisy! You keep waking me up." Muttering, I leaned against a tree and was only able to nap.

After an early start in the morning—since Fred and I were already packed to the gills before the king and queen came out of their tent—we ambled down a long descent through cool forests and meadows strewn with fluffy lambs. We'd finally shaken the winds, and I found it impossible to stay grumpy in the bright sunshine. Villages, as we passed, looked like bouquets—flowers spilled from every garden and window box. I kicked up my wheels and tossed my handlebars, then ran ahead a few steps to give Fred a friendly nudge in the rear. We raced each other for a bit, then slowed to a roll to conserve energy.

That night, we couldn't find either a market for food or a farm for shelter, but settled into a small fenced meadow. As Susan burrowed into my food pack for lentil beans, Fred and I played tag to use up our leftover exuberance from the easy day.

It was cool in the morning, and as Clarke cinched the tent to Fred, we turned at the sound of a bell to see cows moving through the open meadow gate. When they caught sight of us, they stopped, then stared. "Excuse us, girls," I said as Susan pushed me toward them through the deep grass.

It was Saturday, and because the markets would be closed both Sunday and Monday due to the anniversary of the end of World War II, Susan filled the basket on my head with veggies and fruit right to the top while Clarke tied five long loaves of crusty French bread on top of Fred's spirit trees. Hey, you two, haven't you heard of French restaurant cuisine, I groused as I staggered out of town under the weight of three days' supplies. Maybe Susan heard. "Let's eat out Monday night," she suggested. Because of their ten-dollar-a-day budget, they planned only one restaurant meal per country.

That afternoon, as Fred and I trundled up and down through pine forests that were a kaleidoscope of shade and sun, Clarke stopped to study the map.

"We're almost out of the mountains, Susie. I'll bet your knees will be happy about that."

The four of us stood quietly for a moment, imagining how it would feel to scamper through flat yellow grain fields instead of struggling up aching grades in the hot sun. Hard as the trip had been so far, however, I was sure that I'd miss the screaming freefalls down long, cool passes. I always felt like an eagle, then, floating down out of the sky.

As we walked through a pretty town full of fancy glass porches and awnings, Fred started to limp. "I feel terrible," he announced.

"Is it your bracket again?" I asked, afraid that the weight he carried was probably too much.

"I'm not sure."

As music filled the morning air from a public address system, Clarke stopped to examine Fred, then shook his head. "I think I may have to replace the whole bottom bracket this time, Susie."

"Can you make it to Paris?"

"I don't know," Clarke answered, tightening up something with a wrench as Fred winced. "I'll see what I can do tonight to patch it up."

Outside of town, the map showed a 300-meter drop in elevation over the next fifteen kilometers. After sixty mountain kilometers and with an injured team member, a long descent to finish the day was exactly what we needed. "Do you want to lead the plunge, Fred?" I asked cheerfully as we rounded the next corner.

"What plunge?" he said, tipping his handlebars to look up at a hill that looked like the first dip of a roller coaster—from the bottom.

"Rats," I said.

"Rats," Susan said.

"Rats," said Fred.

"Do you want to take this hill today or tomorrow, Susie?" asked Clarke.

"Neither," she answered, worried about Fred and her knees. "But what the heck, let's get it out of the way."

She and Fred made it up the hill without incident, one after the other, with Clarke and my help, then we settled down between two meadows on an unused dirt road. While Clarke fussed over Fred's injuries, I helped Susan reorganize her food pack: thirteen containers of yogurt and pudding, cheese, onions, tomatoes, rice, three kinds of pasta, lentils, soup mix, bouillon cubes, sugar, tea, carrots, green peppers, mushrooms and chocolate bars. Fred carried the overflow: ketchup, mustard, vinaigrette, flour, seasonings, oil, salt—two pounds of it, the smallest size available in the market—and five liters of wine. The end of the holiday weekend couldn't come soon enough for these two pack bicycles!

About noon on Sunday, half way up a steep hill on the other side of Eymoutiers, Fred finally seized up, too sick to continue. I hurried to his side as Clarke tried to dismantle his lower bracket without the right-sized wrench. "Ouch!" Fred complained as the tool slipped.

"It's eleven-thirty," Susan pointed out. "If we coast back down to town, maybe we can find a bike shop that's still open. In another hour, everything will be closed until Tuesday because of the holiday."

Always one to fix things himself, Clarke reluctantly agreed and we coasted carefully back into Eymoutiers. Although both bike shops were already closed, we found an open auto garage. After Clarke drew Fred's problem on paper, the correct wrench was offered along with advice and commiseration in French, which only I could understand, and we were back on the road in an hour. "Do you feel better, Fred?" I asked.

"Much!" he said, rolling down the highway smooth as silk.

Susan hoped to watch the Armistice Day parade in le Grand Bourg the next day, but Clarke made up some flimsy excuse about not wanting to cool off his muscles and pedaled away from the city—he and Fred sure never mind cooling off their muscles during lunch, I thought as we grudgingly followed. At noon, Susan and I shared a silent moment with the farm animals in memory of the war, wondering how many had been killed in the bombings.

Later, we crossed a small stream on a stone bridge. "We're eating out tonight, Susie," Clarke reminded her, parking Fred and pulling smelly clothes out of his panniers. I nosed in behind and Susan grabbed her own laundry and their dirty towel and headed down the embankment. As Fred and I chatted, glad for the rest, we heard splashing from the culvert below us, and eventually two wet heads with arms full of dripping clothes emerged from the underbrush.

As Susan tied a pair of nylon underpants into a bow above my tail, Clarke saddled up Fred with his own laundry, then groaned. "That figures," Clarke said, hands on his hips. "I get all cleaned up to go out to dinner, but first I have to fix a flat."

After eleven hours and a hundred kilometers, we found a little restaurant below the Hotel du Nord in la Trimouille. By then, our riders were so hungry that they left Fred and me to look after each other, loaded with everything they owned, and bundled inside for their first meal in France cooked by the French.

Fred and I leaned against the wall, shifting our weight from one wheel to the other, bored, wishing there were someplace to lie down—after all, we'd lugged them the hundred kilometers while Susan and Clarke just sat on our backs. Hours later, they strolled out of the restaurant, arm-in-arm, weaving just a little, then pushed us across a short bridge to the town park, where they finally unpacked us, pitched their tent in the dark and ushered out the last mosquito as Fred and I stretched out with a sigh.

Chapter 8

EAGER FOR CONVERSATION WITH someone other than each other—after all, since we were all sharing the same experience day after day, the four of us didn't exactly have news to relate around the camp stove in the evenings—we turned down a tiny road in search of a house or farm with a flat space big enough for a tent and two bicycles.

Something was wrong. Away from the main highway, the air felt heavy, foreboding and scary. I rolled faster. Fred caught up, glancing nervously over his handlebars. Side-by-side, close together, we hurried down the road, our tires hissing too loudly on the pavement. Oh, please, Mom, I thought, don't choose one of these places!

The farms were rundown—neglected and sick, maybe dangerous, rather than poor. In front of each one, Susan and Clarke would pull us to a halt, hesitate, and then go on. "This doesn't feel right, Clarke," Susan said finally.

"You feel it, too?" he responded, surprised. "Let's get out of here!" Whirling—Fred and I needed no command—we raced back onto the highway, looking back once or twice to make sure that nothing followed us. On the main road, the air seemed just fine but Fred and I hustled anyway, to get some miles between us and whatever-it-was before we laid down our tired heads to sleep.

A beautiful manor house appeared on the horizon, enticing us to safety. It had nothing to do with its grandeur or beautiful flat lawns just made for tents and bicycle beds. It somehow actually invited us to stay.

After introductions, the owners and their three children escorted us to a soft area of thick grass next to a row of tall trees and flowering hedges. The children stayed to help put up the tent and then returned after dinner with their own bicycles. Clarke let the boys take turns riding me until dark—I'm smaller than Fred—while Susan showed the little girl the tent, which she called their *petite chateau*.

Fred was grazing in the thick grass when I nudged the boys off to bed. "Odd day, wasn't it?" I commented, nibbling a bit myself even though I knew that bicycles aren't supposed to eat.

"Mmmph," Fred answered, mouth full.

At Chinon, we were disappointed to discover that bicycles aren't allowed inside the chateau, so Fred and I were locked to a post outside the tall stone walls while our riders went in to sightsee. "Take care of each other and our stuff," Susan said, patting me on the rear.

"Stupid old castle," Fred grumbled, left out.

I shrugged. "Hey, it's a rest." Occasionally, I'd look around to make sure that no one was sneaking up with a knife in his teeth, but mostly I dozed, leaning against the cool wall.

"Look, Daisy!" My eyes popped open to see two brand new bicycles rolling up the hill toward the castle. Fred shook himself, sending dust in a cloud around his frame, then leaned toward the beautiful touring bikes, thin and sleek as needles, clearing his throat self-consciously. "Hello," he said to the girl as soon as their riders walked away. "My name is Fred. How long have you been in France?"

The young bicycle shyly turned her handlebars away. "Two days," the boy bike answered for her, looking curiously at me. "How about you?"

Suddenly conscious of my muddy tires and scratched frame and faded panniers, I stared at him, struck dumb. Shiny and new and unscathed, brand new packs clean and bright red, he was gorgeous. Fred answered for me this time. "We've been in France almost a month," he bragged, "but this is our twelfth week in Europe."

"Oh, goodness." The girl bike looked dutifully impressed. Come on, Fred, I thought, she's just a pretty frame. It's obvious she has no stamina—look how skinny she is!

"We've even been to North Africa," Fred went on, staring at Miss Sweet

Young Thing. "We were threatened with knives there, and people threw rocks and sticks at us!"

"Oh, my!" she exclaimed, all legs and elbows. Oh gag, I thought.

The boy rolled toward me. "Is that true?" he asked softly, eyes bright.

"Actually," I said, preening a bit, "it *was* pretty scary." All of a sudden, my scratches seemed more like battle scars than age and clumsiness, and I felt proud of what I'd accomplished in the last three months.

When Susan and Clarke returned from their sightseeing, they found four bicycles clustered together, jabbering like magpies, comparing war stories and battle plans. The new bikes were New Yorkers, we'd discovered, in France for two weeks of castle tours with a stringent itinerary and hotel reservations for each night—they couldn't believe that we were on a year's sabbatical with no plans at all. "Fred and Daisy definitely need a bath," Susan remarked as she extricated me from the tangle and compared my scruffy appearance with that of our sophisticated new friends.

"Good luck!" I called as we rolled away. The boy bike winked at me, and the girl shyly waggled a handlebar at Fred.

An hour later, the rain bath that Susan had wished for arrived, driving us off the road to the leeward side of an old barn. "I wonder what those bikes will do if bad weather interferes with their itinerary," I said to Fred.

"I was just thinking the same thing," he answered, a little too dreamy. "She sure was pretty, wasn't she?"

"I didn't notice, Fred. *He* was to die for, however." But Fred wasn't listening.

Outside the chateau at Saumur, we met a pair of Germans—people this time—who had a fit when they heard that we were rolling around the countryside unarmed. "Absolutely, under no circumstances, should you camp alone in the forests!" Christa insisted in English. "I can't believe that you've been in Europe three months and haven't been robbed." Susan and Clarke looked at each other. "Here," the woman continued, "take this mace. And you should leave your airline tickets in a safe deposit box somewhere. How will you get home when they are stolen?"

"There's no place to leave them," Susan explained. "We plan to fly out of Munich and have no way to send our tickets there."

Christa sniffed. "Well, please call us if you get to Frankfurt." She made it sound as if we probably wouldn't be alive that long. "Good luck."

"So much for sleeping in the woods, Clarke," Susan said as we left the concerned Germans.

Clarke shrugged. "We've been fine so far," he pointed out. "I don't know why anything should change." While it was certainly true that Susan and Clarke had two watchbikes to look after them, I was unnerved just the same. What did this German woman know that we didn't?

Not far from Saumur, we turned east off the highway onto a tiny road. It was a dead end, however, so we retraced our tracks back toward the highway. Two men stood next to a black car. As usual, Susan greeted them with a friendly wave and a cheerful, *"Bonjour, messieurs!"* The men glared, then yelled something in Arabic that sounded not the least bit friendly or cheerful.

"Whatever they said to you, Susan, I don't like it," Clarke called over his shoulder. I didn't like it either, on any of our accounts, and hurried to close the gap between Fred and me.

I heard the car behind me but couldn't outrun it. Squeezing past, the driver swerved to cut us off, forcing us to stop on the deserted road. The man in the passenger seat yelled something at Clarke, staring at Fred's packs, then at Susan, then at my packs—choosing, I guessed. Should we try to run away? Could Fred and I kick them hard enough to make them leave? Undecided, I didn't do anything but wonder what the men would do when they got tired of Clarke's insisting that he couldn't understand what they were demanding of him in Arabic. I couldn't understand either.

Suddenly, two more cars pulled up behind us, blocking our escape. Reinforcements! I scanned the area for farms or houses, to no avail, and the main highway was out of sight. "Fred, what will we do?" I whispered. He didn't hear me, jostling nervously as Clarke, stalling for time, repeated again in English—who would possibly think to learn to say 'don't rob me!' in a new language—that he didn't understand what the men wanted.

The driver of the car behind me honked his horn impatiently as the men in the first car continued to argue with Clarke. Could it be that these people weren't together? Finally, the driver of the car that had cut us off drove away in a spray of dirt, shouting curses. The other two cars followed, impatient to be on their way. "Get back to the main road, Susan!" Clarke screamed as Fred bolted toward the highway, packs bouncing against his sides.

"Hurry, Daisy!" Fred's voice shook but I didn't need encouragement. Streaking down the dusty road like a race horse, I scrambled straight up a ravine without slowing, struggling through the brambles to the main highway just as the black car, doubling back, passed below, unable to follow up the gully.

I stood shaking, too frightened to move. "Come on!" Clarke yelled. "It'll take those robbers about thirty seconds to drive the long way up to this highway!" Fred, eyes wide, raced off, sweating, and I followed, hoping Susan could hold on.

"Do you think they'd have killed us?" Fred asked that night as our riders visited with a lovely family that had tucked us safely into the back garden of a flour mill that had been converted into a residence.

My wheels were sore from running. I let out a long breath, deciding how to answer. "Not you and me," I said. "We're worth too much money. But I'm not so sure about Susan and Clarke."

"Holy cow," whispered Fred.

"Joy of joys, our first hot water, Clarke!" Susan ran out of a restroom in a small park near Tours late the next morning, and grabbing the soap from my side pack, she and Clarke appropriated the women's restroom to wash. Hair dripping, they plopped down for lunch at a picnic table among several French families, happy as flowers. My, how things change, one minute to the next, I thought, stretching out in the warm sun.

The next day, after another lovely evening with a French family east of Dierre, Fred and I rolled up the long drive to the famous chateau at Chenonceaux. Inside the car parking area was a special place just for bicycles; Susan and Clarke locked us together and walked toward the castle, holding hands.

"Look pretty, Fred." I nudged him half an hour later. "It's your girlfriend from New York."

"Huh?" he said, struggling from sleep.

The shiny bikes were sauntering up the road, sleek and groomed for their royal visit. Embarrassed that I hadn't had a bath since it last rained, I shook off as much road dirt as I could, covering Fred with dust, then called brightly, "Hi, there!"

"I can't believe we've run into you again!" the boy said, touching my front tire with his. The smooth rubber felt like velvet.

"Uh," I answered, flustered.

"Didn't we go two different directions after Chinon?" Fred asked, straining against our cable lock to get closer to the girl.

She batted her eyes before answering. "Why, yes, I think we did," she said, looking deeply into Fred's dirty eyes.

What a phony, I thought. Well, even if she's a Rockefeller, I'm a Rockhopper! I stomped my front tire, then turned to the boy bike and nuzzled him. "Hey," Fred growled under his breath.

"Jealous, Freddy?" I hissed.

After an hour of listening to Fred flirt, I was relieved when Susan and Clarke came back with our sophisticated friends' riders, chatting about where we'd see each other next. Back at the highway, we all waved goodbye; we were going east and they headed west. "See you at Chambord," Susan said anyway.

Chapter 9

A VERY BIZARRE SERIES OF events began with an odd feeling of Susan's. I didn't feel anything; Fred and I were too busy being jealous of the gorgeous bikes from New York. "Something's telling me to stop, Clarke," she said in a strange voice not long after we'd left the castle.

"Huh?" Clarke continued to pedal.

We continued on, maybe a quarter-kilometer. "I mean it, Clarke. Something's going to happen—I can feel it. We're supposed to stop, and stop now!" She was more than serious.

"Let's take a break over there, then," Clarke suggested, bewildered. As they sat on the bus stop bench in silence, Fred looked at me for translation. I shrugged. How would I know?

Finally, Susan spoke. "I have no idea what that was all about, but I feel better now. Let's go. I don't feel like we're in danger anymore, just that someone—or some *thing*—wants to be in control of our actions." Now I began to feel something odd in the air. Fred shook his head in disgust.

After a few kilometers, Clarke said, "I feel it, too. We're going to meet someone." Sighing, Fred rolled his eyes.

"I hope they're friendly," Susan said softly.

Remembering our encounter on the little road north of Saumur, I shivered. "Nagle?" But the spirit dog didn't respond. This was creepy!

We stopped for lunch at a deserted train station near Bourre. Afterwards, Susan packed away the trash, but instead of climbing on my back to continue, sat beside Clarke on a rusty metal bench. "We're not supposed to leave here yet," she said.

"I know," Clarke responded. Now Fred shivered; even he was beginning to feel something weird.

Two hours later, Susan and Clarke stood up. "It's time," they said in unison.

"Stop at the next farm, wherever it is," Clarke called after half an hour on the road. The next farm was surrounded by cars. As we picked our way up the dusty road filled with people, we found ourselves in the middle of a little farmer's market.

"This isn't it, Clarke," Susan said, turning back, then stopped and greeted one couple out of the dozens who walked up the road.

"Where are you going?" the man asked in English.

Susan took a deep breath. How would she know? As far as I knew, anyway, whatever was leading us had neglected to share its plans for our destination. She answered with yesterday's plan. "We were thinking of seeing the chateau at Chambord on our way to Paris."

"Ah," said the man, nodding. "Perfect. Régine and I live thirty-five kilometers from here on the road to Chambord. You must stay with us tonight."

"We can be there in two hours," Susan said happily.

"These people were the ones, weren't they?" Clarke said as we hurried toward Vineuil.

"Yup," she replied, and I finally started breathing again.

At a renovated sixteenth-century monastery, Fred and I were tucked into a garage—joy of joys—after being stripped of our heavy packs. "We had the strongest feeling all day that we were being led to meet someone," Susan said to our hostess as they left the garage.

"We know," the woman answered, shutting the door.

"Susan is weird," Fred said.

"All humans are weird," I responded. But hadn't we felt it, too?

The next morning, Fred and I went without our packs to Chambord, led by Gilles and Régine's son on his own bicycle. Flying through the forest, we chased each other and the French bike, glad to feel slender and lightweight for once. Catching our first glimpse of the giant castle through the trees, however, we staggered, undone. "It's got four hundred and forty rooms," the teenager explained, "and it's only a hunting lodge."

"How could they ever find each other inside?" I asked the French bicycle, amazed. The bike just shrugged philosophically.

Régine was pulling Susan and Clarke's now-dry clothes from the line as we returned to the house a few hours later. "Lunch is ready," she announced.

"Oh, please, no," Susan said. "The fabulous dinner last night was more than generous—and the hot showers and the bed and now our laundry, for heaven's sake. Please, don't do any more!"

"The food is already prepared," said the Frenchwoman, ending the debate. "Besides, the markets are closed. It is a French holiday."

Fred and I lounged in the back yard. Yawning, Fred looked up at the blue sky. "Ah, this is the life, eh, Daisy?"

"It's not bad, Fred, not bad at all." It was noon and we hadn't broken a sweat. Running naked twenty kilometers back and forth from Chambord had been nothing.

Several hours later, we stood patiently while Susan and Clarke packed, all four of us refreshed. "Stay at the Bois de Boulogne campground in Paris," Régine called as we rolled down the drive.

Susan got teary-eyed. "I feel like an orphan," she said to Clarke. "My heart literally aches. What an incredible family!"

"If we hadn't listened to our intuition, we'd never have met them," Clarke replied. "It will be hard to sleep in someone's field tonight after sleeping in a real bed, won't it?"

"Especially since we still have no food and it's a holiday."

"Ouch. And it's already five o'clock. But keep your eyes open, Susie, just in case. We seem to be well taken care of at the moment."

Fred and I rolled down the tiny road just two bicycles wide, not caring one way or the other whether they found a market. After all, since we'd started eating grass, supper was always at our feet. Fred pulled up next to me. "Do you think that something really guided us to those people?" he asked as the tent posts that were packed across my backside caught hold of one of Fred's side packs. "Watch out!" Fred yelped, losing his balance. Over we went, all four of us, with Susan on the bottom.

"Our first accident, and it's with each other," Susan laughed, unscathed. "Not a car in sight! Get off me, you three."

After sorting out our body parts and belongings, we trundled through the wheat fields on a narrow road like a part in a giant head of blond hair. South of Vendome, Clarke pointed to a tower in the distance. "We'll stay there tonight," he declared.

"What is it?" Susan asked.

"I have no idea," Clarke replied. Fred and I looked at each other. We didn't know what it was either.

Later, as we passed the tower, which was behind an old farm, a gray-haired woman pedaled toward us on an old black bicycle. Susan greeted her, as always, and the woman stopped, so we stopped also. From our right, another woman approached on foot, arms full of fresh lettuce.

The women spoke no English, but Clarke tried out his French as three heads popped over a wall across the road. One of the heads spoke a few words of English, so all three joined us in the dusty lane. Then a car stopped and its occupants joined the throng around us. While Susan and Clarke tried to visit with the seven villagers, I chatted in French with the old bicycle and the car.

Susan asked if we could camp at the farm. The lettuce woman, once she understood the request, smiled broadly. "Of course you may sleep in my field," she said in French, laughing, "but you will have to share it with the sheep and the geese and the chickens!"

As the woman led us across the road, I glanced up at the tower where earlier Clarke had announced that we would spend the night. Susan looked at Clarke; it was his turn to shrug.

After the tent was pitched and Fred and I were making friends with the farm animals, a man crossed the yard and stuck two handfuls of ice cream bars into the tent flap. Then another group of villagers marched across the field to invite Susan and Clarke inside for coffee and calvados. "How come nobody ever invites *us* inside?" Fred groused.

"You couldn't talk to them anyway," I pointed out, quite proud of my French.

For hours, laughter and singing floated through the open windows of the French farmhouse, and it was midnight before Susan and Clarke crawled back inside their tent, hands full of eggs and apples for breakfast.

In the morning, after our riders had coffee with half the town, the whole village gathered to see us off. Not used to the attention, Susan fumbled with the tent and my panniers, loading me crooked, then walked arm-in-arm with the lettuce lady across the field. While Susan and Clarke kissed each villager on both cheeks, Fred and I said goodbye to the chickens and geese but, without lips, of course couldn't kiss them; then our riders urged us gently to move on. The villagers, most of them crying, waved until we were out of sight.

Susan and Clarke decided to travel only sixty kilometers that day because of their late start and a leisurely visit to the pretty church at Vendome. Late in the afternoon, as we stopped at an intersection to study the map, a gray Citroën passed, its occupants waving. Stopping briefly up ahead as if to offer help, it continued on down the road and Fred and I rolled slowly after it, feeling lazy and relaxed.

Later, as Susan stopped to check her odometer in front of a large, wooded yard—exactly our goal of sixty kilometers for the day—she noticed a handsome man at the gate who promptly invited us in French for a cold drink. As he opened the gate, we spotted the gray Citroën that had passed us earlier. André had been waiting for us, he explained. Here we go again, I thought.

Sure enough, after beer and wine and mineral water on the patio, Susan and Clarke were given permission to camp in the garden and invited to dinner with the family. "I could get into this lifestyle," I said to Fred after Susan unpacked her long cotton pants from one of my panniers.

"This is certainly gourmet grass," Fred said, chomping the lawn.

"I wonder who will kidnap us next," I said as we rolled out of the driveway after breakfast in the morning.

"Who cares?" Fred answered.

This time, it was an old man. As Fred and Clarke passed the village market, the man ran into the street, staring open-mouthed at the 'U.S.A.' sign on Fred's rear. I almost ran over him, but as I swerved, Susan said, *"Bonjour, monsieur,"* and the man spun around.

"Okay, adios," he replied.

I caught up with Fred at the next intersection. "A man just chased you into the street and yelled 'okay, goodbye' in Spanish," I said.

Just then a battered old car overtook us, then continued slowly out of town, turning left on the road we planned to take. We followed. Finally, it turned onto a dirt road and Fred and I continued on our way. "Wait, Clarke," Susan called, twisting around to see the same man who had chased us into the street, waving his arms. "He wants us to come back."

"Do you want to?" Clarke asked. I don't know about you, Mom, I thought, but I think we've been lucky enough this week.

She ignored me. "I'm curious," she said to Clarke. As she turned me around, the old man got back into his car and led us slowly down the dirt road into the woods, to a tiny shack by a small stream. I signaled to Fred, preparing to bite or kick or whatever bicycles do in order to protect my nutty mother.

The man got stiffly out of his car and shook hands with Clarke and then Susan, motioning them inside the shack without speaking. Susan followed as Fred and I crowded outside the small window to keep an eye on the proceedings.

Gesturing for our riders to sit, the old man pulled a bottle of red wine and three dirty glasses from a tiny cupboard, then sat down carefully on a wooden crate. Ceremoniously, he opened the bottle, and filling the three glasses, still without speaking, raised his in a toast. *"Salut,"* he said, drinking deeply, then poured again, toasting Susan and Clarke.

He started to explain. "Wait," Susan cried. *"Dictionnaire!"* Bounding outside, she pulled her dictionary out of Fred's front pack and raced back inside.

I didn't need translations to understand. The man had been a pilot in World War II, and when his plane crashed over England, the Brits had pulled him from the wreckage, saving his life. Seeing Clarke's 'U.S.A.' sign, he must have decided that this was a chance to acknowledge the kindness that our English cousins had lavished on him almost fifty years earlier. Inviting Susan and Clarke to stay as long as they wanted, he pointed to a small rowboat tied to a willow and placed a rusty tin of sardines on the little table next to the dusty wine bottle, then solemnly shook hands once more and drove slowly down the dirt road back toward town. "I can't believe this," Susan said.

"I can't either." Clarke had tears in his eyes.

Fred and I just shook our heads and flopped down in the dust for a three-hour nap while Susan caught up on her writing and Clarke floated down the river in the rowboat.

That night, a church bell rang as we crossed a tiny road to a house. "This is it," Susan said, turning me into the drive.

This time, a tiny old man offered tent space in the grass, lettuce from his garden for dinner, oil and homemade vinegar and a large chunk of fresh bread—and in the morning, coffee and calvados with his daughter-in-law at the kitchen table for Susan and Clarke while Fred and I slept in. Boy, did we love France!

Chapter 10

"I HOPE SUSAN AND CLARKE decide to stay in Paris a few days," I said to Fred as we neared the city.

"Me, too," Fred agreed. "A little grazing and sunbathing while those two sightsee will be *superb*." He used the French pronunciation. "If I recall, we had our tour of Gay Paree three months ago." Although our hair-raising race through the city during rush hour after our arrival in Europe seemed like years ago, I remembered every moment of it.

"Look, Fred! The Seine!" The famous river led us toward Paris, afternoon sun sparking off the water like tiny smiles.

We found the campground late in the afternoon. Adjacent to the giant Bois de Boulogne park, it was perfect. "Did you see any markets nearby?" Clarke asked Susan as they constructed their tent for the zillionth time.

"*Non, monsieur*, but I'm pretty tired tonight after all those midnight visits. Do you think we could find an inexpensive restaurant?"

"Probably not, but what the heck. After all, Paris is supposed to have the best food in the world. I guess we shouldn't miss it."

After washing their faces, they locked us to a tree and walked off arm-in-arm, leaving Fred and me in charge of all of their worldly goods. "If somebody tries to steal Clarke's camera out of the tent," Fred whispered, "how am I going to get loose to attack them?"

"Mmm," I said, eyes droopy. If it wouldn't do any good to watch, why stay awake?

In the morning, Susan and Clarke bustled together a quick breakfast while Fred and I made our own lazy plans for the day. Then Clarke popped out of the tent and attached his camera to Fred's backside. Fred looked stricken. "Daisy! What's he doing?"

Susan unhitched me and swung her leg over my back. No way, Mom, I said, scooting sideways; I refuse to tangle with Paris traffic again. Absolutely not. No, thanks anyway, no. Fred argued with Clarke, with zippo results, and off we went toward the campground entrance. I gave it one last try. Who's going to guard your stuff in the tent, Mom? "Cripes," I said to Fred when we didn't turn back.

"Cripes," he agreed.

"I can't wait to see the Eiffel Tower," said Clarke.

"And pedal down the Champs Élysées," Susan added.

Grumbly, we set off through the Bois de Boulogne, hungrily eyeing the rich, fancy grass. Our hearts had been set on a gourmet picnic while Susan and Clarke were at the Louvre, so we'd had only a mouthful of coarse campground grass for breakfast.

Fred and I were still snarly when we rolled under the Eiffel Tower. "The whole thing looks like it's made of wire," Clarke decided, amazed.

Susan consulted a guidebook. "It weighs seven thousand tons."

"Who cares?" Fred muttered.

But by the time we had lunch in a park—the grass was pretty wonderful, even Fred had to admit—we were all ready for a little more sightseeing. "Time for the Champs-Élysées," Susan announced.

Without our heavy packs, Fred and I darted in and out of traffic like thin little racing bikes as Susan called out the names of the buildings and monuments. At the Louvre, we circled back around for a dash to the Arc de Triomphe, the famous arch that sits like a hole in a phonograph record in the center of twelve streets that spike out from its edge like the rays of the sun. "Where are you going?" I yelled as Clarke pedaled Fred like an old-fashioned phonograph needle onto the outer edge of the asphalt disk.

"To the middle!" Fred called back, eyes huge.

"No!" I screamed, but he couldn't hear me above the sound of honking horns. Deciding that we needed to be there to pick up their pieces, Susan and I followed, at least one of us with closed eyes, maybe both.

Around and around we went, dodging through vehicles that gave us just enough room to slip through, until we reached the arch in the middle. Clarke, who's an artist, leisurely examined the sculptures along the faces of the arch, oblivious of the rest of us eyeing with alarm the swarm of traffic circling our island of safety like sharks. "Ready?" Clarke asked calmly after a few minutes.

"Absolutely not," replied Fred.

"Does it make any difference?" Susan asked. Unwilling to live the rest of our lives at the Arc de Triomphe, I followed Fred back through the speeding cars to the edge and spun off onto a street, surprised to be alive.

"That was fun!" Fred decided.

"Maybe," I conceded after my heart rate slowed.

For five days, Fred and I escorted our riders through the streets of Paris, each day starting with an invigorating dash through the traffic circle at the Arc de Triomphe. By the time we left the city, we were masters in the art of Parisian road racing, ready for the Tour d'France. Day six, however, was another story, as our slim little bodies were once again padded with heavy panniers. Our broad beams crowded the cars driving along the Seine, and I kept listing to the left. By the time we got up the hill to Versailles, Susan and Clarke were both huffing and puffing even though they'd pedaled at least thirty kilometers a day in Paris.

As they shared a baguette of fresh bread on a park bench in front of the palace, Fred and I rested against the curb, too tired to eat, then Susan called her sister. After the briefest of greetings, all I could hear was a great deal of mumbly buzzing at the other end of the line. Susan's eyes got bigger and bigger, then there was silence. Finally, she said, "Are you sure?" More buzzing. "How far can they bicycle?" Buzz, mumble. Sigh from Susan, then, "Tell Kelly they'll have to ride at least thirty miles a day by the time they arrive." Buzz. "Teenagers would probably hate this trip. We sleep on the ground every night, you know, and wash in rivers. Pedaling eight to eleven hours every day is no picnic." Buzz-buzz. "If they're sure," Susan replied reluctantly, then rang off and we gathered around. "My niece and her best friend are meeting us in London for ten weeks of bicycling," she announced.

"It will make things more complicated," Clarke replied, "but we'll manage."

"Kelly and Megan can bicycle only eight miles a day."

"Uh-oh," Clarke revised his enthusiasm.

Fred and I stood tied together outside the palace wall as our riders went inside, deep in conversation. "What do you think, Fred?" I asked when they were out of earshot.

"If those bikes can't do more than eight miles a day, they must be girls," he sneered. Then, after a moment of thought, "Hmm, I wonder if they're cute."

"C'mon, Fred," I snapped, "don't be a chauvinist. The issue here is not extra-curricular anyway. We've got big plans for this summer—England, Scotland, Denmark, Belgium, Holland, Germany and Austria, all before the weather gets bad." Feeling up to anything after my Paris road racing class, I wasn't pleased about having to train two infant bicycles, boys or girls, no matter how cute they were.

We had eleven days to get from Paris to London. Anxious to cover as many kilometers as possible before having to cut back for two new bicycles, Fred and I hurried along, hour after hour, enjoying each other and the French countryside immensely.

One night, after a horrendously long day, Clarke for some reason rejected a dinner invitation with a wonderful young family whose children thought Fred and I were the neatest things they'd ever seen, and we ended up in a field of long wet grass next to a cow pasture. Fred and I fell asleep against the pasture fence, too tired to care that our riders hadn't unloaded us. Just before dawn, a cow nose woke me up, slobbering and nibbling at my packs. A whole row of them leaned against the fence, watching Fred and me with soft brown eyes.

Later that day, Susan was attacked. After hours of cold wind and rain, Clarke chose a farm built around a courtyard, hoping the owners would allow the tent inside the walls for a windbreak. As I trotted up the drive, attempting to look friendly, a white streak caught my eye.

"Ouch!" said Susan, looking down. Standing at her right foot was a fuzzy white dog, staring up. "Why did you do that?" Susan asked gently. "I wouldn't hurt you." The furry culprit that had bitten her wagged its tail uncertainly as blood oozed out of the back of Susan's knee.

I growled, baring my own teeth; then the dog licked Susan's extended hand in apology. "Daisy, be nice," Susan warned. "He was just doing his job."

I wasn't mollified but couldn't do anything further because the dog's owners rushed out of the house, apologizing profusely for its manners. The woman took Susan inside and washed her wound, but they wouldn't let us stay in the courtyard; I couldn't tell whether they were afraid that Susan would get bitten again or that Fred and I would bite back. Instead, we slept in their hay field down the road, where we were attacked all night by wind and rain instead of dogs.

The next night, we had much better luck. At a pretty white house with its own pond, Susan and Clarke were offered tent space and drinks on the patio while Fred and I made friends with Jo and Pierre's much nicer white dog, Stasi, whom we called *petite mouton*, or little sheep.

Drinks extended to dinner, then breakfast in the morning, and then lunch. "Do you know what they're eating?" Stasi asked as Fred and I happily nibbled around the pond.

I shrugged. "Probably wine."

"No, silly, *cheval.*"

"What's that?" I asked, not really listening.

"Horse."

I stopped chewing. "No, no. You are wrong. Susan would never eat a horse." Would she? "Fred!" I called, trotting off with the bad news as Stasi barked with laugher.

It was our last day in France, and except for people eating pack animals, I would be sorry to leave the country, particularly since our next project would be dealing with the youngsters from America. That evening, while a French engineer and his family fixed dinner for Susan and Clarke, Fred and I rolled in the grass. I stood up and shook, then asked Fred, "Did you like France?"

"*Oo-la-la,*" he said, rolling his eyes and trying unsuccessfully to kiss his fingertips, "the grass was *magnifique!*"

During seven weeks in France, we'd traveled over 2500 kilometers; for the whole trip, almost 5000 kilometers or 3000 miles. We'd been in Europe fifteen weeks.

Chapter 11

Lashed to the ferry's hold with ropes, Fred and I huddled next to the transport trucks as the ship lurched across the English Channel. "These guys are giants," I said to Fred, looking up at a hubcap on the truck closest to me. "Excuse me. Hey, you up there! Hello!"

The truck turned its head, round eyes staring. "You talking to me, luv?"

"Uh-huh," I said, stretching my neck to look taller. "I just wondered if you and your friends would try not to step on us going up the ramp."

"No problem, ducks. Glad you called it to my attention. You do look a bit like big mosquitoes at first glance."

"Trust me, I hate them as much as you," I huffed, offended.

After the ferry docked, dozens of trucks started their engines. The noise was terrifying. "Easy, Daisy," Susan said, stroking my handlebars.

"You first, mates," a uniformed worker motioned us to the front of the line, and I glanced behind my shoulder at the fire-breathing dragon that had been next to me, black smoke billowing above its head.

It winked its headlight. "Go on, luv. We won't hurt you." It gave me a little nudge. "Atta girl!"

Fred and I raced up the ramp, followed by swarms of trucks and cars whose drivers honked at us and waved, careful to give us a wide berth. My new big friend tooted its horn as the Customs officer directed Fred and me to the front of the line.

"Welcome to England," a rosy-cheeked woman said from her glass booth, pencil poised to take notes. "How long will you stay?"

"We don't know," Clarke answered.

"What cities will you be visiting, luvs?"

"We don't know that either."

"What address will be your home base while you're here?"

"Our tent," Susan said.

The woman chuckled, giving up. "Well, have a pleasant visit," she said, waving us on.

"I guess she decided that if we do anything illegal, it won't be hard to catch us," Susan said as we rolled into Dover.

"We certainly can't steal anything very big."

"Wrong, Clarke. I'm going for a refrigerator if I go for anything." Don't you dare, Mom!

We reached Dover along with the rain, huddling under the eaves of a bookstore while Clarke bought a map of the area. "This will be fun," Clarke groaned as they crowded next to us under the roof. "The roads in England look like spaghetti."

"So which strand do we follow out of here?" Susan asked, peering over his shoulder.

"Let me find an end first," he replied, tracing with his finger a pattern backward from Gatwick Airport.

"Left, Fred, left!" I screamed as he veered to the wrong side of the road again. Traffic was heavy, and Clarke was so busy trying to understand the squiggly map that he let Fred roll along on his own, which was a rotten idea.

The roundabouts confused us both because the lane we needed to be in for our spin-off onto another road seemed to always be the fast lane, and we weaved and wobbled uncertainly from the right side of the unmarked lanes to the left and from one lane to another. To make matters worse, it was raining hard, making us all squint, and the cars splashed water on us up to our bellies.

Somehow, we managed to get out of Dover and onto a road that hopefully pointed toward London, spending our first night at a farm but getting lost again the next morning. Fred and I headed toward a small village, looking for someone to help with directions. "Hello!" Susan said to a man who was washing a car in his driveway. "We're lost."

"You sound lost," he said, chuckling, no doubt referring to her American accent. "I'll give you directions if you'll join us for tea. It's going to rain, you know."

Susan and Clarke popped into the house for tea and biscuits while Fred and I leaned against the house and watched the clouds gather into a storm, like a fist. Although tea time came and went, no one came outside. Then it began to rain. "I wish someone would invite *us* in out of the weather," Fred complained, water dripping from his handlebars.

I shrugged. "We're probably too wide to fit in the door even if they did, ducks." Flopping ungracefully on my stomach, unable to roll onto my side because of my heavy packs, I tried to get comfortable enough for a nap. Fred was already snoring.

Hours later, the back door banged and Fred and I each opened an eye as our riders came outside with the Englishman. "You must go through Canterbury," the man was explaining. "You're in Shepherdswell now, in case you didn't know." We didn't, I was sure. "Go straight on to Woolage Green and then either right then left to Womenswold or left, right, left to Womenswold. Then right and another right with an immediate left to Aylesham."

"We'll keep asking," Susan laughed. "And thank you for lunch. It's a bit cold and damp today, you know." Indeed. "May we refill our water bottles?" she asked as I struggled upright, stiff and wet.

"Here, let me," the man offered, then looked inside them. "No, no, this won't do. Won't do at all. Eileen," he called, trailing inside to confer with his wife.

She met him at the back door. "They're positively green inside," she said. "What did you do to them?"

Susan and Clarke looked inside the bottles. "Mold," Susan said. "Yuck."

"Why aren't their teeth green?" Fred asked.

"Let me soak them in baking soda for a bit," Eileen suggested, and Fred and I were left out in the rain again for another hour.

"Should we bother to get up?" Fred asked when the back door opened again.

"Beats me," I answered, but lunged to my feet.

"If you come back this way, please come see us," Eileen said as Susan and Clarke added full water bottles to our burden.

"We may be back for dinner," Susan laughed, "if we can't find our way out of town."

Six kilometers and one village later, we were lost again. A pretty woman stood on a grassy town square. "Excuse me," Clarke said. "Is this the way to Womenswold?"

"Turn left," she smiled. "But first, come home with me for tea."

Fred sighed. "Think of it this way, luvy," I pointed out. "Wouldn't you rather stand under a tree than be out in the rain? Look at the sky." Sure enough, no sooner had Susan and Clarke gone into the woman's house than the clouds turned into a waterfall.

Our riders didn't come out of this house until morning. "How far did we get yesterday?" Clarke asked as he swung his leg over Fred.

Susan consulted her little journal. "Eleven kilometers."

"When in doubt, turn left," their hostess called as we rolled off into light rain.

All day, we bumped around the little roads like pinballs, reaching Canterbury almost by chance late in the afternoon. "Let's see if we can find some better maps," Clarke suggested as we passed a bookstore.

"What we need are better roads," Susan grumbled, following him inside. Fred and I leaned against the stone wall outside the shop, taking care not to step on the pigeons that hopped around our feet.

Susan came outside to wait with us a few minutes later. Suddenly, an old lady with thin white hair floating around her head trotted up, eyes sparking with anger. "Are those your bicycles, young lady?"

"Yes, ma'am," Susan answered, looking at me to see what mischief I'd gotten into while she was inside.

"How dare you!" the woman snarled. "They're in the way of the pigeon food I scattered."

Fred and I looked down at our feet. As far as we could see, the birds didn't seem the least inconvenienced by our presence as they happily pecked at the food scattered on the ground. Honest, Mom, we didn't touch them. Apologizing profusely, Susan tried to coax Fred away from his wall just as Clarke came out of the store. "What are you doing?" he snapped.

"Hush, Clarke, he's standing in the pigeons' dinner," Susan explained, nodding toward the tiny woman who continued to glare, hands on her hips, chin jutting forward, absolutely furious.

We couldn't even get out of Canterbury without getting lost. Once, Fred cut in front of a car in a roundabout and almost got run over. "Watch it!" Susan and I screamed. "If you're getting off at the next road, Clarke, stay on the left—don't get in the middle and then cut across all the other cars!" she continued, frightened. I was scared, too—big as Fred was with all his packs, he'd looked awfully small compared to the speeding car.

As we trotted out of town, it started to rain again. Half an hour later, holed up under a tree during a cloudburst, Susan turned to Clarke. "I think you're going the wrong way."

"Fine. You find our way then, since you seem to know everything today." Fred and I looked at each other.

Susan led us to a dead end. "At least I admit it when I'm wrong," she said sarcastically, referring for the umpteenth time to the roundabout.

South of Maidstone, on Gravelly Bottom Road, we found a neat house with a beautiful garden. The hard rain had finally stopped; we were down to drizzle, and Fred and I at least were more than grateful. Susan and Clarke were still snarly.

"Here?" Clarke asked, nodding toward the house.

"I don't care."

The white-haired owner showed us a nice spot in the garden for the tent, then offered showers to Susan and Clarke. "I'll be right in," Susan answered gratefully.

"No, thanks," Clarke said sullenly. "I'm hungry," he complained after the Englishman went inside

"So cook while I shower," Susan retorted. "You don't need an audience."

Fred and I cringed. We didn't automatically take sides in Susan and Clarke's fusses anymore—most of the time when they argued, both of them were being stupid—and we rolled a few yards away from the tent. Susan left with a sigh, then returned in ten minutes, wet hair wrapped in their dirty towel. "I've accepted an invitation for tea after dinner."

"Without consulting me?"

"I'll go alone, then. Their company is better than yours anyway."

They tromped off through the grass after dinner, not speaking, and Fred and I stood close together for warmth, glad that we no longer felt that we had to be mad when our riders were. Later, Susan and Clarke rolled us to the garage without a word to each other, finally stripping off our wet packs. Ignoring our owners, the two of us leaned contentedly against a workbench, happily listening to the rain instead of being in it for a change.

In the morning, apparently still peeved, Susan opened the big door of the garage as our host came outside. "Surely you're not leaving yet?" he asked with alarm. "I've called all the bicycle shops in Maidstone and think I've found the parts your husband needs." Fred had been breaking spokes right and left, for some reason. "I'll drive you there. Please." Then shyly, "Winnie is already cooking breakfast."

Fred and I settled back down for an extra snooze as rain pelted the roof of the garage. "Thanks for breaking your spokes, ducks," I said to him, yawning.

"Easy for you to say, Daisy." Fred rearranged himself into a more comfortable position. "You're not the one with a wobbly foot."

The garage door opened again just before lunch. "Let me help you fix your bike, son," the old Englishman offered eagerly. Clarke hesitated. "It's raining," the man added, as if it hadn't been raining all week.

Ken and Clarke handled the minor surgery on Fred in a flash, then trundled inside for lunch. When everybody returned, Susan and Clarke were finally speaking to each other again. "Thank heavens," Fred whispered to me.

"No kidding," I agreed.

Although our bicycling day didn't start until after lunch, a whole afternoon of being doused by English rain was more than enough. By the time we waded through a muddy pasture at a dairy farm about five o'clock, we were all a little testy. Susan and Clarke untied only the packs they'd need from our dripping frames, then covered the other soaked panniers with what was left of their tattered orange rain jackets. It wasn't much. "Do you think we'll get to the airport in time to meet the other bikes?" Fred asked.

"I don't know," I replied. "I guess it depends on how many tea parties Susan and Clarke attend from here to there."

All night, Fred and I huddled in the cold rain with Nagle and the spirit ark, trying unsuccessfully to shield each other and our belongings from the deluge. In the morning, Clarke crawled out of the tent into a cloudburst. "Why don't you stay here and write, Susie, while I bicycle into town and find a laundromat?"

"Don't get lost," I called to Fred as he picked his way across the slimy cow pasture a few minutes later. It felt funny to be separated. I didn't like it. Exasperating as he was sometimes, Fred was my buddy and I relied on him for moral support and conversation, particularly when Susan and Clarke were being snitty.

Half an hour later, our hostess sprinted across the pasture from the house, huddled under a big umbrella, inviting Susan inside. Hunched over her laptop to keep it dry, Susan hurried through the cow dung and disappeared into the warm house, leaving me alone to guard the tent. But who would want it? I couldn't imagine anyone camping in English rain on purpose.

By the time everybody returned, the troops were at war again. "I can't believe that you didn't pack the tent while I was gone," Clarke complained.

He was pulling on a pair of new waterproof pants. "Did you buy some for me?" Susan asked hopefully.

"Of course not. I'd never pick out clothes for you."

It rained harder and harder with each hour on the road, and got colder and colder. As we neared London, the traffic got worse and worse. Trucks and cars, unable to pull out around us on the crowded roads, drenched us with waves of muddy water. It was almost impossible to see, and Fred and I waded along in silence, eyes squinched. Every now and then, we'd pull up under a tree during a new cloudburst, but the break was purely psychological; we were already as wet and cold as we could get. "I've had enough," Susan said near East Grinstead. Looking jealously at Clarke's waterproofed legs, she wiped rain from her bare thighs as effectively as if she were submerged in a swimming pool.

In a little settlement of large stone houses set deep in the woods, Susan spotted a spectacular garden after we'd rolled up and down the little lanes without finding anything inviting. "If there's a house at the end of this drive," she suggested, "let's try here."

There was, and we swam to the front door, streaming water. When it opened, Susan said, "I have no idea how we found your house or how to get back out to the main road, but may we put a tent in your yard tonight?" Fred and I huddled together, looking as pitiful as we could. It wasn't hard.

"I'll help you find a nice place in the garden," the woman answered. "Let me get an umbrella." Get four more, will you, I suggested silently. Jackie led us around the back, to a garden shed. "You can sleep here out of the rain," she offered, moving a large bag of plant food to one side. Thank you, thank you, Fred and I said.

An elderly woman trundled out under a big, black umbrella. "Listen, luvs, my name is Win and you both look horrid. Come inside and take a nice hot shower, both of you." Susan's eyes lit up in gratitude. "If would be very nice," she continued shyly, "if you would join my daughter Jackie and me for dinner." She looked at Clarke hopefully. "Do say yes."

As our riders sprinted into the house, Fred and I shook off as much rain as we could, wishing we could wring each other out, then flopped down on the floor of the shed, scattering the ark among bags of seed and garden tools. Fred sneezed, then fell asleep instantly. I was tired but couldn't sleep, worrying about Susan and Clarke's grumpiness, about how the two new bicycles would do in the rain, about catching cold. Nagle snuggled next to me.

Later, I saw a light go on over the back door of the house and tiptired to the window as Jackie came outside to put a plate of sandwiches on the steps. Within seconds, a red fox peeked her head around the corner of the house, then trotted to the plate, bushy tail straight out in back, and grabbed a mouthful of sandwiches. Scampering back the way she came, she dropped a sandwich in the grass as she hurried to deliver dinner to her babies, whose tiny heads I could see peeking over the flowers at the edge of the garden.

Chapter 12

F RED AND I FIDGETED outside the passenger terminal at Gatwick Airport. It took forever for Susan and Clarke to retrieve Susan's sixteen-year-old niece Kelly and her friend Megan, along with two flat boxes similar to the ones we'd flown in across the ocean. I sniffed the edges, trying to decide what the bicycles inside might be like. They smelled of clean metal and new rubber.

When the boxes were opened, introductions were made all around, then Fred supervised Clarke's attaching pedals and handlebars to our new protégées, who looked clumsy as newborn foals and as innocent. "Aren't they cute?" Fred whispered, turning to me as Kelly's bicycle struggled to stand on her own next to the curb.

"Ask me again after we've nudged them down the road a piece, ducky," I replied, not nearly as enamored with the new bikes but knowing that I'd have to make the best of the situation.

Megan's bike stood next to the curb, wobbly and nervous. I sniffed her tentatively, and when Clarke fastened one of her pedals too tightly, I nudged his hand until he loosened it. "Thank you," Megan's bike said sweetly, eyes sparkly with wonder, clearly overwhelmed. My heart softened, just a bit, as I remembered how scary it had been to arrive in Europe. At least this time we weren't in the middle of a hurricane!

The teenaged riders weren't overwhelmed at all; bright and shiny with new clothes and stylish haircuts, they chattered in admirable imitation British accents as they packed their panniers on the curb. "How far can you bicycle now?" Susan asked when she could get a word in.

"Twenty-five miles yesterday!" Kelly replied proudly. Clarke looked up from Megan's bicycle, surprised and pleased, and Fred and I glanced at each other, equally delighted. Tough little pips, I decided, then felt a bit jealous of their eagerness.

"Mail, madam." Kelly tossed Susan a big brown envelope.

Susan fell ravenously on the envelope, hugging it tightly. "I'll save it for tonight. Did our first packet ever get returned?"

"Nope. Here's your peanut butter, Clarke." Kelly extricated two four-pound cans as big as oil drums.

"Oh, my gosh, how will we carry all that?"

"That's your problem," she laughed, then turned to Susan. "You wanted M&M's? Catch!"

Two huge bags flew through the air. "These will definitely be gone before I'm tired of carrying them," Susan announced.

"Mother made you some of her world-famous brownies," Kelly said, her head in a box.

As candy bags and peanut butter drums flew back and forth across the sidewalk, Fred and I talked quietly with the new bicycles, both Treks like Fred, testing their mettle. They seemed more than willing to do what it would take to keep up, particularly Megan's bike, who positively wiggled with excitement. "What's your name?" Fred asked her.

"Betsy. And this is Zelda," she nodded toward Kelly's bike, who was trying to answer my questions and stare at Fred at the same time.

Next to these sweet young things, I looked like a battered old plow horse. Why did Fred's scars make him look more noble, more capable, more mature? "That's okay, Daisy," Susan said as if reading my mind. "These two babies have lots to learn, don't they?" She patted my rear and turned to Kelly. "Did you sleep on the plane?"

"Nope. Or the night before, either. We were too excited."

"Great. Your first day of bicycling is on the left side of the road, into London, and you're half asleep. Well, you'll be fine if you pay attention—your parents will be more than a bit upset, ducks, if you get run over on your first day."

Clarke strapped the eight pounds of peanut butter on Fred's head where the wine jug normally was, and we trotted off in single file, Fred leading like a general, peanut-butter helmet held high, followed by Betsy and then Zelda. Susan and I brought up the rear, like a pair of dumpy old sheepdogs herding cute little lambs.

Once off the main highway, the youngsters raced ahead, Kelly and Megan screaming and laughing and telling jokes in their best British accents. "Adrenaline does wonders," I said to Fred.

"We're not there yet," he pointed out.

"Hey, you guys, thanks for the sunshine," I hollered. "This is the first day it hasn't rained since we left France."

As the afternoon wore on, so did the newcomers. The laughter and singing stopped, and the young bikes panted up the long hills like the rest of us, sun burning their backs. Fred was back in the lead, with Betsy close behind—was Megan trying to keep up with Clarke, or her bike with his?

On another long, steep hill, Zelda began to lag. "Take a break if you need to," I suggested. "Susan does it all the time." Finally, Kelly pulled Zelda to a stop, and they both glared ahead at Megan and Betsy, who rode like a pair of Mary Poppinses, pert and perky, crowding Clarke and Fred.

"I thought England was flat," Zelda ground out between her gears.

"Nowhere is flat," I replied. "Trust me."

By the time we got to the outskirts of London, Betsy was worn out also. Naturally, based on our luck in big cities, it was rush hour. Fred and I weren't used to trailing through heavy traffic with two other bicycles, and we kept getting separated at stoplights as we wove in and out of bus lanes. "You have to keep track of us, Fred," I complained when we found a market for groceries. "If the rear end of this mule train misses a light, we have no idea where you're going. Clarke has the only map."

"Just keep up, Daisy. It's too dangerous for me to turn around to count noses."

"We try, but four bikes take awhile to get through a light in this traffic. Just make sure that Betsy gets through, then she can keep track of Zelda, then Zelda can watch for me, okay?"

On the last hill to the campground, Zelda tripped, dumping Kelly onto the sidewalk, but we finally herded the bicyclists into Susan and Clarke's tent to cook supper and then lined up the transportation team one after the other along the fence. Fred sandwiched himself between the two youngsters, of course, and I stayed on the end, a little apart. "Not as good as in France," Fred announced after ripping up a big mouthful of the dusty grass, chewing noisily.

"It's gauche to talk with your mouth full, Fred," I snapped, irritated at his pretending to be a connoisseur for the little fillies. Refusing to roll in the grass in case I might look clumsy to these delicate creatures, I let the sweat dry on my back and ended up itching all night.

For three days, I watched Fred flirt with Betsy and Zelda while our owners toured London on foot. From morning to night, it seemed, he bragged about our experiences—somehow, he always ended up being the hero, rescuing me and our riders from one peril after another, single-handedly. Betsy and Zelda soaked up his words like sponges. Oh gag, I thought, but decided not to lower myself to his level by setting the record straight.

Clarke had unilaterally decided to let Kelly and Megan—presumably with input from their bicycles—choose our route for the whole summer. Susan and I hated the idea, but Fred was so taken with Betsy and Zelda that he would have followed them anywhere, with the possible exception of Morocco again.

The teenagers agreed on four weeks in England and Scotland, one week each in France, Belgium and Holland, and three weeks in Germany because Kelly was studying the language. "I know you've already spent seven weeks in France," Megan had pleaded, "but I've taken five years of French and I'm dying to hear it spoken." Susan and I had our hearts set on flat Denmark—the last thing we wanted to do was go back to France—but it wasn't to be.

"We loved France," Clarke assured Megan. "Whatever you two choose is fine with us. So. What would you like to see in England?"

"Stonehenge, Sherwood Forest, and Brontëland," came the replies in quick succession.

"The Cotswolds are beautiful," Susan said, giving in but not quite giving up, "and they're on our way to Stonehenge."

Chapter 13

ETTING EIGHT OF US down the road with any precision was more than twice as hard as four. Strung out one by one on the narrow highways, we were more of a hazard to motorists, and while it was easy to communicate with the bicycle just ahead or behind, for Fred and me to talk was impossible because he was always first, leader of the expedition, and I was always last, keeping an eye out for stragglers. Betsy still trotted behind Fred like a tail as he sailed along faster than usual. Zelda complained bitterly about whose fault it was every time her derailleur chain fell off.

We were on our way to Stonehenge, our first day out from London, when Susan stopped to help Megan with a gear problem. Everything adjusted, we hurried to catch up with the others, then came to a fork in the road. "Which way?" asked Betsy.

"I have no idea," I answered. "Clarke's got the map. I guess we'll have to wait for them to come back after they discover we're missing."

"What if they don't?"

"Don't worry. I'm carrying the food."

Glad for a break, Betsy and I rested while Susan and Megan peered off into the distance, looking for the other half of our crew. I wasn't worried—surely Fred would notice sooner or later that he'd lost half of his audience. Betsy, however, seemed a bit hurt that Fred could run off and leave her so easily; after all, she'd been his shadow since her arrival. I was more callous on that subject; because Betsy and Zelda were twins, the same model and year, why should he prefer one to the other? At that point, of course, caught up in their perfectly matched youth and beauty, I wasn't aware that the two had distinctly different personalities. As it turned out, they were as different as night and day, like most twins.

"There they are!" Megan finally shouted, pointing out two dots moving in our direction along the edge of the road's right fork. Betsy scrambled up eagerly, eyes bright.

"Where have you been?" Clarke yelled as we met them halfway. Betsy tried to nuzzle Fred's side while Zelda glared at her; but Fred ignored them both, as irritated as Clarke that he'd had to come back.

"What happened to watching out for the person behind?" I asked. "Zelda, you should have noticed when Betsy disappeared, at least where the road forked."

"I was too busy trying to keep up with Fred." Sighing, I took my place at the end of the line and nudged everybody forward.

Susan and Clarke had worried about whether it would be harder to get permission to camp for a double helping of Americans, but Mark and Sarah seemed happy to have us. After supervising the tent construction, I wandered to the edge of the field, needing quiet for my own thoughts.

The youngsters had done beautifully today, traveling eighty kilometers—almost fifty miles—in hot, muggy weather. But the constant rubbing of eight personalities was stressful—none of us knew where we fit with the rest of the group, but I hoped that when we got to know each other, we'd be able to stop trying so hard. For now, I decided, to heck with company behavior. Plopping down in the soft grass, I wiggled and rolled, scratching my back, spokes waving in the air like pinwheels. It felt so good that I didn't care how ungainly I looked.

In the morning, the teenagers were ready before Susan and Clarke. "How about some help here?" Clarke asked, and soon we were almost buttoned up. "Go see if Mark and Sarah will let you fill our water bottles," he requested of Megan.

"Me?"

"Sure. Susan and I asked for the camping spot last night. It's your turn."

Kelly and Megan returned in a flash, arms filled with full water bottles. "They didn't mind at all," they reported happily, smug in their victory.

"Asking is much more interesting in a foreign language," Susan reminded them. "Enjoy English while you can."

After lunch, Megan and Kelly spotted an old church that they wanted to photograph, and Fred and I let the twins escort them alone while we leaned against each other to visit without two child bikes clamoring to be noticed. I sensed that although Fred loved the attention, it sometimes got old—maybe he missed the easy comfort of our established friendship. As he ripped up some grass for an afternoon snack, I looked over my shoulder to make sure the youngsters were out of earshot before I made any comment.

They were turning down a side road. As soon as they rounded the corner, Betsy and Zelda moved automatically to the right-hand side of the road. Their riders didn't notice, and as Megan turned around to say something to Kelly, who was laughing, a car headed straight toward them.

Susan saw it, too. "Move over!" she and I screamed. "You're on the wrong side of the road!" Kelly and Zelda swerved to the left without looking, cutting off a car that had just come up behind them. As both cars swerved to narrowly miss the two bicycles and each other—a tricky feat—I gaped in horror. Fred stood open-mouthed, grass hanging from his muzzle. Clarke closed his eyes.

Susan was furious. "You could have been killed!" she shouted when they returned a few minutes later, pedaling carefully on the left side of the road, the twins white as sheets, which was astounding for two bicycles. "Megan, did you remember the permission letter from your mother? Without it, if you'd been hurt, Clarke and I would have no authority to arrange for treatment."

"We'll be fine," Megan answered breezily, apparently oblivious to the close call.

"I'm sure you will, ladies," Susan said icily, "but accidents do happen."

"Quit treating us like children," Kelly snarled.

Susan sighed. "You two are not adults, like it or not. If you want to be treated like adults, however, then act like adults." The girls glared at each other, majorly irritated, and their young bicycles looked embarrassed. Come on, everybody, I said in my mind, let's get on with the day.

"I'm ready to quit," Kelly said late in the afternoon, wilting over her handlebars.

"Megan, can you go farther?" Clarke asked.

"Sure," she said, not overly enthusiastic. Betsy, I noticed, looked exhausted. "Susan?"

"Of course." I wondered whether Susan really meant it or just didn't want to be outcycled by Megan. If so, I understood—if Betsy could go farther, by gum, so could I! We went farther.

Nobody seemed to want us that night. One man even had the audacity to suggest that we couldn't camp in this yard because he had rare plants in his garden—did he think we'd eat them, or what? Come to think of it, I did notice a greedy look on Fred's face as he inventoried the man's foliage. "Let's try this house across the street before we give up," Susan suggested. Zelda groaned at the prospect of having to cross the road, let alone roll a few more kilometers to the next village.

Our riders straggled to the door of the quaint little house, dirty, tired and dejected. An elderly woman, tiny as a tick, answered their tentative knock. "Yes, I think that would be all right," she said to their request, then hesitated and added, "but let me check with my husband." She returned in a moment. "Would you mind waiting outside for a few minutes? My son is on his way over, and I'd like to make sure he thinks it's all right."

Goodness, did we look like bandits? As far as I was concerned, anyway, I couldn't have been a getaway vehicle at the moment if my life depended on it, and I knew that at least Zelda and probably Betsy felt the same way. Fred, of course, still had a few miles in him. The eight of us waited on the curb until we'd passed muster with the son—but our tiny hostess made the wait more than endurable, for the bicyclists at least, with a tray of tea, English style, with milk and sugar. "What about us?" Zelda groaned.

"Hush," I replied. "We're bicycles, silly. We don't drink tea." Or at least I didn't think so.

In the morning, we learned from the woman—whose husband had died ten months earlier but she was too afraid of us to admit it until she'd survived the night unmolested—that her neighbors' hesitation resulted from the summer solstice celebrations at nearby Stonehenge. Apparently, vandalism and burglary had become enough of a problem that campers were the least-favored folks in the universe, at least in this part of England at this time of year.

Later, Susan and I kept an eye on Fred and the twins while the other three toured Stonehenge. From where I stood, I wasn't impressed; maybe it was the fence around it. "We'd better put some miles behind us," Clarke suggested as we left, turning north.

Between meadows of red poppies, we huffed and puffed up steep hills in blistering sun. About three o'clock, we refilled our water bottles with cool water from a farm kitchen, then Clarke started a water fight. With heavy packs, it was hard to play an adequate game of attack and run, but none of us really wanted to get away anyway. Clarke squeezed the last drop out of his second water bottle. "If they're having a drought here, maybe we should conserve," he said too late. It was the first time we hadn't. Susan and Clarke could each bathe and wash their hair in a half-liter bottle from our frames, and all of the dishes were washed in a half-liter also. Fruits and vegetables weren't washed at all—water was too precious.

Chapter 14

SUSAN THOUGHT THAT THE Cotswolds were beautiful and I guess they were, but as we rolled up and down the hills in the hot, humid sun, I got a bit tired of quaint and cutesy limestone villages strung one after the other like identical paper dolls. I wasn't the only one. "I don't like these roads," Fred announced. "They're too narrow."

"I love them," I lied, jumping to Susan's defense. "They're peaceful."

"But they don't go anywhere."

Zelda spat out a mouthful of bugs. "I'm hungry, but not this hungry. Yuck!"

"It's too hot," Betsy complained.

"Let's quit," Kelly agreed, perhaps overhearing.

"I'm not ready to quit," Clarke replied. "At this rate, we'll never get anywhere."

Susan proposed a compromise that was too far for the four youngsters and not far enough for Clarke and Fred, and eventually we spent the night in a lumpy field.

In the morning, Fred and I were packed and ready before the twins even woke up. Clarke was impatient, and to avoid another argument, Susan offered to help Kelly and Megan load their bicycles. "No. Let the girls do it," Clarke told her. "They have to learn to be responsible."

"You asked them to help us the other day when they were ready before we were," she reminded him.

"That's different. Our cooking gear can't be packed until we've all eaten."

"Why does everything have to be the way Clarke wants it?" Kelly hissed as she strapped their tent to Zelda's backside.

Our riders snitted at each other all morning while the patient transportation team trotted them up hill and down, between one village and the next, and even once, back the same way we'd come. "Let Clarke lead, Susan," Megan said. "I'm not pedaling up this hill again."

By lunchtime, the bicycles were pretty disgusted with the bicyclists after listening to an entire morning of arguments about the route, about the weather, about the hills, about bicycle maintenance, about shifting properly, about what was for dinner and who would cook it—they fought like a bag of weasels, yet we still were the ones doing all the work!

Just past the turnoff to Moreton Morrell, we gathered at the foot of another long, steep hill. "No. Absolutely not," Kelly announced. "Over my dead body. Airmail me home. Now!"

"You're about three hundred kilometers from the nearest airport, luvy," Susan said sympathetically, and I nudged Zelda gently to let her know that I knew how hard she'd been working.

At the top of the hill, a large farmhouse stood behind a luscious garden. I turned into the driveway without consulting anyone, deciding that fifty difficult kilometers were enough for beginning bicyclists and bicycles. If Fred complained, I was ready to bite him, and I'm sure that Susan was more than prepared to take a chunk out of Clarke if he said one more word about not getting enough mileage.

We gathered in front of the farmhouse as a formidable woman with beautiful eyes emerged from the side door. "May I help you?" she asked, drying her strong hands on a flowered apron.

"You could stuff a sock into Clarke's mouth," Zelda whispered, and Betsy giggled.

Seconds later, four bikes and two teenagers flopped on the grass, delighted to be not moving, while Susan and Clarke put up their tent and decided, in the interest of peaceful coexistence, that Kelly and Megan could choose start and stop times every day. "How come nobody consults with the beasts of burden?" Zelda grumbled. "All the humans do is sit on our backs!" I looked at her. "Well, maybe that isn't *quite* true," she decided, "but true enough."

Accompanied by three dogs happily running about her feet, our hostess came across the grass with her hands full of fresh strawberries and eggs. Nestled in the carton with eleven brown eggs was a pale green one.

After a perfectly lovely night in a bed of soft grass surrounded by beautiful flowers, Susan and Clarke were cinching the last of their packs on Fred and me when Megan approached, yogurt cup in hand. "I don't care for this flavor yogurt," she said. "Would either of you like it?"

Susan shook her head. "I'm too full of brown and green eggs."

"I'll eat it," Clarke said, swallowing a big spoonful. "Uh-oh, it's got nuts."

Susan snatched the container from his hand. " 'Brazil nuts,' " she read.

Clarke is allergic to nuts, and his reaction was immediate. "My throat is swelling," he rasped. Within seconds, his voice was unrecognizable and his face grew red and puffy. "I itch all over."

"Fred, do something!" I nudged him. Eyes wide, wheels pinned to the ground, Fred watched Clarke inflate like a red balloon. We stared openmouthed, immobile, amazed, then Susan finally streaked for the house. Running back to Clarke, she grabbed his fat red hand. "Get out of the sun until the doctor comes." He followed her willingly into the house, unable to talk.

The rest of us watched for the doctor, whose little car finally puffed up the driveway twenty minutes later. Clarke's inside, I told the man, but he didn't seem to hear me. Susan met him at the door, and the bicycles crowded to the window.

Five injections later, Clarke began to breathe more easily. "That's quite an allergy you have there, young man," the doctor said. "It could have been fatal." I laid a comforting handlebar on Fred as he let out his breath.

"Thank you for coming so quickly," Susan said to the doctor.

"You're lucky I was home. But your husband's not going anywhere today. At most, he's to walk around a little this afternoon." He turned to Clarke. "I think you'll be all right now, but it's possible you could have a relapse."

The bicycle half of the group rested under a lofty shade tree while Susan and the girls watered the big garden for our hostess. "What if this had happened while we were hidden in a forest somewhere, or someplace with no phone?" I wondered out loud.

Fred, clearly shaken, had another thought. "What if it had happened someplace where they don't speak English?"

Zelda groaned. "I can just see poor Kelly flipping through her German dictionary to find out how to say that Clarke is fatally allergic to nuts!" I could pose the question in perfect German, of course, but it wouldn't do any good because humans—except maybe Susan—couldn't seem to understand me in any language.

Betsy had been very quiet. "Do you suppose that Megan thinks that this is her fault?" she asked now.

"Why would she?" I asked, puzzled.

"She gave Clarke the yogurt."

Fred raised up on his front wheel, ready to sock Betsy for her owner's part in Clarke's close call. "No, Fred," I said, restraining him. "It's Clarke's allergy, and his responsibility to read labels. She didn't do it on purpose."

In the morning, after difficult goodbyes, we trotted off, Clarke only a tiny bit wobbly. And instead of the horrible hills and heat of England, the human conversation turned to its wonderful, warm, generous people, much to everyone's delight.

It was our eleventh day with the youngsters and already I couldn't remember what it was like without them. Life seemed much more conversation than action now, and much more complicated. There was less scenery and more talk. Like a short chain of paper clips, we wound up through the English countryside toward Rugby. Every once in awhile, one of our riders would drop off to fix a derailleur chain or drink water or take a photo, but for the most part, we stayed clipped together, pulling and pushing each other up and down the roller coaster roads. Traffic was light.

During lunch in a tiny park, Clarke spread out his map of England and Scotland. "We're still a couple of weeks away from Edinburgh," he estimated. "At the rate we're cycling, we won't have time to go much farther than Edinburgh, and that doesn't count bicycling back to Dover. We'll have to take a bus unless we turn back now."

Susan and I were more than unhappy. Everyone we met had told us of the beauty of the Scottish Highlands. The terrain was difficult, they said, but well worth it. Now, not only had we given up Denmark but now also most of Scotland, and I'd lugged Susan all the way from Morocco to get there! "Let's go on to Edinburgh at least," Kelly suggested. "I still want to see Sherwood Forest."

"And Brontëland," agreed Megan.

It was nine o'clock and almost dark when we found a large, bare dairy farm off a dirt road. Behind the main house, a man pitched hay up in a storage loft in the dim light. "Hello," Clarke called up. The man glared down at us, pitchfork in hand, and I rolled backwards, a bit afraid. "We're Americans bicycling for a year," Clarke explained hurriedly. "May we put two tents in your field tonight?"

Coming to the edge of the two-story hay pile, the man looked us over sternly. I edged behind Fred. "You must be very wealthy," the man said finally. Clarke laughed. "Hardly," he said. "We've sold everything we own and still can't afford a campground."

The farmer shook his head. "Well, go around the front and put your tents on the grass," he said after thinking a moment. "When I'm finished with this, I'll bring some fresh milk."

The heat and humidity lay over us like a blanket the next morning, setting record temperatures all over England. By the time we arrived in Nottingham, all eight of us were overheated and irritable. "I assume you want to see Nottingham Castle, Kelly," Susan called over her shoulder

"Of course," she snapped.

"I don't," Clarke snapped back.

"The Robin Hood stuff is the only thing Kelly's asked to see in England, Clarke," Susan reminded him. "You can watch the bikes and sit in the shade while we go inside."

While Clarke sat under a tree, the bicycles were stacked against the castle wall head to tail and tail to head, so crowded that even if there had been a breeze it wouldn't fit between us. Fred, as usual, I thought, was being much too chummy with the young ladies. "Quit pushing the twins against me," I growled. As the wall side of the sandwich, I could hardly breathe.

"Oh, hush, Daisy," Fred replied. Clarke looked up briefly as we kicked and squirmed into a better arrangement, then went back to writing postcards.

Chapter 15

A S IT TURNED OUT, Sherwood Forest is just a sparse wood, nowhere much for Robin Hood or anyone else to hide. After trussing us all together in a small picnic area, our riders visited the exhibits. We didn't get to see a thing.

The weather had turned—it was overcast and windy. On the outskirts of Budby, Fred came to a screeching halt. "Look!" Clarke pointed to a small mole that trundled back and forth across the road, little pink feet scuffling, bumping into the verge and then wandering back into the traffic lanes. "Let's give him a hand before we have to add him to the spirit ark."

Susan and I held up Fred while the twins held up traffic and Clarke followed the confused mole to the side of the road. As Clarke tried to nudge him over the edge, the fuzzy gray animal snapped blindly. "Whoops," said Clarke, quickly pulling his hands away. Finally, as the little guy bumped up to the edge again, nose snuffling, Clarke gave him a fast boost and sent him safely on his way, then waved to the patient motorists. How sweet, Clarke, I thought.

In Worksop, we talked with half a dozen bicycles and their owners. Susan mentioned the mole. "I tried the same thing a few years ago," one of the bicyclists said, "and damn near lost my fingers. Nasty little beasts, aren't they?"

"I think they're cute," Susan replied.

John and his son Roger gave us permission to camp under their apple trees just south of York, which they said was the oldest city in England. The next day, after risking life and limb to deliver our riders to the middle of the big city, we discovered that bicycles aren't allowed on the pedestrian-only streets called snickelways, narrow as arrows. "Not nice," I complained as Susan hitched me to a bike rack and left Megan in charge until she returned for her own watchperson shift.

We were allowed to see York Minster, from the outside only, of course. It was a beautiful cathedral, and I could hear the London Festival Orchestra practicing inside for a concert. Susan and Clarke came outside together, arms linked. "Let's ask to stay at John's another night," Susan suggested, "so that we can come back for the performance."

"Rats," I said to Fred as we hurried to John's. "If we'd known about the concert earlier, we could have left these heavy packs at the farm this morning."

Back at the tent, I put Nagle in charge of the spirit ark while the rest of us scrambled to clean up, sponging off our faces in cold water, then raced back toward York for the concert. Without packs, I felt emaciated, thin as a stick, like just a bone or two of a skeleton. In front of the cathedral, crowded together with Fred and the twins in a bike rack, I felt claustrophobic—without our packs, we stood too close together. "When was your last real shower, Zelda?" I asked.

"Exactly the same time as yours," she snitted back.

The concert was over at eleven. Our headlights weren't bright enough to illuminate the highway and Betsy and Zelda didn't have any; but we hoped that cars could see us, or two tiny lights anyway, as we carefully picked our way back to the farm.

"We're backtracking a bit from here if you still want to see where the Brontë sisters lived, Megan," Clarke said in the morning as he studied the map and stirred oatmeal on the one-burner camp stove. "Anybody want to leave our packs this morning and see more of York? We didn't have time to see the Castle Museum yesterday."

"Or York Dungeon," Kelly added, delighted.

"I'd rather see the National Railway Museum," Susan said.

"So we'll split up," Clarke suggested.

As we neared the city an hour later, Clarke asked Kelly if they had remembered their bike lock. "Nope," she replied, unconcerned.

"How were you planning to protect your bikes? Did you think that Susan and I would stay outside while you saw the museum?"

"We didn't think anything, Clarke—obviously," Kelly responded sarcastically.

"The bikes will be fine," Megan said breezily.

"I'm not sharing our cable lock with Betsy and Zelda," I announced to Fred. "It's too short." We managed anyway, mashed together, front wheels unprotected. "Can't you train your riders better?" I growled at the twins as the steel cable cut into my neck.

"We don't like this any more than you, Daisy," Zelda said as she poked my back wheel with her pedal.

After everyone saw the Castle Museum, Fred and I took Susan and Clarke to the railroad exhibit while the twins, without a lock, headed to York Dungeon with Kelly and Megan.

I'd forgotten how easy it was to travel with just one other bike. Fred and I breezed through town, delighted with our compactness. "Betsy and Zelda are great," Fred told me, "but this is so much easier!"

I agreed, and felt a bit disappointed two hours later when we collected the rest of the crew and rolled away in a long procession to pick up our packs. I'd enjoyed having Fred to myself and not being burdened with everything that our riders needed for a year.

Soon I felt fat again, with four panniers front and back on my wheels, a giant duffel strapped to my rump and a stupid basket on my head. Betsy and Zelda only carried two bright new panniers each, perched on their cute little back wheels like fanny packs, accentuating their sexy sway as they pranced down the highway. Fred, of course, looked more like a bulldozer than a bicycle, but because he was male, appeared brave and strong.

Pulling into a village for groceries, I cringed as I saw myself reflected in the plate glass windows of the stores—a lumbering ten-ton Tillie followed by two petite ponies and then Ironman protecting our rear flank. There was only one brick building on the street, so we leaned carefully against the bricks, not wanting to scratch the windows of neighboring stores.

Before Kelly and Megan had joined the trip, Susan and Clarke went into the markets together, trusting that Fred and I could take care of ourselves. After all, they said, if someone could pedal off on a bike loaded with a hundred pounds of equipment without falling down, they were welcome to try. Now that there were four bicyclists, however, one always kept us company while the others shopped for supper. Today, it was Susan's turn to stay outside. "Young lady!" A woman stood at the door of the brick building. "This is a private residence. Remove your bicycles!"

Susan scurried to our rescue. "I'm sorry, ma'am, we were afraid that they might scratch the windows."

"I don't care. I've the only residence left in this neighborhood and I won't have bicycles leaning against my house!"

How rude, I thought. We're probably the nicest bicycles that woman will ever meet if she'd just take the time to get to know us. "We'll leave immediately," Susan said, not introducing us.

"See that you do!" The door slammed.

In Haworth, it was girls only to the Brontë museum. Clarke and Fred wrote letters on the curb while the rest of us ooh'd and aah'd at the old Brontë house and wandered around the hilly town.

It was almost dark before we found a house with room for the tents. "Why did you pick here?" asked the owner, a tall man with bushy gray eyebrows. His small wife huddled behind him at the door.

"Because we need a place to sleep and because you have a flat field next to your house," Clarke answered.

"But we didn't expect you," the man said.

As the elderly couple questioned our motives, my tired teammates and I shifted from tire to tire, anxious to unload our heavy burdens. It had been a hilly day again. As the man formed yet another question, fuzzy eyebrows bunched together in concentration, his wife broke in. "You can stay over by the garage." Her husband frowned but closed his mouth.

I was almost asleep when a tiny old man with wild white hair appeared on the other side of the crumbling stone wall dividing our camping spot from the lane. "Do you have permission to stay here?" he asked Clarke in a horrendously broad accent.

"Yes, we do," Clarke answered, introducing himself.

"My name is Dick," the man said. "Originally owned this farm, lived in that house over there." He pointed to our hosts' home. "Sold the house when the farm got too much for me. Live down in the little house yonder."

He looked over at the long-suffering transportation team, then back at Clarke. "Would you like to put your bicycles in my barn? It may rain, you know. You're lucky—any other year and you'd have drowned by now."

My head popped up. What a lovely man, I thought, nodding politely as Susan led me down the lane to an old dairy barn and slipped me into a private stall between Fred and Zelda. "Some hotel, huh?" Betsy said, shaking off dust.

"I hope it rains tonight just so we won't have to be out in it," Fred added. It didn't, but we still enjoyed the luxury of knowing that if it had, we'd have been warm and dry.

We'd been on the road less than an hour the next morning when I got a cramp in my front wheel. "My wheel sounds like it's full of gravel," Susan called to Clarke.

Fred hurried to my side. "Daisy! What's wrong?"

I was scared. "I don't know, Fred. I'm getting paralyzed, I think. My wheel barely turns and it's numb. What if I'm having a stroke?"

"It's probably your bearing, Susan," Clarke said, not very sympathetic.

I hobbled into Skipton, where we found a bike shop. Mom pushed me inside, reassuring me with gentle hands that I'd be all right. I didn't believe her. "It's a cracked bearing, all right," the bike doctor said, "but I can't replace it because the bearings in your wheel are sealed. You can buy a new wheel but it won't be as good as the one you have, or I can rebuild your old one. It won't cost any more, but it will take all afternoon." Although I didn't want inferior parts, an all-afternoon surgery didn't sound fun at all. What if they didn't give me an anesthetic?

"My God, look at those packs!" a voice boomed behind us. "You should be reported to the Society for the Prevention of Cruelty to Bicycles. If your bicycles were horses, they'd have to be put down!" We whirled around to face the bike shop owner, who stared at our overloaded frames in amazement and then wanted to know all about our trip while Mom and I discussed my injuries.

"Good news!" The bike doctor ran out of the storeroom. "I've found a new wheel as good as your old one. It's more expensive, of course, but I can put it on in a jiffy." Please, Mom, I said, trembling, don't let him cut me open.

"We'll take it," she said before Clarke could object to the expense. "Daisy's been a champ so far on this trip, and I don't want her downgraded."

I pranced away from the store, shiny new wheel rolling smoothly. "How do you feel?" Betsy asked.

"Great," I said.

"You were lucky you didn't need surgery," she said breathlessly.

"No big deal," I lied.

It started to rain for the first time since the girls had joined us eighteen days earlier, and Susan distributed what was left of the tattered orange rain gear, usually tucked on our rumps like bunny tails to make us more noticeable to drivers, to cover the essential packs—cameras, food, clothes. Betsy and Zelda were skittery, afraid of the lightning and thunder, but Fred and I ambled along without complaint to set a good example.

Having climbed toward the Lake District through dales and moors for the past two days, the hills were again steep and the air was cold. The scenery was spectacular in spite of the black sky and clouds, and although we all grew silent and soggy, the twins and their riders didn't complain. At a small village, hands shaking with cold, Megan asked to stop for tea. "Not fair," Zelda complained as we waited outside in the cold, leaning in a row up against the courthouse, dripping, while our riders dried out in a cozy restaurant and drank hot steamy tea laced with sugar and milk.

After fifty very cold and wet kilometers, the teenagers decided that enough was enough, but we couldn't find an occupied house with flat fields. Finally, we spotted a little house with a tiny garden. Smoke rose from the chimney in wisps as we waded up to the porch; I shook, flinging rainwater over everybody. Susan asked the woman who answered the door if we could put two tents in her garden for the night. "How much will you pay?" the old woman inquired, eyes narrowed.

"No one has ever asked us for money before," Susan responded, surprised. "We ask for nothing except water." How could this woman possibly resist us?

But she did. "There's a caravan site down the road," she said, slamming the door. Susan brushed off my wet saddle with dripping fingers and climbed aboard as dusk began to darken the already dark gray day.

After another half hour, off to the left, two farms faced each other like mirror images. Clarke knocked on the door to the right. A trim man with graying hair peeped around the edge, holding a pipe in his hand. "Yes?" he said as Kelly and Megan hugged themselves for warmth, teeth chattering. Clarke asked if we could camp in his field. "Do you have any ulterior motives?" the Englishman asked. "I mean, are you Jehovah's Witnesses or something?" Fred and I looked at each other, shrugging, as Susan and Clarke burst into laughter and the man joined them. "They're getting quite creative, you know," he said. "Well, you can stay, then, if you're not trying to convert me." Kelly and Megan jumped up and down. "Surely you don't want to sleep in a wet field. Let's see if there's room in the garage."

The man backed his car out in the driveway and moved some boxes so that four people, four bicycles, two tents and Susan's spirit ark could fit inside the warm, dry garage. I thanked the car for giving up its house for the night, then scooted inside the wooden building, way in the back, as far from the rain as possible. Betsy and Zelda snuggled close beside me, shivering. Fred squeezed in between the twins, nuzzling them gently. "You two did great today in the rain," he told them.

He was right, of course, but I was irritated that he hadn't noticed my contribution to the cause. "What about me, Fred? I was the one who was injured."

Fred dismissed me. "Oh, you always do fine, Daisy." I do not!

Finally, after we'd dripped dry, huddled in a clump at the back of the garage, our combined body heat warmed us into a blissful drowsiness and I only noted briefly the sound of the heavy rain on the roof before I fell into a deep sleep, surrounded by my smelly traveling companions, Nagle tucked up at my feet, keeping my tires warm.

It rained all the next day, and the next. Then we had to climb Kirkstone Pass, a sixteen-percent grade. It was horrid. Supposedly, the view was fabulous, but we only saw rain and clouds and fog. For some reason, I did better than usual—part way up the steep pass, Fred asked me to slow down because I was getting so far ahead of everybody. I decided to bring up the rear then, encouraging the others as they struggled past. "You're doing great, Betsy. Come on, Zelda, you're half way up. Way to go, Fred."

By the time we got to the top, the twins and their riders were shivering uncontrollably. A tiny inn beckoned. "Can we stop for tea?" Kelly asked.

Susan hesitated. "We really can't. I can't, anyway. If I stop pedaling, my muscles will get too stiff."

"May we at least use the bathroom?"

"Of course, Megan, but hurry, okay?"

Kelly and Megan raced inside the little restaurant while the rest of us stood outside in the rain. "Which way are you going?" asked a young man under a big black umbrella en route inside from his warm car.

"North," Clarke answered.

"You're lucky. That side of the pass is a twenty-percent grade."

Fred and I rolled our eyes. "Our sixteen-percent side was bad enough," Clarke replied.

"Where are Kelly and Megan?" I asked Zelda and Betsy after twenty minutes. "I'm freezing."

"How would we know?" the twins responded, no doubt unhappy themselves that they'd been deserted.

Finally, Susan went inside to retrieve the teenagers but returned empty-handed. "They're drinking coffee," she explained to Clarke.

"They hate coffee," he said.

"I know, but the restaurant is out of tea. They must be desperate. I told them that we'd meet them at the bottom of the pass. My knees are stiff as poles already."

"What about Zelda and me?" Betsy asked as Susan and Clarke mounted up. "What if someone steals us?"

"Who in his right mind would want to bicycle in this weather?" I reasoned.

"Good point," Zelda replied. "But I hope they hurry."

Fred and I flew down Kirkstone Pass through the heavy rain and fog, struggling to stay in control on the slippery road. Although I was miserably cold, my thoughts were with Zelda and Betsy, who would have even more trouble if Kelly and Megan let them cool off any more.

At the bottom, we pulled to a stop in front of a little cafe to wait for the girls. "I can't believe how well you cycled up that pass, Susan," Clarke said. "The wind was blowing so hard that the rain was horizontal! I couldn't keep up with you—how did you do it?"

Susan patted me, then started toward the restaurant, trailing water. "For one thing," she said thoughtfully, "I concentrated on myself instead of everyone else for a change."

"You did great, too, Daisy," Fred admitted after they'd gone inside.

"It was actually fun today, except for the weather." Although I was pretty proud of myself, my mind was on the twins, who should have caught up with us by now. Where were they? Although they were a pain in the neck sometimes and I was jealous of their youth and beauty, I certainly didn't want anything to happen to them.

Half an hour later, they emerged from the fog and clattered to a stop at the cafe. "Don't ask," Zelda said, her head drooping to her front hub. "We don't want to talk about it." Fred and I looked at each other, then snuggled close to warm them with what body heat we could muster as Megan and Kelly dripped through the door of the cafe.

Chapter 16

I N THE MIDDLE OF our nineteenth week in Europe, Fred and I crossed the border to Scotland after carrying Susan and Clarke 6000 kilometers, 3600 miles. It was our fifth foreign country, but except for having to travel on the left side of the highway, England hadn't felt foreign. Scotland did. Instead of American supermarkets and lots of cars, we were back to tiny villages and narrow roads. It was a relief to see more lambs than vehicles.

We stopped for the night at a large old farm in Newcastleton. Its owner, a handsome man with twinkly blue eyes, tucked us under a big open barn in case of rain, then invited our riders inside his house for tea and cookies while he finished his supper. Afterwards, they piled into his little truck and headed toward town. "Where are they going, Daisy?" Betsy asked.

My foreign language skills shouldn't have been needed in Scotland, but this man's brogue was as unrecognizable as Arabic until I got used to it. "I think he's taking them to meet his wife," I answered. "He said something about her owning a restaurant."

After chatting with the man's cows and sheep for a bit, we settled down in the fragrant straw for a good night's sleep. It was raining when I woke up at dawn—I knew that I had time for a few more winks before Susan would want to get wet, but the day was well on its way toward noon when Megan came to get Betsy. The rain had stopped, at least for the moment. "What's going on?" I asked Fred as they rolled away.

"We're staying two more nights," he explained. "Apparently, there's some music festival in town that Clarke wants to see. Betsy's taking Megan to buy groceries."

"How lovely," I said, stretching. "Wake me for dinner, would you?"

The next morning, we were pressed into service to escort our owners into the village to see the festival. Although the bicycles were allowed to watch the bagpipe competition in the town square, I was disappointed that they wouldn't let us inside the competition hall for the tin whistle contest.

We stayed in town for dinner because everyone wanted to hear the winners' concert later in the evening. It was still light at ten-thirty when Megan appeared alone, unlocking Betsy from Zelda. Then Kelly arrived, out of breath. "Clarke says you can't bicycle back to the farm alone," she announced. "It will be dark before you get there and you don't have a headlight on your bike."

"So?" said Megan.

"He said to bring you back, Megan. Argue with him." Our hostess appeared then, offering to drive the bicyclists back to the farm a bit later in her car. Her husband could take the bikes in the back of his van, she said. Megan walked off with Kelly, muttering.

It turned out that only three bikes would fit in the van. "I'll ride back," Clarke offered. "I seem to have the only working headlight at the moment."

"If it's not safe to bicycle at night," Megan snarled, "why is Clarke riding?"

"Because he has a headlight," Susan replied. "Mine's burned out. And because he's bicycled more than you. And because he's unlikely to get hassled by a carload of drunk men after the festival."

"So there, Betsy," I said for good measure as we were lifted into the back of the van. "Be careful, Fred," I called as he rolled away, his tiny headlamp illuminating nothing on the unfamiliar road. Back at the farm, I waited nervously until he arrived, but when he tried to brag about his adventures on the dark highway, Betsy and Zelda weren't the least interested and, to be honest, I was too sleepy to listen.

North of the farm, the road was narrow and quiet and the open fields were dotted with fluffy white sheep as the emerald green landscape rolled peacefully past mile after mile. This far north, it was daylight until eleven o'clock and dawn came only four hours later. For those accustomed to being awake when the sun was, Scotland was a marathon. Houses were sparse, and a refusal somewhere meant miles to the next opportunity and many more to the next.

Our first night out of Newcastleton took five tries and a couple of hours before we found shelter, and I was grateful for the late summer daylight.

The next morning, Megan did the supper dishes while Clarke made oatmeal and Susan went up to the house to wash up and fill water bottles. Kelly grabbed the first bowl of food, then washed only her own bowl after breakfast. Clarke didn't comment but was grouchy all morning.

The eight of us had been together three weeks. At this point, the plan was for the bicycles to stay on the outskirts of Edinburgh while our riders toured the city, then we'd all take a train to London. From there, we'd bicycle back to Dover via the home of the women who fixed sandwiches for the wild foxes, then take the ferry to France.

As we neared Edinburgh, we stopped in a parking lot for lunch. Clarke was still in a snit and the girls asked Susan what was wrong. "Ask him," she suggested.

"Are you kidding?" they groaned in unison.

"Will you lead, Susan?" he asked after eating in silence. "I could use a little help from the rest of the troops for a change."

"Sure," she replied, "but I may need help reading street signs. I'm only wearing one contact lens today."

"Forget it, then." Clarke pedaled off down the street but eventually returned when no one followed.

"I said I'd lead, Clarke," Susan pointed out through gritted teeth. I snarled at Fred, then pulled away from the curb before he could get ahead of me. Every time anyone led but Clarke and Fred, it didn't last—after a few minutes, they'd pass us, back to the front. The twins thought that Fred felt that they didn't do a good job; I assumed that it was just habit. Today, however, I wasn't about to let them ahead of me. If Clarke wanted a new leader, he was going to get one, like it or not.

It took four tries to find a place to camp. "Is it us or is it because we're so close to a big city?" Susan finally asked.

"Both," was the consensus.

The best we could do was the backyard of someone's mother who was on vacation. The next door neighbor girl, however, brought a bucket of warm water when she saw Megan washing her hair with a garden hose.

"Since no one's at home," Susan said early the next morning, "we'd better not leave the bikes here. I'll watch them while you all see Edinburgh Castle, but let's check train schedules to London first."

Megan and Kelly kept us company while Susan and Clarke went into the American Express office in downtown Edinburgh. "Bad news," Clarke said when they returned. "A rail strike is scheduled for midnight, which means no late trains. And, even worse, the ferry workers may go on a sympathy strike. We could have trouble getting out of England after today." I'd heard that it was possible to swim the English Channel, but hoped that we wouldn't have to.

"So let's get out tonight," Kelly suggested. "Can't we take the train all the way to Dover instead of just to London, then take the ferry across tonight?"

"I suppose," Susan said, "but we'd planned to see those wonderful women who feed foxes. They offered to give us a party if we brought you back." Kelly shrugged, and Susan and Clarke disappeared back inside the travel office. Bursting back through the door, Susan said, "We have five minutes to get to the train station if we want to get to France before midnight. So much for Edinburgh Castle, ladies."

As it turned out, only three bicycles were allowed per train, so Fred and Clarke waited for the next express and the twins and I crowded into the allotted spot on the baggage car. At a hundred and twenty-five miles an hour southbound, we compressed our three-week northbound odyssey into five hours, like a fast-forward movie, then met the boys in London and packed all eight of us into an unattended baggage car for the short trip to Dover, arriving at the dock ten minutes before the last ferry to France.

It would be midnight when we arrived in Calais. "How will we find a place to stay?" Susan asked as we waited in line to board. Considering France, when I was mentally still in Scotland, was too much. I couldn't have understood French at that moment if my life depended on it—I was still changing my language gears from Scottish to British, amazingly different languages, I'd decided.

"Let's use the radio phone on board to call the people where we stayed our last night in France," Clarke suggested. Luckily, they'd invited us back if we returned to the Continent. "May we sneak into your garden about one o'clock tonight?" Clarke asked after three unsuccessful connections.

"We'll leave the light on," they promised.

Chapter 17

THE STREETS OF CALAIS were wet with rain, and mercury lights made shiny streaks on the black pavement by the ferry dock. It was midnight, the Fourth of July, Independence Day for Americans, a loss for the British, nothing for the French. Echoing through the deserted streets from streetlight to streetlight, we looked for the road to Frethun, eight kilometers southwest of the city.

At the edge of town, we were pitched into total darkness. I couldn't see a thing. There was no moon and I trailed Zelda, frightened, certain that I'd fall into a pothole or veer into a ditch if I didn't stay right on her rear. "Stop it, Daisy," Zelda said once, kicking backward. "You're making me nervous."

"Sorry," I said, "but I'm night blind. I wish you had a tail so I could hold onto it with my teeth."

"Well, I don't. Besides, I'm having enough problems of my own."

An hour later, I recognized a light over a garage behind an open iron gate. "Stop, Fred!" I called ahead. Creeping up the gravel drive to the side yard, we leaned against a fence while our riders stripped us of their tents and sleeping bags. Still bulky with packs, we slept standing up and I had horrible nightmares about falling off the edge of the earth into a black void.

Our riders had breakfast the next morning on the patio with our French hosts while Fred and I introduced the twins to French grass in the pretty yard edged with roses. "Boy, did I miss French bread for the last month," Clarke said.

"Boy, did I miss French grass," Fred echoed. Betsy and Zelda were too busy munching to comment. Since when do bicycles eat, I wondered yet again, chewing contentedly.

We hurried back to Calais to exchange English pounds for French francs, but the markets closed before Susan could buy white cheese, onion and tomatoes to go with the fresh bread that our French family had sent along for lunch. In a little park, the bicyclists settled down to peanut butter sandwiches, sitting cross-legged around a map of Europe. "You planned a week in France," Clarke reminded Kelly and Megan, "but it won't take that long to ride along the coast to Belgium. We're also ahead of schedule since we took the train all the way to Dover yesterday. So. Where to?"

I was mildly interested in what they'd come up with and guessed that they'd choose a few days at the beach somewhere, or to dawdle along the tiny roads of northern France. Kelly and Megan looked at each other briefly. "Paris," Kelly announced.

Memories of the traffic at the Arc de Triomphe raised the very cables on the back of my neck. "Paris?" Susan croaked, thumbing through her daily journal. "It took Clarke and me nine days to get to Calais from Paris. Even if we could get back in a week, by the time we reach Belgium, we'll have spent two weeks in France. You agreed on just one."

"Kelly and Megan get to choose the route, Susan," Clarke reminded her. "If they want to spend two weeks in France, we'll spend two weeks in France."

Although I loved France, I agreed with Susan that seven weeks had been enough when there were so many places we hadn't seen. Besides, I was looking forward to the flat countries of Belgium and Holland. Fred, I knew, would be happy to stay in France because of the grass, and Betsy and Zelda would side with the girls. Susan and I were clearly outnumbered. Two more weeks in France it would be.

After a brief dip in the ocean, we started up a steep little pass in the hot sun. "France isn't flat either," growled Zelda. "I thought it would be, at least near the coast."

"For bicycles," I reminded her, "nothing is flat, at least not for long."

Minutes later, we were at the top and over we went, hurtling down the curving road with whoops and hollers, flat out, enjoying the hot wind in our faces. Fields of grain shimmered in the sun, then faded into the horizon near the ocean. Delighted now, Fred and Zelda and I gathered at the bottom of the pass. "Where's Betsy?" I asked Fred.

He shrugged. "She was behind me a minute ago."

Finally, Clarke walked back up the road to look for Megan. Then he started running, and Kelly scrambled after him. Susan stayed with the rest of us and paced back and forth, worried.

A few minutes later, Clarke and Kelly appeared, walking back down the hill with Megan riding Betsy, wobbling, behind them. When Megan saw us, she pedaled ahead, arriving with a bloody shoulder, elbow, hand and knee, plus a torn halter top and tennis shoes. Betsy's saddle had been torn up, and she had several gashes along her side. "Oh, dear," Susan said when she saw Megan.

"Oh, dear," I said when I saw Betsy.

"I was going too fast and hit some gravel," they both explained.

As Susan cleaned Megan's cuts, the bicycles gathered together. "Did you break anything, Betsy?" we asked.

She was shaky. "I don't think so. But I was really scared that a car would run over me. Ouch!" she yipped when Zelda gently examined a scratch on her side.

"I'm just trying to help," Zelda said, hurt. "Don't be a baby."

Fred and I stood apart, talking quietly. "What would happen if Betsy had broken a leg?" he asked me. "Would they shoot her?"

"I don't think so, Fred," I assured him. "When I got hurt in England, remember, they fixed me. We're not exactly real horses, you know."

"What if Megan had broken a leg?"

I smiled. "Well, they certainly wouldn't have shot *her*. But I'm not sure how we could have gotten her to a hospital, or what we'd do about Betsy since one person can't ride two bicycles. We'd better be really careful, Freddy."

That afternoon, we rolled slowly toward St. Josse, solicitous of Megan and Betsy's injuries. The people who had fed Susan and Clarke horse for lunch had invited us to return if we could, and although Fred and I had enjoyed their dog Stasi, the *petite mouton*, we were concerned that the family might want to eat Betsy if she weren't up to par by the time we got to their house.

As it turned out, instead of eating our buddy, they gave a dinner party for thirteen friends and family in honor of the Americans while Stasi found the best grass near the pond for the transportation team. It was a delightful evening, and even Megan and Betsy felt better after we cleaned them up with hot, soapy water. Lying in the cool grass, tummies full, we listened to everyone converse in French and English on the patio. "Where do you go now?" our hosts' son asked.

"Back to Paris," Susan sighed.

"Ah, to the Bicentennial?"

"No," Susan said quickly. "We will leave long before then." In Calais, Kelly and Megan had agreed to spend only one or two days in the city; today was Thursday, and we planned to arrive in Paris no later than Tuesday. The Bicentennial celebration, Bastille Day, was on Friday, the 14th of July.

"Ah, no," the young man said. "The two hundredth birthday of the French Revolution will be very special. Where will you stay in Paris?"

Susan shrugged. "The Bois de Boulogne campground again, I suppose."

"You will never find room there," announced the young Frenchman, turning to his father. "Papa, do you think they could stay with Coco?"

"Ah, but of course," the man said in French. "*Superb.*"

"My father's brother lives south of Paris," the son explained. "We'll ask him if you can camp in his yard."

Although the family begged us to stay for the weekend, we decided to move on, knowing that the longer we stayed, the harder it would be to leave. Early the next morning, I nuzzled little Stasi, sniffing back tears, and trundled off down the driveway knowing that I'd never see her again. "Don't get eaten," she barked as we rounded the corner.

It was Clarke and Megan's birthdays, forty-one for Clarke and sixteen for Megan. In spite of a full day's dousing of cold rain, Susan and I were determined to find someplace special to stay for the night and ignored Kelly and Megan's decision to stop early. An hour later, we spotted a long gray wall, and although we had no idea what was behind it, somehow we both knew that it would be wonderful. A fancy car came out of the gate as we turned to go inside. "What's behind that wall?" Susan asked the driver in English as if certain that he could speak her language.

"My house," the man responded in English, amused.

"May we camp on your property tonight?" For the first time, Susan didn't explain who we were.

"Of course," responded the Frenchman. "Tell my wife that you've already spoken with me."

Confidently, Susan and I coasted down the long drive followed by our bewildered buddies. When the woods opened up, we spotted a chateau. Our companions gasped, but Susan and I weren't at all surprised. "Is a castle good enough for a birthday celebration?" we asked smugly.

Soon we were tucked inside a large square of sparkling white outbuildings adjacent to the main castle. Protected on all four sides from wind, with empty stalls if it rained and even a bathroom for those who needed such things, it was glorious.

As Susan and Kelly made onion soup for dinner, our French hosts marched across the yard with a homemade birthday card and candy and flowers for the birthday boy and girl. Megan was stringing wet laundry on the barbed wire fence that separated the castle from the sheep. "I have a clothes dryer. Please, let me take care of your things," our beautiful hostess offered, picking a piece of ragged cotton underwear from the sticky fence as carefully as if it were silk.

In the middle of the night, I heard someone cross the courtyard. It was our hostess, carrying bags of neatly folded laundry tied with pink ribbons. No doubt about it, I decided, snuggling with Fred, Susan and I had chosen the perfect birthday house.

The next day didn't turn out as well. First, we lost half a day while Megan installed a new derailleur chain on Betsy as Clarke worked on Fred's still-troublesome lower bracket. Then, to make up for lost time, the teenagers decided to pedal fifty hilly kilometers after lunch; Susan's knees looked like balloons and I was still worrying about Betsy's cuts and scrapes when Kelly called up to Clarke, "There's something wrong with my bicycle. It sounds awful in low gear." All we need, I thought, is another sick bike.

"What do *you* think is wrong?" Clarke asked Kelly. "Be more specific than 'fix it, Clarke,' would you?"

"I haven't a clue," Kelly snarled.

We kept going. In a large backyard in the small village of Grandvilliers, the teenagers pitched their tent as far from Susan and Clarke's as possible. Megan started dinner while the other bicyclists shared drinks on the patio with our host family and I tried to find out what was wrong with Zelda. "Where does it hurt?" I asked.

"It's just a gear ache," she replied. "I probably just climbed too many hills this afternoon."

Suddenly, a scream pierced the still air and Kelly and Susan raced to the teenagers' tent to discover that Megan had spilled a pan of boiling water on her feet. As we regrouped to assess the extent of Megan's injuries, it started to rain and our host ran out under a big patio umbrella to invite the bicyclists for dinner and to sleep inside. While our riders spent the night dry and warm, their poor beasts of burden huddled under drippy trees. It was a long night for us.

The next day dawned under clear skies that darkened to brilliant blue as we rolled briskly in the bright sunshine north of Paris. "Stop, Kelly!" Clarke suddenly called from behind her. "Your freewheel just fell apart!"

Zelda grimaced in pain. "See, Clarke?" Kelly gloated. "I told you there was something wrong with my bike."

He ignored her outburst. "You're lucky that Susan brought a spare freewheel from home. We'll need a vice, however. We'll have to walk back to the last village and try to borrow one."

"Take Megan," Kelly retorted. "I don't speak French."

"It's your bike," Clarke pointed out. They walked back down the road pushing Zelda, who was crying.

"Will she be all right?" Betsy asked after we'd waited by the roadside for an hour.

"I'm sure she will," I answered with more confidence than I felt. "How's your lower bracket, Fred?"

"It hurts some. I think it's cracked again, but Clarke can't find the right wrench to replace it. It doesn't hurt as much as it did in Spain, though."

"How are your cuts, Betsy?" I figured that I might as well take inventory of the whole group as long as I'd started.

"Pretty oozy," she answered, craning her handlebars around to examine her backside. "Megan's used up all the antibiotic cream, and I can't keep clean with just cold water from a garden hose. Look, there's Zelda!"

Zelda looked much better, erect and bright. "All set?" I asked, touching her shoulder with my handlebar.

"Fit as a fiddle," she said, grinning happily.

"We don't have time to ride into Paris tonight," Clarke decided. "Let's find a post office and ship home our used maps."

Anything that would lighten our burden was fine with me, and I rolled along happily, humming. At the post office in St. Ouen, Clarke and Megan waited in a long line to buy two boxes, then were told that the boxes were too big to go by boat and had to be airmailed for more than a hundred dollars.

"Airmail!" Susan shrieked when she heard. "If they can ship cars by boat, why not two small boxes? Forget it—surely we can find a rational postal clerk somewhere else."

Clarke loaded our box onto Fred's head under the wine jug, but Kelly and Megan had more trouble finding a place for their box because the twins didn't have front racks. As they rearranged their rear gear to fit around the box, camping equipment strewn all over the sidewalk, a young Frenchwoman stopped to chat. "You are American?" she asked in English. "Where are you going?"

"Paris," Susan answered with a sigh. "Eventually, Belgium and Holland and Germany and Austria and Italy and Greece. We've already been to Morocco and Spain and England and Scotland. And France, of course. We stayed seven weeks and liked it so much that we've come back for another two," she added, glaring at the teenagers.

"Are you going all the way into the city tonight?" the woman asked, ignoring the sarcasm.

"We'd rather go in tomorrow," Clarke answered. "We've been camping in people's fields all through Europe."

"My boyfriend's sister has a garden," the woman said with a smile. "If you'll come home with me for a drink, I'll find you a place to spend the night. I'd love to hear about your trip. I teach English and I've traveled in your country."

It was a challenge to keep up with her car in busy rush-hour traffic as it turned this way and that and then into a driveway behind a wall just as I thought we'd lost it in the stream of autos hurrying somewhere or other.

"Might as well take a nap," Fred said, leaning against a low wall. "No telling how long they'll be."

As it turned out, we never had to move that night at all. The woman's boyfriend arrived, then Susan and Clarke drove with them to the store for dinner groceries, and then the French couple left to spend the night with his sister, giving their house to the Americans. "Wow, that was nice," I said as they drove off.

"Mmm," Fred said, his eyes already closed for the night.

In the morning, the woman returned to say goodbye, inviting Susan to go with her to a steam bath in a Muslim mosque in Paris on Thursday, ladies day, which would ensure Kelly and Megan's two days in the city without sacrificing Mom's escape before the Bicentennial festivities the next day.

Chapter 18

"WHY CAN'T WE EVER arrive in a big city when it isn't rush hour?" I groused as we weaved through the Place de la Concorde, its periphery stacked with bleachers for the Bastille Day celebration, and down the Champs-Élysées behind a double column of horses sporting rumps shaved like checkerboards.

"Cool!" Betsy said to Zelda, "I want to shave my rear end like that!"

"You don't have hair," I pointed out. "Come on, you guys, pay attention or you'll get lost. I'm not coming back for either of you."

"Yes, *ma'am!*" Betsy said sarcastically and I couldn't blame her. After all, it wasn't her fault that Megan was so engrossed in the Paris streetscapes that she didn't pedal fast enough to keep up. Squeezing between cars and pedestrians, we were a strange little procession as we made our way out of the fabled city toward L'Hay-les-Roses, where the brother of Stasi's master lived.

Coco's house, old and narrow and crumbling, sat like a thistle between million-dollar new homes in a fashionable suburb. Leaving us alone on the street, our riders climbed a narrow staircase and knocked hesitantly. The door opened, arms reached out, and our traveling companions disappeared inside amid welcoming shouts. Then a jumble of men bounded outside to lift my teammates and me up the steep stairs to a garden in back of the house. The garden was small, like the house, and consisted of straggly overgrown weeds in a long-unattended vegetable garden. "Yuck," Fred said, nibbling a dead root.

Leaning against the back of the whitewashed house, I soaked up the last of the afternoon sun, glad to be out of the Paris traffic. "I'm not looking forward to running through the Arc de Triomphe again, especially with four of us," I said to no one in particular. "Maybe they'll sightsee on foot this time," I added wistfully.

Fred was looking around the small garden, measuring it with a practiced eyeball. "Two tents and four bicycles aren't going to fit here tonight," he decided. As it turned out, they didn't have to. After preparing a grand dinner party for his friends and our riders, Coco gave his bed to Susan and Clarke, an attic bedroom to Kelly and Megan, and allotted himself the living room couch.

My dreams came true—the next morning, Megan and Kelly took the subway with a handsome young friend of Coco's to see the sights of Paris while Clarke visited with our host and Susan caught up on her writing. The transportation team snoozed in the sun, snacking a bit on the dry garden vines—we didn't need much as we weren't using up any energy. "Let's play some games," Betsy suggested after lunch. "I'm bored."

"How about spin the bottle?" Fred suggested, leering.

"Shame on you, Fred," I admonished him. I'd been hoping that the youngsters' new battle scars and dirty frames were making them less attractive to him. Apparently not, the lout. "How about pin the tail on Fred-the-donkey?" I suggested to Betsy and Zelda, who giggled. Let Susan worry about Kelly and Megan and their attractive young escort; my hands were full here in the garden.

After dinner, Kelly and Megan left again with their Frenchman and one of his friends. "We'll be back by midnight," Megan called over her shoulder.

"*Oo-la-la*," Betsy said, rolling her eyes.

"Uh-oh," I said when the girls tiptoed up the stairs at three in the morning, then I decided I'd better check the whereabouts of Fred. He was fast asleep, innocent as a lamb.

The next morning, our riders left the house together on foot. If I'd counted right, this was the day that Susan was to go to the Muslim mosque with her friend from north of the city, so I turned over to bake my other side, stretching. "I need some decent grass to eat," Fred complained.

That evening, when the bicyclists got ready to attend a street dance in the park, Fred got very bright of eye. "Park?" he said, lunging to his feet. "Park means grass. Are we invited?"

"No, Fred, you'd eat their whole party," I chuckled. "You're not going to starve to death. Ask Clarke to bring you some bike kibble. We're leaving tomorrow anyway; it's Friday, you know." I wasn't looking forward to the Bastille Day traffic and hoped that Kelly and Megan wouldn't decide to pedal back through the center of Paris to head toward Belgium.

As it turned out, Clarke misplaced his money belt and wouldn't be able to replace his travelers' checks and passport until after the weekend. Whether we liked it or not, we were staying for Bastille Day. Coco and his friends seemed to be delighted and so were Kelly and Megan, of course. While our riders and their new friends went into the city for the parade, the backyard bunch celebrated quietly, unsure of the proper way for bicycles to honor a major French holiday. We ended up drinking a toast out of a dirty bucket full of rusty rainwater.

After Clarke found his money belt under a pile of papers in Coco's living room the next morning, Susan came outside to begin packing. Oh well, I thought, the lazy days were nice while they lasted. Inside, I could hear Coco talking to Clarke. "*Non, non, non,*" he said when Clarke explained that we were leaving.

"He wants you to stay until Monday," translated one of the young Frenchmen who'd stopped by for coffee. "He's been diagnosed with cancer and hates to be alone."

Our riders gathered in the backyard. "How can we stay?" Susan asked, an empty food pack in her hand. "Coco refuses to let us cook and he's given us his bed. He needs his rest."

"Please," Kelly and Megan begged.

"I'm still not caught up on my writing," Susan finally admitted, then followed the rest of them inside to tell Coco that we would stay the weekend. We could hear his yelp of delight all the way out in the garden, and soon Clarke brought an armful of wet laundry outside to hang in the trees.

Mom wandered in and out of the yard, restless, checking on the laundry and the rest of us, worrying about taking too much hospitality from Coco while I worried that Fred would have too much time to flirt with the twins. Did I like him more than a friend? Of course not. Any woman would be jealous of two beautiful young ladies in Paris for a week with her male buddy!

After dinner, everyone except Coco and the bicycles went into the city for the Bicentennial fireworks display, getting back at two-thirty in the morning to be greeted by an exotic feast prepared by Coco. The next night, Chef Coco hosted a big goodbye dinner party that lasted the whole night, then convinced our riders one more time to stay over. They agreed only if they could cook dinner. "I hope they cook something for us," Fred complained, dusty from digging holes in the dry garden. "There aren't even any more roots."

Without munchies, Fred had no interest in anything, including women. "Did we do something wrong, Daisy?" Betsy asked after Fred turned away, eyes haggard, to nibble bark off of a dead tree.

"Not really. You'd have better luck if you bring him take-out from the Tuilleries Gardens, however. If I recall, that's his favorite grass."

Zelda flopped down in the dust. "He can get his own lunch," she said, angry that food was Fred's number one priority.

By the time the yet-again farewell dinner party was over, I was fast asleep, unconcerned for once about Fred and his pretty friends, who were still pouting.

Mom woke us early in the morning so that we would be ready to leave before Coco tried to tempt us again to stay. The four of us were lined up against the house, ready to roll, when Clarke went inside to wake our host for a goodbye breakfast. "Please stay until after lunch," Coco begged one last time.

"I'll starve if we stay one more minute," Fred said.

Susan's eyes filled with tears. "*Non, monsieur,* we cannot," she said gently. "But we love you very much." Coco cried, and so did everyone else. Then even Fred got a little misty—probably at the thought of real food again.

Chapter 19

"Holy Moley," I said to Fred late in the day. "Only a week off and I'm totally out of shape. My shins hurt and I have ankle cramps! How far have we gone today?"

Fred thought. "Seventy-five kilometers, about."

"No wonder. And all this afternoon. We've only been traveling fifty kilometers a day since the twins arrived."

It was a struggle to get up the next morning, yet Betsy thundered up the road at a furious pace. Were the twins still upset with Fred? I limped along at the end of the train, sore from the day before. A few kilometers into the day, Betsy stopped. "I'm not leading anymore," Megan announced.

"Why not?" Clarke asked.

"I don't like to lead."

"Neither do I, Megan. So what?"

"I don't know how fast to go, Clarke. Kelly just yelled at me because I was going too fast. But how would I know? She was right on my tail."

"Kelly," Susan sighed, "if Megan is going too fast, don't worry about it. Just go at your own pace. She'll either slow down or wait up ahead when she notices that you're not right behind her. Whoever leads needs to set her own pace." And please make it nice and slow, I added.

"I won't lead anymore," Megan insisted.

"Kelly, how about you?" Susan asked.

"No way."

Susan sighed again. "Then I will. My knees are so sore from yesterday that no one will have trouble keeping up."

With Mom and me in the lead, we traveled thirty kilometers before lunch, then another fifty in the afternoon before Kelly and Megan called a halt at a ragtag farm owned by a widower and his fuzzy dog.

The twins flopped on the grass next to Kelly and Megan's tent while Fred and I visited with the dog, more concerned about our responsibilities as American ambassadors than about how tired we were. "If the twins can travel fifty miles a day after a week off," I said to Fred after the dog went inside with the farmer to help make coffee for Susan and Clarke, "why can't they help us visit with our hosts?"

"Betsy and Zelda aren't the ones deciding how far we go," Fred reminded me, sticking up for his girlfriends. "It's up to Kelly and Megan."

"Right," I said, but didn't believe him. Susan and I had gotten so close in the last few months that I couldn't imagine that Betsy and Zelda didn't have input into their riders' decisions. As for Mom and me, when she hurt, I hurt; when she felt good, so did I. I trusted her absolutely, to never push me farther than I could go, and I would never do anything to injure her knees, no matter what. Certainly, at least Clarke and Fred had the same close relationship by now, didn't they? Surely Betsy and Zelda talked to Megan and Kelly—didn't they?

Our departure from the farm the next morning was accompanied by cheers from a dozen villagers who had stopped by the farm for a visit after dinner. At the first turn, Susan said, "Since nobody likes to lead, why don't we take turns?"

"Okay," Kelly said. "You first."

"I led yesterday and Clarke led the day before. You and Megan decide between you." We waited in silence while the teenagers and the twins looked glumly at each other.

"All right, all right," Megan said finally. Betsy nipped at me as she pushed in front.

Mid-morning, we stopped at a service station to top off our feet with air. As soon as the mechanic saw the 'U.S.A.' sign on Fred's backside, he ran to assist. "Thank you for liberating France," he said in French.

"Pardon?"

"During the war. America liberated France. If it weren't for your country," he continued with a shudder, "we would be Germans."

We were nearing the Belgian border. While the others shopped for groceries the next morning, Susan and I sat on a sunny curb and waved at some school children. Pointing at Fred and me, they exclaimed over our heavy packs, then engulfed us in greetings and smiles. An old lady stopped to pat Susan lovingly on her head. "You know, Daisy," Mom said softly, "I'm glad we came back to France. What a wonderful country—it actually feels like home now. I'm sorry this is our last day." I nodded my handlebars in total agreement—I'd live in France in a heartbeat!—then wondered what Belgium would be like. Because Belgians speak French, I'd heard, at least nobody would have to worry too much about language—I, of course, was fluent, and with Megan's five years and Susan and Clarke's ten weeks of French practice, the only tough adjustment in this border crossing would be the new currency.

As Susan gathered orange peels and yogurt cups after lunch in a little town park, an old Frenchman trotted across the grass with a large trash can. "If you would like, here is a can for your rubbish," he said in French. "And please, come into my house and wash up. You are Americans. I was ten years old during the war, and I will never forget the Americans who died to save France. Thank you," he added shyly.

Normally, Susan carried our trash in a plastic grocery bag until we found a trash receptacle, and everybody's hands stayed sticky and oniony until they sweated off the remains of their lunch. Surprised and grateful, our riders followed the man back to his house while the rest of us finished off our own delicate lunch of July Frenchgrass. Fred was in hog heaven. You smell good, Mom, I thought when she returned. "Thank you, Daisy," she said out loud.

I was chatting with Betsy, healing nicely after her rest in Paris. Really, she was quite a sweet girl and I liked her a lot. Zelda, too. It was Fred who was a pain with all his flirting.

"The girls are leaving in a month," Susan said to Clarke. "Airfares will probably be cheaper with thirty days' notice. Okay if we call a travel agent today?"

"We don't have time," he answered.

"Why not? Do we have a dinner reservation somewhere?"

"So call," he replied, fuming. "You're going to anyway, so why ask my permission?"

Betsy and I looked at each other. "What's the matter with him?" she asked me.

"Who knows?" I answered, wondering why anyone had to ask permission to make a phone call. Humans are weird.

In a fair-sized little city, Susan inquired at the town hall about travel agents. There weren't any, and we were still several days from Antwerp. "I think we'd better have your mother reserve something, Kelly," Susan suggested.

"Hurry up," Clarke snarled.

Susan crowded into a little phone booth with Kelly and Megan to call America as I looked over at Fred. Maybe he knew what was wrong with Clarke. He looked away, shrugging. "If there are penalties for changing the dates, don't book anything," Susan was saying into the phone. "We have no idea if we can get to Munich by August twenty-first. We'll call you back in a few hours."

Later, as Clarke paced impatiently back and forth in front of another phone booth, Kelly's mother reported that any reservation that could be changed would cost three times Kelly and Megan's airfare to London. "We might as well book at the last minute, then," Susan said. "In the meantime, let's all see if we can come up with something better."

By now, we were on the border of France and Belgium. "Anybody want a French pastry before Belgium?" Susan asked.

"Yes" and "yes," replied Kelly and Megan. "No," replied Clarke. But it was three against one since their trusty steeds hadn't been asked, so we rested patiently against the bakery window while our riders indulged in gooey cream pastries.

"You're going to get fat," Susan teased slender Megan as she went back for seconds, writing down Megan's purchase in her little journal to make sure that the extra treat would be paid out of Megan's allowance. Every Sunday, Susan tallied up all the expenditures and figured out who owed what. It must have been a pain, especially when we changed currencies, and I was glad that bicycles didn't have to worry about such nonsense. This week's expenses in French francs, for example, would have to be settled in Belgian francs, which had completely different exchange rates.

"Can we stay on the French side of the border tonight?" Megan asked Clarke, licking her fingers.

"I guess so. We can follow the river for another ten or fifteen kilometers."

Half an hour later, we spotted a red brick house next to a small pond. The owner's son spoke a little English. "No, it is not possible to stay here," he said after consulting with his father. "We are afraid that our dogs will attack you. But Father says that maybe you can sleep in the soccer field next door." I knew that Susan would be disappointed if our last night in France didn't include conversation with a family, but what could we do?

Susan grimaced as she helped Clarke put up their tent on the edge of the soccer field in shouting distance of Belgium. She'd pulled a muscle in her back somehow, and I could tell by the way she walked that her knees always ached. We were four nights out of Paris and the eighty-kilometer days with no breaks were taking their toll.

Now that we were on flatter ground, Zelda and her rider Kelly seemed to have settled their differences, turning into incredible long-distance runners. When they led, they never rested, burning up mile after mile with total focus on the road. When they followed, they kept so close to the bike in front that we were all afraid that we'd be trampled. "Don't you ever look at the scenery?" I'd asked Zelda.

"I'm too busy."

"Have you seen how swollen Susan's knees always are?"

"Get that spirit ark of yours to pull its weight, then," Zelda replied.

I mulled over her words. Wouldn't it be nice if the squirrels and hedgehogs and birds and chicken feet would get off and pull sometimes? The only one whom I'd felt had given us a boost was the spirit dog Nagle, who occasionally would jump off my top tube to run alongside, barking happily, cheering us on. I decided to talk to him later about asking the others to give us a hand—or, more appropriately, a leg. Surely I could work out some sort of harness arrangement with a few bungee cords. Besides, it would be nice for my handlebars not to be crowded by dead animal feet all the time.

Feeling that I'd had a helpful idea, I relaxed near the tents while our riders ate dinner and Clarke complained about how hard it was to wake Kelly and Susan in the morning. "Maybe you should try a gentler approach, Clarke," Susan suggested. "When I took off a semester from college, I wrote poetry until three-thirty in the morning, then had to get up at five-thirty for work. My dad would bring me hot coffee every morning and light a candle on my nightstand." She laughed. "Of course, I don't know where you'd get a candle or, for that matter, the coffee, but it's still a sweet idea, don't you think?"

Clarke didn't answer, and after dinner went inside the tent without a word. Susan followed. "Listen, Susan," I heard him say, "that really hurt to be compared to your father."

"I wasn't comparing you to my father, Clarke."

"Tell me, do you think your father did those things for you because he felt guilty for something?"

Oh, for heaven's sake, Clarke, I thought. "Some people do things for others," Susan replied, "just because they want to, believe it or not. If you're jealous, that's your problem."

"Be quiet, Susan, or I'm sleeping outside." Followed by his sleeping bag, Clarke crawled out of the tent wearing only bicycle shorts.

"No way," Susan said, yanking the bag back inside. "If you don't want to work things out between us, then sleep in the dirt!"

"Ouch," I said to Fred.

"Ouch," he said back. Betsy and Zelda had long ago rolled closer to Kelly and Megan's tent.

Furiously, Clarke strode over to me and I skittered away, afraid that he'd hit me and wondering if Fred would do anything to protect me if he did. Yanking open one of my back panniers, Clarke pulled out his black sweatpants, then jerked a water bottle off of Fred and stomped across the soccer field. I could hear Susan crying inside their tent.

Once, in the middle of the night, and again in the bare light of pre-dawn, she walked all over the field looking for Clarke, but it was too dark to see him, wrapped in black. Kelly and the twins stirred at seven. "Have you seen Clarke?" Susan asked them, embarrassed. They shook their heads. "Get Megan up and pack, Kelly, while I look for him again."

Finally, as the mist lifted, Clarke was visible at the far side of the field, an immovable black object. Relieved, Susan strode across the grass with long steps. "Uh-oh," I said to the others as she stood above where he lay. She said something but he didn't respond. She spoke again, poking him with her foot. Clarke curled into a tight ball, arms wrapped around his chest. Susan grabbed an arm and pulled it loose from the Clarke bundle; Clarke wrenched it back and curled up tighter. Picking up the water bottle, she poured it on his head.

"Jeepers," I said as Clarke uncoiled like a snake, jumping up, ready to strike. He grabbed Susan's arm and she shoved him away, then followed when he retreated.

"I don't want to watch this," I said, turning away, scared.

"I do," Zelda said, getting comfortable. "Darn," she said a few moments later. "They aren't hitting each other. They're just yelling."

Megan, meanwhile, leaving Kelly in charge of us and the fight, had gone to get yogurt for breakfast, the cooks being otherwise occupied. When Susan and Clarke finally returned to the group, bedraggled and embarrassed, Kelly and Megan were seated like spectators at a soccer match, cross-legged on the grass, empty yogurt cups scattered about like flowers. "We've been to the store twice already," Megan announced.

"I liked it when you poured water on him, Susan," said Kelly, licking her spoon. "That was good."

"But we cheered for you, too, Clarke," Megan added hastily.

Susan and Clarke looked at each other, mortified. "The first time you two get up at a decent hour," Susan said, "and we still aren't ready to leave until nine."

"That's okay," Kelly replied happily. "I wouldn't have missed this for the world."

Susan repacked Clarke's damp sweats in her pannier, hands trembling. Her sadness was apparent in each of her moves and in her hands as she stroked me. "It's okay, Daisy," she said. "I think we're okay now." My heart ached for her and for Clarke. How can people who love each other act like that, I wondered. Boy, I sure don't want to love anyone!

Chapter 20

W E CROSSED THE BORDER into Belgium at noon, our sixth country, sixth currency, and as it turned out, fourth new language—Flemish, the Belgian dialect of Dutch. After Clarke and Megan unsuccessfully tried to ask a Belgian housewife in French for water, they found themselves back to hand signals and gestures in the air. "Daisy, can you understand these people?" Fred asked as Susan tried to explain to the woman's husband where we were going and where we'd been.

"Pretty much," I responded, "but the dialect's a little tricky."

Susan tried to speak with the elderly man. *"Antwerpen,"* she said. He looked astounded. Susan laughed. "France, Scotland, England, Spain and Africa," she said slowly, making up what she thought might be a Belgian accent. The man took a step backwards. "Then the Netherlands, Germany, Austria, Italy and Greece." The man's mouth dropped open. I didn't blame him—Fred and I had lugged Susan and Clarke 6800 kilometers over the last twenty-two weeks, over 4200 miles, and Betsy and Zelda had carried their riders 1000 miles already. I hardly believed it myself.

As we rolled along the deserted road in the blazing sun, I felt like a chocolate chip cookie burning in a too-hot oven. No, worse than that, because it was humid as well as hot. "I feel like steamed asparagus," I said, dropping back to see how Fred was doing.

His frame was wet with sweat. "Me, too," he groaned. Behind him, the twins dragged along, handlebars wilting, sweat running into their eyes. The sun glittered across the flat fields like a mirror, bleaching everything white.

After two hours, we stopped for water again at a neat, square house surrounded by flowers. Clarke and Megan spoke in French to the tiny old woman who answered the door, Kelly tried out her first-year German, Susan held up one of my water bottles for illustration, and the rest of us demonstrated our request with lolling tongues and heaving sides. The woman understood somebody, gesturing for Megan to follow her inside with all eight water bottles.

The afternoon stretched into the sun in endless waves of stifling heat. "I'm through," Zelda announced.

"At least the roads are flat," Betsy pointed out to cheer up her friend.

"Like a frying pan," Zelda snorted.

Fred and I were too hot to talk. Even the spirit ark was soaked with sweat. About four o'clock, Kelly spotted a little market. "Can we at least get a Coke?" she wailed.

The four humans slid off their panting mounts and traipsed into the store, leaving us alone to bake our brains in the sizzling sun. There was no shade anywhere, or even a tiny breeze. I pondered the irony of my surviving the mountains of Morocco, Spain and France, and the steep Lake District of England, just to die of heat stroke outside a grocery store in a perfectly flat country.

Our riders were gone a lot longer than it took to buy something to drink. "I'll bet that store is air conditioned," I muttered to Fred. Mad with jealousy, I was ready to storm the doors to see for myself when the bicyclists bounded out of the market, rejuvenated, and gently rolled us to a little yard behind the building, where soft drinks and Belgian beer were waiting on a little table alongside a big bucket of cool, clean water and four towels. An attractive woman stood at the back door of the market.

"Feel free to clean up a bit," she said in perfect English to Susan, pointing to the bucket of water. "I'm so glad you'll stay the night. I know that my daughters will love to meet you, and this will give me a chance to practice my English."

I stuck my head in the bucket as soon as she turned away, slurping more than my share before Fred nudged me aside. "Glutton," he grumbled. Zelda and Betsy hovered anxiously next to the bucket, ready to sneak a sip as soon as Fred raised his dripping muzzle to take a breath. Finally, he relinquished the bucket to the twins.

Susan wandered over to freshen up after finishing her beer. "Didn't Nicole bring us water to wash?"

"Yes," Clarke answered. "Why?"

"The bucket's empty," Susan said, puzzled, then turned suspiciously toward Kelly and Megan.

"Don't look at us," Kelly said, draped in a patio chair, licking the last drops of Coke from the top of her bottle.

By now, the transportation team had rolled silently away from the scene of the crime, backs to our riders so they couldn't see our wet noses. Betsy and Zelda innocently cropped dainty mouthfuls of the lawn as Fred carefully examined a bright bunch of flowers in the garden and I hid a grin by rubbing the side of my face against my front wheel as if to scratch an itch.

It was a national holiday in Belgium, and while the rest of us relaxed in the cooling day, Susan and Clarke went off with Nicole's daughter to a Catholic mass and a procession to each of several chapels in the town, returning about eleven that night. The rest of us were already asleep underneath a cloudless sky, the bicyclists' clean clothes drying in a neat row on Nicole's clothesline. Two hours later, our world exploded in thunder as lightning struck daylight into the yard. Fred and I scrambled to our wheels. "Are you guys okay?" we called in Betsy and Zelda's direction.

"Yikes, what was that?" Zelda said as another bolt of lightning flashed so near that we smelled it, setting off rolls of earsplitting thunder. The town fire alarms went off, then rain literally poured from the sky. Fred and I huddled together, soaked, waiting for the storm to pass or to be hit by lightning, whichever came first. It was a long night.

Nicole was in the back yard at first light. "Are you all right?" she asked. "I was awake most of the night worrying about you."

"You weren't the only one," Susan assured her as Kelly crawled out of her tent dragging a soaking wet sleeping bag.

"There's a foot of water in there," Kelly said, pointing toward the tent with dripping fingers. "I would have drowned if I hadn't sat up all night. My nose was below water line."

Megan emerged, hair dripping, to wring out her own bag. "Eeeeoo, eeeeoo, eeeeoo," she said as cold water oozed between her bare toes.

I surveyed my bicycle buddies and decided that we were all intact—in fact, as clean as we'd been in months. "You poor dears," Nicole said, and I assumed that she included us in her sympathies. "Here, let me hang your sleeping bags on the line to dry. I've already moved your laundry into the garage and set up a little table for your breakfast."

Although the bicycles weren't invited inside, we enjoyed a fresh breakfast salad of tender grass dressed in rainwater, then stretched out on the damp lawn while clothes and sleeping bags baked dry.

"The secondary roads have been deserted," Clarke said outside of town later, studying the map. "Let's try the big roads to Brugge." Traffic was light, but it wouldn't have mattered—the main highway boasted a bicycle lane separated from the roadway by a parking lane. We sailed along, two by two for the first time, safe and secure.

The first thing we found in Brugge was a whimsical fountain, and we stopped to cool off our feet together with more people than we'd seen since entering the country. My favorite part of the fountain, of course, was an iron sculpture of bicycles. "Hello," I called up to them, but they didn't respond.

A young man approached. "Hi, there!" he said to Clarke. "I'm a Canadian on a year-long bike trek. Just broke down outside of town and hitchhiked in on a truck." He took a step backward after examining Fred. "You're certainly carrying a lot of stuff."

"We're camping," Clarke explained. "How about you?"

"No way. I stay in hostels every night. After eighty or a hundred kilometers a day, the last thing I want to do is cook. I'd rather eat out and sleep in a bed."

The young man's comments made me proud of my own little group. Our record was still 118 kilometers in one day, but Betsy and Zelda's eighty-kilometer days since Paris were nothing to sneeze at either, particularly since we had to set up camp and cook every night and cook and clean up every morning. And this guy was much younger than Susan and Clarke. I wished that his bicycle were here so that I could brag.

"This is without a doubt the most beautiful city I've ever seen," Susan said later, leaning over a bridge to watch the reflection of pastel buildings shimmer on the still waterway like an impressionist painting. Inside a tiny store, she bought me a present – decals from every country we'd been in and those we planned to go to, in silver, gold, red, yellow and blue. They didn't have one for Morocco. "I can't put these on you now, Daisy," Mom explained after she showed them to me. "You're too dirty."

I twisted my handlebars around to look. Hadn't I just had a rain bath the night before? Even so, I was already sweaty again, with dirt to my knees. Disappointed that I couldn't wear my fancy new decals, I nevertheless mentally nuzzled Mom's hand and looked forward to the next rainstorm or river.

"You guys want to try to make it to the beach tonight?" Clarke asked Kelly and Megan.

"I'd love to sleep on a beach," Kelly answered.

"I think we can afford to spend a whole day there," Clarke laughed. "The way you two are cycling, we'll have no problem getting to Germany in a month."

"The way you two are cycling, we'll probably be there in two days," Susan grumbled.

We made it to De Haan on the North Sea before dark, but 'no camping' signs were posted all along the shore. Turning inland, we found a house surrounded by roses and flowering bushes. The eight of us lined up outside the front door and Clarke knocked. *"Goedenavond,"* Clarke said in Dutch because his phrasebook didn't include Flemish.

The woman who answered the door looked carefully at each of us. "Are you British?" she asked in English, "or American?"

"How did you know?" Clarke breathed a sigh of relief at not having to muck about in tongue-tangling Flemish or Dutch.

"Your accent," she laughed. "I'm an English teacher."

While we relaxed in the garden, our riders enjoyed fresh coffee with cookies and big ripe strawberries dipped in sugar, compliments of the nice Belgian woman and her husband. I thought about the Canadian, too tired to even pitch camp at night after bicycling all day. "It must be really hard for Susan and Clarke to visit with strangers every night," I said to Fred after I rolled in the grass.

"I don't know," he answered. "They don't work as hard as we do, of course. I think I could visit with anybody who fed me."

"Maybe," I said doubtfully, then fell asleep.

The next day, we left our packs in the garage while we went to the beach. It was fun to roll along the highway, light as a feather, and to lie in the sun with our human companions.

Zelda led the next day at a blistering pace of thirty kilometers an hour. With my heavy packs, I struggled to keep up, thankful for the flat terrain. "If we can find a place to stay near the city," Clarke proposed as we neared the outskirts, "Susan and I can ride into Antwerp to pick up our mail and get her computer looked at—again." He glanced at Susan sternly. "Kelly, you and Megan can come with us—it's only another thirty kilometers—or you can shop for groceries and start dinner."

"We'll stay," they replied. Can I stay too, Mom?

Downtown Antwerp was on the other side of a wide river, which we crossed via an underground tunnel. Because the elevator wasn't working, Fred and I were forced to manage four flights of steep escalators. I was scared to get on the first step, but Mom held me tightly. Halfway down, I decided to roll the rest of the way to get it over with and struggled to get Susan to let go of my front and rear brakes. She wouldn't. Three more escalators, then we all walked through the tunnel and climbed on the four long escalators going up the other side. That was even worse—I was sure that I'd roll backwards all the way to the bottom; this time, I wanted Mom to hold on.

Antwerp is paved in cobblestones, which hurt our feet; grumbling, we picked our way carefully through the old part of the city. Clarke and Fred went to the American Express office for mail and money after unsaddling the laptop at the computer store, where I waited alone outside for Susan. She came back after a few minutes looking disappointed. When Clarke returned, she explained that the technicians weren't able to work on her computer. He sighed. "We have to take it to Deurne," she continued.

"Who's Deurne?"

"A town north of Antwerp. I have an appointment with a technician between eight and noon tomorrow."

Bumping back through the city, we hung on down the escalators, hurried through the tunnel, negotiated up the escalators on the other side and returned to the farm where Kelly and Megan were fixing dinner while the twins lounged in the grass. I flopped down next to Betsy. "Goodness," I said, "ninety kilometers today. Wait until you have to go down and up eight escalators tomorrow. We did sixteen today!"

"What's an escalator?" she asked, nervous.

"Only a moving staircase," Fred responded, glaring at me for trying to scare her.

Clarke was the last to be ready in the morning and had a tussle with Megan about who was supposed to cook breakfast while Susan fretted that we'd be late for her computer appointment. By the time we left the farm, we had no time for sightseeing in Antwerp and hobbled through the cobblestone streets as fast as we could, everyone snarling.

When we finally found Deurne and the computer company, Susan raced inside. It was five minutes before noon. "I misunderstood," she said, returning. "My appointment was between eight and nine, not eight and noon. The technician is in Brussels until three-thirty."

"This is just another example of your stupid computer holding us up," Clarke groused.

"Come on, Clarke," Susan replied sharply, "if you hadn't held us up this morning, we'd have been here by nine. Let's just make use of the wait by doing some errands. I need stamps, and we can go to the market and fix lunch."

After clattering all over the suburbs, we returned at four but the technician was still in Brussels. Another engineer, however, had been found who could take a look at the computer, so Susan hurried into the building, laptop in her arms. Returning half an hour later, she smiled sheepishly. "He couldn't find anything wrong," she explained. "It malfunctioned the first time he tried to turn it on, but after that, it worked perfectly."

"Why didn't you try more than once?" Clarke asked.

"I tried dozens of times, Clarke."

"So what did they charge to fix a working computer?"

"Nothing. Just wished us a safe trip and asked me to send a postcard." She laughed. "They also told me that the bike paths in Belgium are lousy, that the ones in Holland are better."

Clarke laughed, too. "These are the only bike paths we've had in five months! I think they're fabulous."

"That's what I told them. Well, anyway, you guys, I'm sorry I made you wait for nothing."

It was five o'clock. The homes northeast of Antwerp were beautiful, spread out under large trees and formal gardens. They all had room for us, of course, but since we hadn't really gone anywhere yet, we wound around the narrow roads toward Holland for another forty kilometers until the bike path disappeared and we were almost flattened by a speeding car. "Whoops," Betsy said, whisking her slim rear toward the edge of the road as Fred and I lurched our bulky bodies into the roadside grass.

Kelly found us a nice spot, the garden behind the house of an elderly couple whose son's family lived next door. While our riders trooped off after dinner to visit the younger generation, we went to bed early to rest our cobblestone-sore tires.

Chapter 21

A FTER ONLY FIVE DAYS crossing Belgium, here we were in the Netherlands, country number seven, land of bicycle paths, tiny lanes two of us wide wandering through grain fields from one village to the next untroubled by cars, noise and exhaust fumes. Heaven was upon us, I decided, spotting the first bicycle capillary to branch off from the busy main artery.

Mom and I were leading. We stopped. Susan studied the map, then looked up at the sign at the head of the path, a tiny bicycle with the name of a village underneath. She looked down at the map again, then at the sign once more. "I can't find the village where this bike path leads. We'd better stay on the highway."

The same thing happened at the next bike path, and the next. "I don't mind never knowing where we're going," Susan said finally, "but at least we need to know where we are. I guess we'll have to skip the bike paths." Acutely disappointed, we wrenched ourselves from the little bicycle lane tucked enticingly into a tall field of wheat, peaceful and safe, and grumbled back onto the busy highway.

At Zundert, Clarke went into a small bank to exchange travelers' checks for Dutch guilders. "I'm still not used to converting French francs to Belgian francs," Susan groaned. Actually, the currency exchanges were easy—if there are six French francs in one American dollar, for example, and the budget is ten American dollars a day, just spend sixty francs.

Language-wise, I was glad to see our riders begin to let go of the invisible boundary that kept them from fluidly crossing the foreign language barrier. Instead of thinking of the English word for something and then translating it, they'd just holler out whatever word came to mind when they wanted to say something—often, it wasn't the English word, and their conversations were becoming quite delightful, I thought, sprinkled with French and Spanish and British English. Even Fred and the twins were picking up a few words.

Now, in the midst of Dutch, we stopped for groceries in Breda and Clarke and the transportation team rested against a wall while the women went inside. They should have taken me along to translate. "That was a nightmare," Susan exclaimed when they came out later. "We were supposed to ask someone behind a counter what vegetables we wanted. How do you say 'tomato' in Dutch?"

"What did you do?" Clarke asked, grinning.

"Pointed and named vegetables in French and German until someone standing nearby translated one of the languages into Dutch for the clerk. How embarrassing!"

"It worked, though," Clarke noted the bag of groceries disappearing into my left front pannier.

About seven o'clock, we knocked at the door of a dairy farm and were given permission to camp by thirteen-year-old Carin; her parents were out for the evening. She and a friend, themselves planning to sleep in a tent in the garden, scrambled over the pasture fence to move a horse and two calves to an adjacent field, disappointing me, as I would have liked to meet them.

The twins were still asleep when Carin's father carried a bucket of water across the pasture to his livestock early the next morning and waved a greeting to Susan and Clarke, who were packing their sleeping bags. Fred was up grazing; still stretched out in the dewy grass, I was caught between being really asleep and fantasizing about not having to wear panniers every day. Soon enough, I'd be on my feet, fully loaded, trudging through the hot sun to Rotterdam with 200 extra pounds on my back. "Come on, Daisy," Mom said then, wheeling me to my feet against the pasture fence. "Time to get on the road."

Stretching, I patiently allowed myself to be packed as Carin scampered across the field. "My parents want you to come inside for coffee," she told Susan.

"We can't," Clarke said. "We're already getting a late start."

Two minutes later, Carin returned with her father, a handsome man with startling blue eyes. With two or three words in English, he insisted that the bicyclists accept his invitation and then turned to lead them into the house, assuming victory. Our riders followed like puppies, then returned half an hour later to roll us into the barn. "You guys are staying here," Mom explained. "The rest of us are taking the train to Amsterdam for the day. This family says that you'll be stolen if we bicycle into the city."

"Perfect," Fred said, yawning. "I could use some extra sleep."

"I wish we weren't wearing packs, though," I answered, settling down next to a trailer full of windsurf boards. Betsy snuggled next to me, putting her head on one of my panniers, and Zelda leaned against the door.

That night after dark, our riders came into the barn only long enough to unload their tents and sleeping bags, leaving us in the barn for the night. And instead of retrieving us in the morning, they retrieved the windsurf boards and headed off with the Dutch family to a nearby lake. "How come we weren't invited?" I complained to Fred. "I need a bath."

Fred opened an eye. "You certainly do," he answered uncharitably, falling back to sleep.

"So do I," responded Betsy.

"I'm hungry," Zelda said, nosing the closed barn door.

The next morning, it was business as usual in spite of threatening rain. Once again, loaded with our heavy packs, after photographs and kisses all around, we rolled down the long drive toward the highway.

It was raining lightly when our riders went inside a small cafe for a snack because the markets were closed. By the time they returned and we'd traveled only a few kilometers, the rain exploded into a downpour. "I can't see anything," Zelda complained.

"None of us can," I replied, pelted by rain needles.

"Something's wrong with my freewheel," Betsy said a bit later, and we pulled under some trees while Clarke tried to adjust it as rain soaked through the branches and fell in great blobs on our heads.

"Let's get out of the rain for a minute," Susan called ahead at Baarle-Hertog, a strange little polka dot of Belgium set inside Holland for some inexplicable reason. Thanks, Mom, I thought, then slumped in disappointment when she left me and my bicycle friends leaning against a wet wall while our riders ran inside a warm bakery for hot rolls.

They returned a few minutes later. "We shouldn't have gone inside," Susan decided. "Now I feel even worse. Wouldn't it be wonderful if one of these drivers, instead of splashing us with muddy water, would invite us home?"

"Especially if they have a huge house with a fireplace in every room and big, deep bathtubs on feet," said Megan as rain washed her face.

"And bowls of hot, thick stew," Clarke put in his two cents, "or a casserole."

"I'd be happy for another barn," I said to Fred, "or even a big tree."

"Look for a barn," Susan said after seventy-five kilometers as if she'd heard me. "I refuse to sleep in the mud tonight. And believe me, I won't wait until it's offered. I'll ask." Yes, oh yes, Mom. All of us were frozen and wet, through and through.

Soon, tucked into a barn filled with automobiles instead of hay, we rested while our riders cooked supper. "I couldn't be you two on this trip," Susan said to Kelly and Megan. Their tent leaked, their sleeping bags weren't warm and got wet every time the tent did. They had no sleeping mats, and they always managed to leave things out in the rain at night. But then, why not? It was just as wet inside their tent as under a waterfall. Of course, we bicycles didn't have tents or sleeping bags at all. Did anyone appreciate *our* sacrifices?

Megan's clothes had been damp, dirty and stale for weeks. One day, Susan had asked her why. "No washing machine," she shrugged. Apparently, she thought that anything larger than underwear couldn't be washed by hand. When Susan sat on the ground, she tried to sit on one of the tattered fluorescent raincoats to keep her shorts clean as long as possible; the girls just sat, and used their jackets as cutting boards. Even when they did wash something, they forgot to hang it out to dry on Betsy and Zelda or at our next stop, leaving it in plastic bags to mold. Of course, if they'd been bicycles, they wouldn't have had to worry about clothes at all.

The next day, we spotted a bridge over a canal at lunchtime. "Let's duck under there to eat before it rains again," Clarke suggested, then discovered that bike paths edged the canal, flat and straight as arrows toward Maastricht, our destination. As we rolled happily along after lunch, container boats floated up and down the waterways, long barges made homey by white lace curtains and hanging plants and flowers in the pilots' cabins. One even had a big tomato plant tucked up behind the front window.

Late in the day, Betsy got a flat. In trying to fix it herself, Megan ruined Betsy's inner tube. "Why didn't you ask for help?" Clarke asked, irritated, while Fred tried to take Betsy's mind off her injuries by telling stupid jokes.

"Because you always say that you're tired of doing things for us, Clarke. Make up your mind."

After Megan and Clarke finished the job in silence using a tube that was too big for Betsy's wheel, we trotted off again. "How do you feel?" I asked her.

"Like one shoe is too tight," Betsy answered unhappily. Then her freewheel started to rattle again.

"You still owe me a freewheel," Susan reminded Kelly. "I know that you and Megan are anxious to get to Germany, but I think it's time we buy two."

"Tomorrow," Megan replied.

"I hope Betsy stays together that long," Fred whispered to me. "What will we do if she doesn't?"

"Carry her, I guess."

"Not Megan, too, I hope."

I could imagine our dividing up Betsy's pieces and packs, but how could we divide up Megan? "Megan can walk," Zelda announced.

While our riders spent the night inside a little guest house for university students, we crowded together in a cozy shed after an early supper of fresh-mown lawn, happy for our owners that they had their own kitchen and bathroom for the very first time. I was glad that I didn't care about things like that for myself; traveling was easier when you didn't need anything but an occasional tall tree for shelter and maybe a little grass. Maybe.

"Where to?" Clarke asked the group in the morning.

"I'm hungry," Kelly said.

"Me, too," said Megan.

"I think we'd better think about a bike shop today," Susan said, "like it or not."

Clarke studied the map. "It'll take about an hour to get to Maastricht," he decided.

"I can't wait that long for food," Kelly announced.

"Neither can I," said Megan.

Clarke, impatient, said, "Then we'll have to leave the canals and go to Genk."

I didn't want to go to Genk; the flat canal bike paths were wonderful, and struggling through a big city seemed to take forever, no matter how much we hurried. "I hope your freewheel falls off," I said uncharitably to Betsy.

It was almost noon by the time we reached Genk, bought groceries and found a bike shop, which had just closed for lunch. Susan wasn't happy. "We can eat here if you want, but I'm not leaving town without bike parts after riding this far out of our way," she announced. "It's about time we accomplish more than just another feeding frenzy."

As soon as Susan unpacked the food, Kelly and Megan pounced on the Belgian waffles and jam she had bought for dessert. "You two are spoiled brats," Susan snarled. "Can't you wait five minutes for lunch? Better yet, help fix it. I'm not your slave, you know." Kelly and Megan stopped chewing and looked at Susan with big eyes while the rest of us moved as far from her as possible.

"What difference does it make if they eat their dessert first?" Clarke came to the girls' defense.

"Because I'd like a little help. Can't they each peel a stupid egg?"

"I'll do the dishes," Megan offered to appease her.

"You bet you will," Susan growled, piling lunch in front of the girls. "So eat," she ordered, turning away to sit by herself on the wall where I huddled against my friends. I scrunched against Fred, staying out of her way.

Kelly spilled a quart of milk on the sidewalk and used our entire water supply to clean up the mess. "Now I can't wash the dishes," Megan announced smugly.

"Wrong," Susan said, stomping off to the nearest house to get water, then waited in silence, crouched against the wall, for Megan to clean up the dishes. When the bike shop finally opened, Clarke went inside to buy replacement parts while the teenagers wrote in their journals and Susan fumed.

After trotting single file away from Genk at three o'clock, tool kit complete and no one complaining about hunger, it rained off and on all the way to Maastricht. Instead of taking an hour to get there, it had taken a day; and we rolled through the beautiful city on the western edge of Holland's apostrophe between Belgium and Germany in silence.

Just short of the border into Germany, we stopped for the night at a dairy farm in order to avoid the city of Aachen at rush hour. Unfortunately, rain from the past few days had made the pastures a mire of mud and manure but the young farmer offered a tiny shed for the bicycles. "Eeeeoo, eeeeoo, eeeeoo," Megan said as she squished through the slimy mud wearing the tennis shoes that had split when she fell off Betsy near Calais. "There's cow poop oozing between my toes."

Tucked into the shed with old farm implements and dusty hay, my friends and I were nonetheless more content than our owners, I decided after hearing Kelly scream when she found a dead blackbird stuck on the electric fence as she chased her mucky tent across the field in the wind.

Chapter 22

W E CROSSED THE BORDER into Germany at Aachen on
August 2nd. The plan was for the younger half of the
group to leave from Munich on August 21st. We'd have to
hustle. Fred would be bereft when Betsy and Zelda left, I was sure. I had mixed
feelings—although traveling with eight was so much more complicated than
with four, I had learned to enjoy the twins and their riders.

As usual, it took hours to get through the big city; in addition to navigating
through the busy streets, the bicyclists had to exchange money—this time,
Belgian francs for Deutschmarks—memorize the new exchange rate, learn
part of a new language before their first trip to the grocery store, and buy maps
of the new country.

It was three o'clock before we left the city and Mom and I, who were in
the lead, had a horrible time with the German maps. An hour later, we were
still on the outskirts of Aachen, snuffling blindly around the streets like moles,
when Zelda broke down on a bridge over some railroad tracks. "Stop!" she and
Kelly screeched.

Kelly, our only teammate who knew even one word of German, rifled
through her German dictionary as Susan strode off to look for someone who
could speak English, into efficiency instead of language practice. By the time
Kelly had fashioned a question in German, Susan had directions to the nearest
bicycle store. "I'll meet you at the bike shop," Megan announced. "I'm going to
the post office across the street."

"I don't like splitting up," Clarke said. "What if you get lost?"

"I won't get lost." Susan repeated the complicated directions to the bike store twice and Megan and Betsy left, offended.

Fred and I escorted Zelda to the bike shop, one on either side. There, she was fixed in twenty minutes. While we waited for Betsy, Clarke showed the bike mechanic Fred's still-cracked bracket. "There is nothing wrong with it," the German said in English.

"Yes, there is. See the crack?"

"It is fine." It is not, Fred insisted, it hurts. But the man wouldn't listen.

"What could be keeping Megan?" Clarke changed the subject.

"She's lost, of course," Susan predicted. "I can't believe that we turned her loose alone where she can't speak a word of the language. What now?"

"I'll try to find my way back to the post office," Clarke said, sighing. "You two stay here in case she shows up."

It was six o'clock by the time Fred and Clarke returned with Betsy and her rider; it had taken all day just to dip our toes into Germany. Two hours later, we stopped at a large house at the edge of a forest and were given permission to camp, thanks to translations into German by Kelly and into English by the owner's daughter.

After our riders had breakfast with our host family, we were back on the road, Betsy in the lead, climbing up through a beautiful forest and then down into a meadow, galloping through several kilometers of tiny green frogs that hopped back and forth across the road as we passed. They reminded me of the chicken feet in Spain, except that these guys were attached to their legs. It was a glorious morning.

Mercifully, the spirit ark hadn't grown much in Belgium or Holland or now Germany; apparently, either dead animals were immediately picked up off the highways or maybe, I hoped, they didn't get run over to begin with. Even so, I was still crowded with the spirits of cats and dogs and hedgehogs and birds from other countries, fur and feathers ruffled by the winds and pelted with the rain, just like my own. Although they sometimes felt awfully heavy, they were always good company, especially Nagle, our fluffy French spirit dog.

Betsy kept getting lost, as I had the day before. Although the big autobahns had been built for efficiency, our little roads seemed to go around and about like scribbles, going nowhere. After Clarke grumbled that we'd never get to

Munich if we didn't make better progress, Susan suggested skipping Köln and turning south to Bonn. "As long as I get to ride along the Rhine," Kelly said.

"Coming up," Susan answered, head-to-head with Megan over the map.

"I wish they'd let me navigate," Fred grumbled.

"How could you help?" I answered. "You can't read German."

"I suppose *you* can," he snapped, bristling.

"Of course."

At Widdig, a man directed us to turn left to a bike path. Sure enough, there was the Rhine, all ours, with no cars, compliments of a perfectly lovely paved bicycle path right next to the water. "Let's stop for the day," Clarke suggested. "We've ridden seventy kilometers and there may not be any houses along the bike path."

No one wanted to offer us a garden for the night, but one man suggested an empty field next to a fenced pasture. After leaning Fred and me into some spindly bushes, Susan and Clarke tried to find a level spot in the vacant lot for their tent. "We've gotten spoiled by garages," she said, stringing wet laundry on twigs. I looked up; rain clouds bundled overhead.

Across the pasture, a man watched us in amusement. Finally, he came over to the fence, and in a mixture of German and gestures, explained that it was going to rain. "*Ja, danke,*" Susan answered. But what could she do about it?

"You had better stay in my barn," the man said in German.

Kelly and Megan crowded themselves and all of our packs into a stall full of clean straw; because of Clarke's allergies, he and Susan pitched their tent outside near the doorway while my bicycle friends and I curled up next to the barn after introducing ourselves to the nervous horses now relegated to the small corral. I was exhausted.

By the time we got organized for the evening, the German had returned to the pasture with his wife. Soon, another neighbor appeared, his hands full of eggs, and then another, an East Indian Sikh who said he'd left his country because of religious persecution. As Fred told silly jokes to Betsy and Zelda, I tried to listen to the more mature human conversation but was too tired to be interested. All of a sudden, this whole trip seemed to require a monumental amount of energy.

Rolling in the dirt, I scratched my back, then flopped onto my stomach with my head on the ground. In the morning, I rolled onto my side to sleep some more while our riders went to their new friends' house for breakfast. When they returned, I forced myself to let Mom load me up with panniers, then trudged off down the Rhine, head down, still tired. "What's the matter with you?" Fred asked.

"I don't know, Fred. Leave me alone." It was a cloudy, gray day, and trundling in silence along the quiet bike path gave me a chance to be alone with my thoughts. Something was troubling me, but I wasn't sure what.

A family of white swans nestled next to the path. As Zelda passed first, one of the birds reached out its neck and hissed, ready to grab Kelly's foot. When Betsy crossed in front of them, the swan struck like a snake. "Ouch!" Betsy yelped.

"Don't be a baby, Betsy," I said. "He's just trying to protect his family."

Betsy turned to look at me, then rolled up to Zelda and whispered something; they both looked back and giggled. So what? Maybe I was tired of their company, and of worrying about them and Fred and about Susan and Clarke. Who cared? Nobody but Mom seemed to worry about me.

My grumpiness lifted as the morning turned into afternoon and clouds tattered across the sun to make light and shadow lace across the path. Tour boats from Holland and Belgium bobbed down the Rhine as gray container boats slid flat and silent in the water. A family of ducks cut the current like tiny rowboats one after the other. Try as I might, it was too hard to be grumpy on such a pretty day.

In Koblenz, the market was closing for lunch but a customer directed us to a store that stayed open another half hour. "After that store closes," the German explained, "nothing will be open again until Monday morning, you know."

"If the stores close at noon on Friday in Germany," Kelly groaned, "we'll starve before Monday." Normally, our riders shopped for food twice a day except for weekends, when the markets closed at noon on Saturday and they had to buy enough to keep them for a day and a half. As the bearer of most of the food supplies, I hated the weekends. Now, how could I carry yet another day's food?

After the shopping spree up the street, my bicycle buddies were pressed into service. We looked like elephants. Every corner and crack was filled to overflowing with food— plastic bags hung from our handlebars and packs and the bucket on my head spilled over with fresh fruit and vegetables. Pulling a little notebook from her pocket, Susan started to write down the cost of their purchases. "It's not Friday," she laughed. "It's Saturday. We don't need all this stuff."

"Oh boy, more to eat," Kelly said happily.

"Not funny," I said to Fred, angry that we'd been overburdened unnecessarily.

"Let's hope they eat fast," he agreed.

Whatever day of the week it was, it was beautiful. The sky was a clear, bright blue and the warm sun on our backs pushed us along like a little motor. As we wound through riverside villages, our path threaded through pocket parks like a needle and thread tying town to town at the edge of the Rhine.

At Obserwesel, we found a terraced garden leading up the mountainside and Clarke and Kelly knocked on the door of a white house set with its back against the hill. A woman stuck her head out of an upstairs window, looking stern and suspicious. *"Einen Augenblick,"* she said, just a minute, after Kelly attempted to communicate a request to camp. Closing the front door behind her, the woman came out on her front porch and Kelly's sincere attempts to converse won her over. *"Ja, das ist okay,"* she agreed with a smile and turned to go inside. Then she stopped, her hand grasping the doorknob. It was locked. Cheeks pink with embarrassment, she turned to Kelly, hands over her mouth, eyes wide.

Racing to her rescue, Clarke retrieved a mostly-toothless twenty-foot ladder he'd seen by the roadside and, leaning it against her balcony, climbed up to where there were no more rungs. Then Megan climbed on his shoulders and reached the two remaining rungs, crawling over the balcony, careful not to upset the potted flowers, as our hostess watched, hands clasped in her starched white apron. In a flash, Megan was down the stairs to fling open the front door. "Nice work," I remarked to Fred, impressed. He didn't hear me; he was too busy laughing at something Zelda said.

After dinner, the woman's son invited Kelly and Megan to a disco. "Why can't we go, too?" complained the twins.

"You smell bad," I said, my mood sour again.

"So do Kelly and Megan," they pointed out.

After the girls left, Susan and Clarke climbed into their tent, alone for the first time in two months. Susan started a conversation about their wedding, one year ago tomorrow. "I'm too tired to talk tonight, Susan," I heard Clarke say. Yet when the German woman came to ask if he and Susan wanted to come inside for wine, Clarke readily assented.

"I thought you were too tired for conversation," Susan hissed.

"This is different," he responded, popping eagerly out of the tent. Reluctantly, Mom followed, running a hand over my handlebars as she passed. I knew exactly how she felt.

In the morning, as Clarke made a new 'U.S.A.' sign for Fred's backside, one that included a flag of each country through which we'd traveled, Susan kissed his shoulder. "Happy anniversary, Clarke." He didn't respond.

Hurt, Susan came out of the tent to pack. It began to rain. "Daisy has a leak in her front tire," she called to Clarke. "Will you unfasten my brakes so I can repair it?" Her reach was too small to squeeze the brakes with one hand while unhooking the cables with the other. Without a word, Clarke jerked off my brakes, then pushed past us to return to their tent.

Mom had trouble with the repair. Clarke watched her work from inside the tent, then sarcastically offered a hint or two. Finally, soaked with rain, Susan asked him for help. Ignoring her, he went inside the house for coffee with the German woman and her son. "Irene wants you to come in for coffee, Susan," he announced when he finally came back.

Susan was still struggling with my wet, slippery tube. "When I'm finished, Clarke. Why did you go inside when I asked for your help?"

"Because I wanted to be with Irene," Clarke replied, then pinched my foot as he angrily pushed my tire into its rim.

Susan finally went in for coffee while Megan did the breakfast dishes. "Wasn't that nice of Megan?" Clarke said when Mom returned to finish packing. "What an incredible woman Irene is," he continued as if his wife didn't matter at all. I could have killed him.

Susan looked at him, expressionless. "I'd hoped to spend some time this morning reminiscing about our wedding day," she said finally.

"Maybe later."

"Right." Mom wheeled me away from the group before I could ask Fred what was wrong with Clarke. Hurrying off into the gray, dreary day, we tried to keep as much distance as possible between us and Clarke. Behind us, he chatted happily with Kelly and Megan in a fake British accent, telling stories and laughing as if Susan were nonexistent. Fred laughed along with him, the toad. I pulled ahead in the steady rain, unable to tolerate Clarke's joking with the girls when he wouldn't even be civil to my mother on their first anniversary.

"Stop! I have a flat," he yelled after an hour.

Remembering his not wanting to help with my flat that morning, I took my time going back. "What do you want me to do?" Susan offered without enthusiasm.

"Nothing," Clarke replied, smug. "Megan is already doing everything I need."

"I'm the nurse," Megan said brightly as Fred nuzzled Betsy, the jerk, even with his front wheel in pieces.

"Goody for you," Susan said to Megan, pushing me across a bridge to wait on the other side. As Clarke and the girls crossed over a few minutes later, I hurried on ahead. How could Fred let Clarke be so awful?

The bike path turned to gravel and then to mud, which splashed all over us. We strung out farther to keep from splashing each other, and all conversation stopped. It was cold. Then Fred got another flat and pulled into a tunnel under a road. "It serves you right," I yelled back to him.

"Shut up, Daisy," he growled, holding up his hurt tire.

Susan and I stood shivering against the cement wall of the tunnel, as far from Clarke as possible without going back out in the rain. Again, we started off before everyone was ready, keeping our distance, ignoring everyone.

About six-thirty, we arrived in Wiesbaden and pulled under an overhang. "Where do you want to stay tonight?" Clarke shouted over the rain.

"I don't care," Susan shouted back.

"I guess we could at least find out if there's a hotel nearby," Clarke said to the teenagers, looking up at the leaden sky. "Kelly, let's see if anyone in that bar knows of an inexpensive hotel."

"You're having a pretty bad day, aren't you, Susan?" Megan said gently after Clarke and Kelly walked across the street.

Hunched on the wet curb, Mom began to cry. "Yes," she answered as I touched her shoulder with my muddy front tire. Fred and the twins stood apart, afraid to come near.

As if they weren't already soaked to their bones, Clarke and Kelly returned running. "There's a Greek hotel down the street," Clarke told Megan, ignoring Susan. "Let's check it out when the rain stops."

Slumped on the curb, unchecked tears streaking her face with dirt, Mom ignored everyone and everyone but me ignored her. Finally, the rain let up just a bit and Clarke and the girls pedaled off. "Rooms are seventy-five Deutschmarks each, about forty dollars, including breakfast," Kelly explained when they returned.

"What do you want to do, Susan?" Clarke asked impatiently.

"I already told you it doesn't matter." Susan finally looked up. "As far as you and I are concerned, Clarke, I could spend our anniversary right here on the curb." Hopping on my back, she pedaled me down the street toward the little hotel.

Eventually, Clarke and the girls caught up. "We've just been hearing about the world according to Clarke," Megan told Susan, rolling her eyes.

"Lucky you," Susan replied.

I spent a lonely night locked in a storeroom with my bicycle buddies, worrying about Mom, unable to protect or console her. Fred had just shrugged when I'd asked about Clarke, and Betsy and Zelda hadn't noticed anything wrong. Why should they? They were too busy giggling at Fred's jokes.

In the morning, Clarke silently shouldered Susan aside when they came to get us out of the storeroom, yet when the hotel owner's son stopped to chat, Clarke was instantly full of conversation. Obviously, he wasn't too tired to talk to strangers, only to the person who was supposed to mean more to him than anyone else in the world, and I decided to knock him flat the first chance I got. Fred too, while I was at it.

Chapter 23

STILL UPSET WITH CLARKE and Fred, I waited with the other bikes outside a shopping mall in Weisbaden, a large city too much like America for me to feel like I was exploring a foreign country. Susan was inside with Clarke looking for new bike shorts while Kelly and Megan kept an eye on the rest of us. I needed keeping an eye on, tempted as I was to run away from all the tension, but of course I couldn't leave Mom. Maybe she and I should run away together.

Kelly and Megan whispered together, then Kelly went into the mall. When she returned, they put their heads together again, chattering excitedly. Susan and Clarke returned empty-handed, walking far apart in silence. "There's a travel agent inside," Kelly announced.

"So?" Susan asked.

"We asked how to sell our bikes," Megan continued. "We want to use that money toward our airfare home. The travel agent told us to take them to the American military base here."

Sell their bikes? I was aghast. How could Kelly and Megan sell their friends, their companions, their loyal beasts of burden? Surely I hadn't heard right. I glanced at Fred for reassurance, but he was staring at the teenagers, incredulous. Betsy, stiff as if bracing for a blow, looked pleadingly at Megan, tears in her eyes. Zelda, lips drawn back, snarled at Kelly, eyes smoking. I scooted over to Betsy and snuggled up close—Zelda could obviously take care of herself. Susan, as surprised as the rest of us, finally stammered, "But how on earth can you deliver the bikes here from Munich?"

"We won't have to," Kelly said excitedly. "We'll leave now."

I looked at Fred. "Wasn't Germany the country Kelly wanted to see most?" I asked. "We just got here."

"Are you sure about this?" Susan was asking the teenagers, shocked. "Absolutely."

Zelda sputtered. "Those horrible little brats," she said. "How can they just ditch us in a foreign country after all we've done for them?"

Betsy dissolved into tears, inconsolable. "Because they don't love us," she sobbed.

"Oh, shut up, Betsy," snapped Zelda.

"Do you suppose that Kelly and Megan want to leave because of Clarke and Susan's fight yesterday?" Fred asked me quietly. I was wondering the same thing but didn't know the answer. I looked at Mom. At least she and Clarke were talking again, but perhaps only because they had to. What if they decided to go home, too, and to sell Fred and me?

Leaving Fred to comfort Betsy and to keep Zelda from tearing off Kelly's arms when she returned from checking airfares, I nuzzled Mom's hand and she absentmindedly rubbed my left handlebar. No, she'd never sell me. Never. I knew that as well as I knew anything in my short life. She knew that I was more than just a bicycle; she talked to me, understood my feelings and how hard I tried for her. No matter how mad she was at Clarke or Kelly or Megan, she'd never been mad at me. She'd sell Clarke before she'd sell me—come to think of it, that wasn't such a bad idea. Except that I wasn't ready to give up Fred, who'd probably be part of the package. Not that he didn't deserve giving up, I reminded myself.

"Will you miss Betsy and Zelda?" I asked him an hour later as our owners ate crackers and cheese in a small park.

"Won't you?"

"Of course." As much trouble as the twins had been, they were fun and I realized that I'd grown very fond of them. After all, it wasn't their fault that Fred was a flirt. I rolled over to where they were standing, hunched together in silence. "I wish you were going on with us," I said. Betsy's eyes overflowed with tears and she put her head on my handlebar. Zelda, subdued now, merely nodded, her eyes dark with sadness. "Maybe you'll both be bought by the same family," I said hopefully, trying to cheer them up.

Betsy's head jerked up. "I hadn't thought about Zelda and me having to split up, too," she wailed, sobbing anew.

"Good work, Daisy," Fred said sarcastically.

"Be quiet, Fred. I'm doing my best."

It was time to start up the hill toward the military base. Kelly made Zelda lead, and Megan followed on Betsy. I brought up the rear, staying close to Fred for comfort. It was a slow procession. Why hadn't I been nicer to the twins when they first came? Who would tell good jokes when they left? Worse, what would happen between Susan and Clarke without the buffer of two funny teenagers and their happy bicycles?

Blinded by my own tears, I shuffled along slowly, sniffling, beginning to lag the others. I'd looked forward to seeing Betsy and Zelda again in America when we came home in six months. Now, I'd never see them again, and maybe they'd never see each other. Trotting to catch up with Fred, I touched his rear tire with my nose as I realized with surprise that I considered him my best friend, no matter what. I vowed that we'd never be separated.

"It's not fair, Daisy," he said over and over. "It's just not fair." I felt a tinge of jealousy until I realized that I felt exactly the same.

Up ahead, Zelda was dragging her wheels. Kelly urged her along, oblivious of the sea of sadness around her. Apparently to her and Megan, bicycles were just pieces of metal, not living, breathing companions—a way home, a way back to America and their friends, money toward airfare, freedom from bicycling and camping and getting rained on, a means to get away from Susan and Clarke's haggling.

The military base stood on the left at the top of the hill, all square corners in tan brick. A young soldier came out of the guard house, his head shorn, very interested in the pretty blond teenagers who'd arrived in shorts. After a great deal of conversation, it was determined that the soldiers couldn't help after all, but they suggested a large bike shop downtown. "A reprieve," Fred whispered hopefully.

"For half an hour," I answered, wishing I could think of a way to save Betsy and Zelda. We coasted down the hill together, staying close, not talking, full of memories and regrets.

We couldn't find the bike shop. "Never mind," said Kelly. "We'll sell the bikes at home if we have to. Let's make plane reservations."

Betsy looked at Zelda. "At least we'll get to be Americans," she said, trying to be brave.

"And I'll have more time to plan my revenge," Zelda replied, but I could tell that her heart wasn't in it.

The travel agencies were all closed for the night. Kelly was undaunted. "I'll have Mother make reservations," she decided. "It's eight hours earlier in America." She obviously wasn't going to waste another day, or another minute, and called her mother from the first pay phone she found. "We want to come home," she said.

"The twenty-first?"

"Now."

"Why? Is something wrong?" I crowded close to the phone booth, anxious to hear her answer.

"We're just homesick." No doubt bewildered, Kelly's mother agreed to make reservations and Kelly said she'd call her again in the morning.

After dinner at a Burger King in downtown Weisbaden—Kelly and Megan apparently were already mentally back in the land of fast food and shopping malls, unwilling to eat another camp stove meal—we found our way out of the city to a nature park and pitched camp as inconspicuously as possible in a deep thicket of trees, hoping not to be caught trespassing. Noticing the bunching clouds overhead, Susan and Clarke put their packs inside their tent and suggested the same to Kelly and Megan. The teenagers ignored the advice, and by morning, rain had soaked everything they owned—again—and they were furious—again.

We went back into Weisbaden and called America. Kelly's mother hadn't heard back from the travel agent. "How about taking a train to Frankfurt?" Susan suggested. "It may be easier to sell the bikes there and maybe your mother can get you on some sort of a charter flight for a better fare."

An hour later, our riders rolled us onto a passenger car of an eastbound train just like we were people, and we arrived in Frankfurt about two in the afternoon. "Let's check with a couple of bike shops and then call the woman who gave us mace at the chateau in France," Clarke suggested.

"Let's not," Zelda grumbled.

We had a scare at the first bike shop when the owner told us that Betsy and Zelda were worth 600 Deutschmarks each. "American mountain bikes are very valuable here," he said, and I was sure that he'd buy them on the spot. "To get that much, however, you'll have to sell them privately," he continued. "I couldn't give you very much."

"We have no way to run an ad," Clarke explained. "We have no home, no phone number." The man directed us to another dealer who might be interested.

"Boy, that was close," Fred said as we left. I glanced over at Betsy, who rolled slowly along the pavement, droopy. Didn't Megan notice how hurt she was? Zelda, much as she tried to hide her hurt with anger, looked just as sad.

The second bike shop refused to purchase Zelda and Betsy. "*Nobody* loves us," Betsy sniffed.

"We haven't eaten at a real German restaurant yet," Kelly said, oblivious of the twins' suffering. "Can we have dinner next door?"

Clarke sighed. "We'll take the train to Christa's village after dinner, then. If they aren't home, we can always find another garden."

"I don't know why you think these people will help strangers," Kelly groused. "Why don't we stay in Frankfurt tonight?"

"Because we promised we'd look them up and because Christa speaks English," Clarke closed the discussion.

Outside the village train station two hours later, Susan reached Christa on the telephone. "It's the Americans, Bohus," Christa called to her husband. "Yes, of course you can stay. We have room for two inside the apartment and the others can stay outside in our garden."

"We dibs inside," Kelly and Zelda said, now delighted with the decision to find these people.

"No, you won't," Mom growled. "You'll soon sleep in a bed every night while Clarke and I will be on the ground for another six months. Respect your elders, missy. Our old bones won't hold out forever, you know."

But when Christa arrived to lead us to her house, she disagreed with Susan's decision. "Two young girls are not safe outside," she stated. "You and Clarke will sleep in the garden." Kelly and Megan snickered.

The garden where Fred and I slept with Susan and Clarke was several blocks from Bohus and Christa's apartment building. It was a community plot, where families rented small patches of land to grow flowers and vegetables.

Most had little sheds and tables and chairs, and the whole thing was fenced, with a lock. Christa insisted that Mom and Clarke sleep inside their tiny shed. "We've slept in forests and fields for months, Christa," Clarke told her. "This is the first time we've even had a locked fence around us. We are fine outside in our tent. The shed is too small—there's not even enough room to lie down."

"It doesn't matter," she insisted. "You will sleep inside the shed. It locks from the outside only, but you will lock it and then climb in through the window and latch it from the inside."

"Christa," Susan laughed. "We never lock our tent."

"I do not care. Do what I say, please. Now lock your things inside and then we will go back to the apartment for dessert. I want to hear about your trip."

Mom and Clarke stuffed their packs inside the little shed and locked Fred and me on either side of a post, then trailed meekly behind Christa, who locked both her garden gate and the big fence around the community plot and strode with long steps toward her apartment.

Bohus's friend who owned a bike shop agreed to consider buying Betsy and Zelda. While Bohus escorted Kelly and Megan with the twins on the train to his friend's shop the next day, Susan and Clarke stayed in the garden and fussed over Fred and me, tuning and cleaning us. With new brakes pads and cables, we felt wonderful; the best part was when Mom decorated me with the colorful decals she'd bought in Belgium, lining them up along my sparkling clean frame like bright flowers: America, Spain, France, England, Scotland, Belgium, Netherlands, Germany. "You look beautiful, Daisy," she said. "I've saved room for Austria, Italy and Greece when we get there. Too bad I couldn't find a sticker for Morocco."

"Wow, Daisy, look at you," Fred said, sidling close. I felt like a garden, proud of my merit badges and what I'd accomplished to earn each one.

"You look pretty spiffy, too, Fred," I said, noting his bright blue paint shining with polish. At the moment, both of us looked better than either of the twins.

Fred stared at me for a long minute. "How about lunch, Daisy, just the two of us?"

"Why, thank you," I answered shyly. "That grass over by the fence looks yummy, don't you think?"

"Yes, I do." He backed up a step. "After you," he said gallantly, and we rolled to the edge of the garden and nibbled self-consciously at the tender grass.

"What do you think is happening to Betsy and Zelda?" I asked after a few minutes, unable to forget the fate of our friends.

"I don't know, Daisy. Try to enjoy lunch, okay? You worry too much about all of us." Fred touched my front wheel with his in comfort, and I rolled backwards, embarrassed, moving closer to Nagle and the spirit ark.

Later, Mom and Clarke returned to the garden. "I can't believe that Kelly and Megan sold their bikes," she was saying.

"They needed the money," Clarke reminded her.

"I don't care. I'd swim home before I'd sell Daisy. Besides, they only got enough to cover a tenth of their airfare."

"Not everybody thinks bicycles are alive, Susan," Clarke smiled.

Fred and I looked at each other. "We didn't even say goodbye, Fred." Tears ran down my clean cheeks.

"Poor things," Fred replied, sniffling.

"I can't believe we'll never see them again. Little Betsy will be terrified in some strange German bike shop."

Fred chuckled. "But Zelda will wreak havoc on the place if they don't sell them together." We ate another mouthful of grass, thinking our own thoughts. "Are you really jealous of Betsy and Zelda, Daisy?" Fred finally asked.

"Um," I stammered.

Fred laughed. "You shouldn't be. They're lovely young ladies, but they aren't you."

I moved closer to Fred's warm blue frame. "Even when I'm mad at you," I said softly, "which is often, you're still my best friend. I could never leave you, Fred."

"I couldn't leave you either," he replied. From the corner of my eye, I saw Nagle wink at the rest of the spirit ark. Blushing furiously, I scooted to the far edge of the garden and lay down with my back to Fred.

Chapter 24

"WHAT DO YOU SUPPOSE Betsy and Zelda are doing right now?" I asked Fred as we rolled southeast toward Wurzburg. Kelly and Megan had left the country the day before.

"Sleeping in, I imagine," he replied, sun sparking from his clean frame. Without Zelda and Betsy's youthful exuberance, even the air seemed heavy; and I kept looking back, hoping to see the twins racing to catch up, out of breath, hurrying to see the rest of Germany as we had planned. Without them, our short little train felt inadequate, incomplete, impossible.

"My bike's too heavy to pedal, Clarke," Susan groaned as we went up a small hill.

"You got soft after a few days of rest," he surmised.

Mom struggled a bit farther, gasping. I assumed that the problem was my heavy heart rather than my rider's physical fitness. "Stop!" Susan shouted after a few more painful kilometers. "I forgot to lengthen the cables when I replaced my brake pads! My back brakes are clamped onto the tire like emergency brakes—no wonder pedaling is so hard!"

They called it a day after sixty-five hot kilometers. "Oh, cripes, Clarke, where's Kelly? We can't speak German!"

"Where's that piece of paper she gave you?"

"What paper?"

"The one with the German phrases."

Susan rummaged in my pack and came up only with a German dictionary. "Rats."

No one was home at the first two houses we tried, then we spotted a one-armed man working in a garden outside a small apartment house. *"Guten Abend,"* Susan stammered, then paused, casting desperately for another German word. *"Amerikanisch,"* she said, pointing to herself and Clarke.

"Nein," the man said, looking up brightly.

"Amerikanisch," Mom said again. *"Clarke und Susan."*

The man shook his head in confusion, then ran off with his one arm above his head. Mom and Clarke looked at each other. "Hello!" A voice speaking English drifted down from the balcony above us as a pretty face popped over the railing and framed a bright smile. "I am married to an American soldier so I speak English. Do you need something?"

"Yes," Susan said, obviously embarrassed. After all, here we were in the middle of Germany, unintelligible. "Neither of us speaks German, and our traveling partners who do flew home yesterday. Forgive us, but would it be possible to put our tent in this yard for one night?"

"I will ask Horst." Horst apparently was the man who had been working in the yard. *"Ja,* he says that it is fine with him," the young woman said after a moment's consultation.

"We've got to learn some German tonight, Clarke," Susan whispered, pocketing the little dictionary as they put up the tent, and I was frustrated for the zillionth time that she couldn't seem to realize that I was fluent in every language so far except Arabic.

Mom and Clarke bought us a present the next day in Aschaffenburg, waterproof bags to cover our packs. After almost 5000 miles on the road, they were apparently tired of damp clothes and damp food and damp everything when it rained. It was two o'clock when we left the city, ready for a downpour, our faded packs trussed with army green rubberized canvas—and spent the next five hours struggling uphill in hundred-degree heat under a cloudless blue sky.

The scenery was beautiful. Rolling hills heaped themselves one after another edged by dark forests, tall tree fingers beckoning us into their shade. Fred and I trudged along in silence, baked to a crisp in the blazing August sun, lonely for the twins and their teenagers but glad for the company of each other and that Susan and Clarke were getting along. It was too hot not to.

Every hour, our riders stopped for water, but ten minutes after filling their water bottles, the water inside would be scalding hot. All four of us were on the verge of heat stroke—dizzy and shaky and wobbly, we wound through the blistering countryside, wordless, concentrating on rolling one foot in front of another, rolling toward sunset and relief from the heat.

Finally, where our small road threaded under an autobahn, we found a service station and dunked all four of our heads under a water faucet. "Can you go farther?" Clarke asked.

"If I don't die," Susan replied, shaking her wet hair into curly tangles as Clarke studied the map.

"How are your knees? It looks like we start downhill fairly soon. We've climbed about thirteen hundred feet in the last two and a half hours."

"I haven't even noticed the hills, Clarke. It's the heat and humidity that will kill me."

Fred came to my side. Ever since our little lunch in Frankfurt, we'd been self-conscious together, aware of a change in our friendship. I found myself wanting to know where he was every minute, how he felt, what he was thinking. Embarrassed by my feelings, however, I felt shy whenever he approached. Fred, although a bit awkward around me, seemed more than happy to make sure that we stayed close together every minute. Now, he said, "Daisy, are you all right? I'm worried about you in this heat."

Sweat poured across my pretty new emblems, streaking my clean frame. How could anyone care about a sweaty old mule? "I'm okay, Fred, thank you. These new waterproof packs are awfully hot, though, aren't they?"

"Heavy, too," he nodded. "Take it easy now. If you need help, I'll push you along with my nose."

About seven o'clock, we found a bike path off the road and followed it to the next village. "That one," Mom said, pointing to a large white house with terraced rose gardens. She knocked on the door. No one answered. "We have to stay here, Clarke. This house is wonderful. Look, a little stream runs right under it!"

They went through a back kitchen and up some outside stairs, knocking on another door. A tall, white-haired man with fuzzy eyebrows stepped outside. *"Guten Abend,"* Susan said to him. So far, so good, I thought. *"Uh, es tut mir leid, ich sprecha kein Deutsch. Sprechen Sie Englisch?"* Good girl, Mom! I'm sorry, she'd said, I don't speak German. Do you speak English? It was the extent of her German repertoire, however.

"*Nein.*"

Susan gestured to Clarke and herself. "*Amerikanisch.*"

"*Nein.*"

She looked at Clarke, then made up a sentence. "*Bitte, ist okay schlafen en Garten ein Nacht?*" I watched the man as he translated her words into his own language for consideration.

"*Petit Camping Gaz und Wasser,*" Clarke added brightly.

"*Gaz* is French," Susan hissed.

Clarke shrugged. "*Wasser* is German," he said defensively.

The German turned to go inside. Mom panicked. "*Ist okay?*" she called after him. "No problem?"

"*Ein minuten,*" he answered, holding up a finger. Two minutes later, the door filled with the shadow of the tall man, then it opened and sunlight flooded his large features. "*Das ist gut, ist okay,*" he said with a smile.

Mom sagged with relief. Putting her hand on her chest, she said, "Susan," then gestured toward Clarke. "Clarke."

The German's eyes twinkled. "Alfred," he said and then followed Mom and Clarke back out to the garden, where Fred moved too close by my side as we watched the proceedings. Embarrassed, I rolled over to Mom, who looked at me curiously.

Clarke found a flat space for the tents under a huge old willow. "*Nein,*" said Alfred, pointing to the large black rain clouds that gathered in the distance.

"I think he's afraid that tree will fall on us," Mom said to Clarke.

"It's probably only been here a hundred years," Clarke chuckled, but paced away the distance of the height of the tree and found another flat spot by the woodpile.

"*Ja, das ist gut,*" Alfred bellowed after he rechecked Clarke's measurements with his own eye.

The back door banged shut and a short, gray-haired woman appeared and nodded her own welcome. Her name was Elsa and she was Alfred's *Frau,* she said. "*Mein Mann,*" she explained, pointing to Alfred.

Then a beautiful young woman rounded the corner. "Hello," she said in English. "My name is Irmgard." Apparently, Elsa had called for an interpreter.

"Alfred thinks you should put your tent under the porch roof. It will rain tonight."

"Danke," Clarke nodded to Alfred, who nodded back and then rolled Fred into an inside workshop. Mom followed with me. I found it hard to believe that clouds could be part of such a blistering hot day; nevertheless, over the last few minutes, they'd gotten fatter and darker. Inside was fine with me.

Fred and I, too tired and hot for conversation, took a nap on the cool workroom floor while Susan and Clarke gathered around a table under the porch with the three Germans. Later, Clarke came into the workshop to adjust something on Fred under the luxury of a light while Mom fixed a light dinner of bread and cheese.

It was too hot to snuggle when Fred and I lay down to sleep, wheels touching. "Goodnight, Daisy," Fred said softly.

"Goodnight, Freddy." Why had it taken me so long to realize what a lovely bike he was?

About midnight, a hot wind blew up through the garden, up through the willows, and slammed against the workshop. I jumped up and rolled on tiptire to the door, not wanting to wake Fred. Rain poured from the sky then, washing the roof, running in rivulets down the side of the house. Mom and Clarke's tent was safely tucked under the porch; because of the sound of the stream running under the house, I wondered if they even heard the rain. It felt odd to be so removed from nature; usually whatever happened to the air outside happened to us also. After watching the storm a bit longer, I went back to Fred and stretched out by his side.

Mom and Clarke were packing Fred and me inside the spotless workshop the next morning at seven. It was already hot and muggy, and we wanted an early start. Alfred trotted in the door, announcing that breakfast would be ready in *"zehn minuten."*

Exactly ten minutes later, Elsa called out, *"Kaffee!"* and our riders obediently followed Alfred from the workshop for breakfast and a tour of the water wheel under the 150-year-old mill house.

Elsa and Alfred watched as we finished packing, amazed at how quickly a whole household folded around our haunches. As Mom rolled me onto the back porch, Elsa held out a huge coral rose, finding an empty beer bottle for a vase. Mom filled it with river water from under the house and tied it with orange twine into the basket on my head as Elsa pointed to herself and to Mom. *"Schwesters,"* she said, then pointed to Clarke and Alfred. *"Bruders."* Mom hugged her, and then Alfred; as we trotted away, I turned to see Elsa wiping her eyes with her apron.

The rain had washed out some of the heat. As I trotted along behind Fred, the beautiful rose bobbled and tipped along on my head, scenting the air with rich fragrance. I felt like a Spanish dancer.

Chapter 25

THE PLAN WAS TO follow the famous Romantische Strasse from Rothenburg to Augsburg, then turn east to Munich. As we backtracked through the cobblestone streets of Rothenburg after lunch in a park, we saw two bicycles, obviously American, judging by their riders' clothes. Sure enough, they were from Los Angeles, on a three-week trip through Germany.

Mom and Clarke visited with the bicyclists as Fred and I talked with their bicycles, skinny touring bikes with small packs. "How far do you go every day?" one of them asked me.

"We average seventy or eighty kilometers, I guess, depending on the terrain."

"We always go a hundred," the Californian bragged.

"If we were on a little three-week trip with baby packs like yours, we'd go more than a hundred," Fred replied, flexing his frame. "But we're carrying two hundred pounds between us, plus our riders, and we'll be on the road for a year. Even so, one day in Spain we covered a hundred and eighteen kilometers."

"Big deal," the second road bike sneered. Fred looked at me and rolled his eyes.

"So how's your marriage faring?" the woman was asking Mom.

Susan chuckled. "This hasn't been easy, Karen."

Clarke told the man that we stayed in people's gardens or fields every night. "At home," Gary said, "we can't even get water or use of a toilet when we bicycle."

"I wonder if Americans would be nicer to foreigners than to their own countrymen," Susan said.

"The Germans haven't been all that nice to us," Karen responded.

"Really?" Mom was surprised. "Do you speak German?"

"Gary does, very well."

I wondered if we'd been lucky or if Mom and Clarke just took more time with folks because we didn't need to cover a hundred kilometers every day. We didn't even have a destination in mind when we started in the morning. Every moment was all we had—we never looked ahead. It was a nice way to travel.

Gary and Karen had been following a bike path along the Romantische Strasse and explained how to watch for the signs. We waved goodbye to the skinny bikes, knowing that we wouldn't see them again because of their faster pace.

Although the bike route was no longer a path of its own, it followed tiny roads through quiet villages, beautiful and peaceful. Late in the afternoon, as our path intersected the main route, Gary and Karen appeared on the main road. "Why aren't you on the bicycle route?" Clarke asked, amazed to see them again.

"We started on it," Gary explained, "but it meanders too much."

They haven't been away from America long enough, I decided. Or maybe we've been gone too long. As the Californians pulled away out of shouting distance, hurrying to the next town, this time we were sure that we'd never see them again. "Fine with me," Fred said. "Those bicycles are snooty."

The next morning, Mom washed clothes and her hair and took a sponge bath in a faucet in the garden of the little house where we'd stayed. As we pulled out of the driveway . . . here came Gary and Karen on their sleek bicycles. This time, they stopped long enough to tell us that Gary was a minister, Karen a painter, and then were off to Donauwörth for lunch. "That's probably where we'll end up for the evening," Clarke laughed as we said goodbye forever for the third time.

A bit later, I turned around to see bicycles behind me. Oh, no, it can't be, I thought. But it was another couple, Canadians touring Europe for three months, and we rolled along together for awhile, pacing the same speed. Their bikes were friendly, laid back and interested in our trip so far. The woman was riding next to Mom and me. "We stay in small hotels and eat our meals out," Ione explained. "I could never cook and camp after bicycling all day."

"Sometimes I feel that way, too," Susan admitted, "but we get the people this way as well as the scenery. I wouldn't trade the experience for the world."

The Canadians pulled ahead when Mom and Clarke stopped for water and we all waved, hoping to see each other again along the way. In Nordlingen,

Susan and Clarke were making sandwiches in a park when the Canadians bumped up the curb to join us. "We've been looking for you," Bob said. "Can we ask about your route?"

While Mom and Clarke pointed on the map to their favorite parts of France, the Canadian bicycles admired my decals and commented on our heavy packs. "I don't know how you can carry those," one said to Fred.

"Part of my load is a laptop computer," he told them proudly.

"You're kidding! Oh, my gosh!"

"Susan is writing a book about our trip," Fred continued. "We're going to be famous!"

"Maybe," I reminded him.

"Let's meet in Donauwörth at the end of the day," Bob suggested a few minutes later, putting on his helmet. "Ione and I will wait for you at the first cafe with outside tables."

When we arrived, however, we could find no cafes that were open, with or without outside tables. It was a pretty town, but the streets were almost empty, most of the businesses closed. Wandering slowly out of the village, we looked in vain for our new friends, then left feeling cheated.

"How about hiding in the woods tonight?" Clarke suggested later as they ate cheese and crackers in a woody park to hold them until dinner. "We haven't been by ourselves one night since Kelly and Megan came."

"Fine with me," Mom replied. "Leaving new friends day after day is getting harder and harder. I'd love to catch up on my writing and not have to say goodbye forever to another lovely family in the morning."

But we couldn't find a place to hide and ended up at a dairy farm near Meitingen. There, Paul and Elizabeth offered eggs and fresh milk and called a neighbor to speak English. "Poor Susan didn't get to write again," I said to Fred as we relaxed near the tent after Mom and Clarke extricated themselves from the friendly Germans a couple of hours later. We nibbled the grass quietly, content just to be close to each other.

"This is the pits, Clarke," Mom said inside the tent after twenty minutes of silence.

"What now, Susan?"

"We never talk to each other any more."

"I'm sick of this conversation."

"Of course you are. So am I. I'm sick of our whole marriage. It's boring." I raised my head, alarmed, staring at Fred, who stopped chewing to listen.

"Yes, Susan," Clarke said after a long moment. "It *is* boring."

Perhaps thinking what I was—that if Mom and Clarke split up, Fred and I would have to also—Fred moved closer to me. "Our egos are so well fed by strangers," Mom continued, "that we don't want each other anymore. Each night, we show up on someone's doorstep and I say something, then you say something else, Clarke—it's always the same because we each know only a few words. We get praised and taken care of then, and in return, are friendly and loving. But we don't give anything to each other."

"I don't need to talk to you, Susan. I already know what you'll say, everything you think. Talking to you takes up energy I could use talking to someone else."

The air filled with a long silence. Neither Fred nor I moved, waiting. I felt a deep hole open up in my stomach, and it hurt. I fought tears. Mom finally spoke, her voice broken and soft. "Our marriage is boring because we make it boring, Clarke. We're like Siamese twins. Everything that happens to either of us happens to us both. We never have anything new to share with each other. The real issue, however, is whether we want our marriage to work. Do you?"

Rolling closer to the tent, I strained to hear Clarke's answer. Fred followed, handlebars forward, grass hanging from his muzzle. We looked at each other for a long time, then Clarke spoke. "I want it to work."

"So do I," Mom replied. Turning away, I hid my tears from Fred. I'd just lost Betsy and Zelda and their teenagers; I couldn't bear to lose Fred and Clarke.

In the morning, I was relieved to see Mom and Clarke kiss after scraping wet slugs off their tent and accepting the fresh bottle of milk that had been proffered as soon as their heads popped out into the misty daylight. They seemed extra considerate of each other as they packed up their tent and sleeping bags, and Fred and I rolled off with renewed hopes that things would be okay. The four of us enjoyed the pretty countryside and each other without incident all day.

The next morning, our short ride to Maisach, where we planned to catch a train into Munich based on Christa's advice, was a fairy tale. The sky was so bright that it was luminous, the deep green forests and quilted fields bathed in buttery light. The roads were almost silent; perfectly smooth, they flowed up and down the gentle hills like silk ribbons. Villages glowed in the sunshine, all quiet, although dazzling white laundry already hung in the yards. I heard a dog bark, and bird songs in the forest, but that was all except for Fred and me rolling softly down the road, one after the other, close together.

After using all of our change to buy tickets to Munich from a machine at the train station, we rushed toward Track Six only to find that it was up two flights of impossibly steep stairs. "We don't have time before the train to unload the bikes," Clarke said from the bottom while Mom looked for other routes from the top.

A man on the platform spoke English with a Texas accent. "Do you know of a way up to this platform other than these stairs?" Susan asked him.

"No, ma'am," he replied.

"We'll carry your bikes up," the woman with him announced with a German accent, descending the stairs without waiting for a reply.

"They're too heavy," Clarke protested, but she ignored him, hoisting my rear while Mom lifted my head and shoulders up the stairs. Clarke and the Texan followed with Fred just as the train arrived, and we crowded together into a passenger car, introducing ourselves after the train left for Munich.

At the Munich station, the couple helped carry us up three escalators. "If it weren't for you," Mom said gratefully, "we'd never have gotten out of this station."

"If it weren't for us," the German woman laughed, "you'd still be in Maisach!"

An hour later, we rolled along the Isar River, hot and tired, intrigued by the nude sunbathers along its banks in the middle of the big city. "I can't stand it, Susan," Clarke said finally. "I'm filthy. Let's join them."

After only a moment's hesitation, she agreed, and stripping off their sweaty clothes, they eased their naked bodies into the cold river surrounded by Germans of all shapes and sizes. "Shall we?" Fred asked.

I shouldn't have been embarrassed, but I was. "Not this time, Fred," I said, then wondered why. Fred had seen me plenty of times bathing in rivers, but I just couldn't bring myself to take off my packs and dive in beside him.

South of Penzberg, we rolled silently in the soft light of early evening. "Daisy, look!" Fred pointed with his handlebars to the right, to a craggy silhouette bordered on the bottom with soft green fields and on top by pale sunshine.

I stopped, staring. "The Alps!" They were breathtaking.

"Holy cow," Fred whispered as Clarke and Mom pulled us to a halt. Susan moved closer to Clarke, emotions crossing her face like shadows—awe at the staggering beauty, of course; gratitude that we'd made it this far in one piece, no doubt; fear, maybe, that she couldn't pedal me over them. Clarke touched her arm gently, his face reflecting her own thoughts, connecting them once again with a common goal and a common experience. They'd shared so much in the last six months that they couldn't give up now, I decided. Fred and I would not have to part after all.

A big yellow farmhouse sat like a hen in a meadow nest just up ahead, the Alps a watercolor backdrop to its fields. Trailed by a dirty, naked four-year-old, a young woman was cleaning up the last balloons of an outdoor birthday party when we arrived. Elfriede welcomed us in English, inviting Susan and Clarke for coffee after tucking Fred and me into an empty garage, a pedal-in hotel just big enough for us and the tent. "We cleaned out the garage this morning because we thought it might rain for the party," she explained.

Later, while our riders visited the young family inside the house, Fred and I snuggled in the garage unaffected by the lightning and thunder outside the little windows, dry and warm thanks to the generosity of strangers who once again gave more than we requested.

Early the next morning, sunlight washed the rain-drenched meadows as we left the garage. It was our last day in Germany, and we trotted and then walked and then crawled up a beautiful, long pass that looked like intestines on the map—steep winding roads that rose almost 800 feet in four kilometers. Fore and aft were lakes, seen from breathtaking lookout points along the way as we stopped to catch our breath in the clean air.

At the south end of Walchensee, we stopped for lunch and then continued on to Wallgau, Krün and Mittenwald, Germany at its most charming: tiny whitewashed villages with red tile roofs and brightly-colored wall murals and the always-present church steeple, sometimes with a brightly-colored clock face, red or blue, contrasting with the clear, quiet air and bright sky; clean farms in velvet meadows; flowers bunched around every window and in baskets and jars and gardens.

We spent the night on the German-Austrian border behind a work barn set in a perfectly-groomed field of grass, the cuttings stacked by hand on shelves to dry in the sun.

Chapter 26

THE ROAD TO INNSBRUCK was a steady five-to-fifteen percent grade, but after six months of conditioning, Mom and I took it in stride and were able to enjoy the view instead of worrying about our knees.

In Austria, not a rock is out of place—the grass meadows are as smooth as fur, bordered by lines of tall pines that look like prickly grass against the rugged Alps blue with distance. Creamy white villages huddle in the valleys, low and cozy except for the red church spires that poke at the sky. "Unbelievable, Daisy," Fred said at the top of a pass. "What a beautiful place to be together."

Nodding shyly, I rolled past, starting down the mountain. 'No bicycles' said a sign, but there was no other road, so we plunged over the edge on a sixteen-percent grade, hurtling along as fast as the cars, all four of us screaming like children out of joy and fear. After all, if either of us lost our balance or tangled our wheels, that would be the end of everything.

Once in Innsbruck, we followed bicycle paths along the river east toward Salzburg, rolling from one village to the next through fields and meadows, the long way from one place to the next but quiet and beautiful.

In that perfect slanting light of just-before-sundown, we stopped for dinner next to a railroad track, then found shelter at a farm across the road. While Susan and Clarke practiced German with the Austrian family and met their new beagle puppies, Fred and I enjoyed a light dessert of Austrian meadowgrass after impressing the farm children with all of the weight we carried.

Later, inside the tent, Clarke massaged Mom's knees with lotion that he'd warmed over their camp stove. "Your knees are always cold, Susie," he said solicitously. "We need to find a way to increase your circulation—no wonder they hurt all the time."

Glad that our owners were getting along, Fred and I hugged handlebars and settled in the grass under a big round moon. That night, I dreamed of crossing the Alps with Fred and Mom in a chariot with soft streamers of pink and peach, pulled aloft by huge white swans, feathers tinged in pale gold. It was a lovely dream, but in the morning I wondered why it hadn't included Clarke.

Mom and Clarke were discussing their route over breakfast. "I'm not crazy about crossing the Alps in snow," she said, absentmindedly rubbing her knees.

"But if we go south from Salzburg, we'll miss Vienna. I'd also hoped to try to get into Czechoslovakia. I'd love to visit a Communist country. Maybe we can sneak into Albania."

"The weather may decide for us, Clarke. Let's wait until Salzburg to choose."

"What do you think, Daisy?" Fred asked as we started down a little bike path in the fresh sunshine.

"How could it possibly matter, Fred? Have you seen anything more lovely?"

Fred looked around, savoring the view. "Only you," he said gently.

I smiled. "You dope. I'm muddy and smelly and all bunged up. I'm as far from lovely as possible."

"I think you're gorgeous."

"Well, thank you. I think you're pretty handsome, too, although you're getting fatter every day."

Fred stood up straight. "I am not. Any growth you see on me is muscle, or extra stuff in my packs."

We continued our lighthearted banter all day, even after getting lost and ending up at an impassable stream. In the big scheme of things, who cared where we were, as long as we were all together, all healthy, all doing what we wanted to do most. "Let's go to Kitzbühel," Mom suggested at Wörgl.

Turning down a narrow highway, watching Fred instead of my own wheels, I tripped on the edge of the pavement and spilled into the roadway with a crash. "Fred!" I screamed. Fred spun around, racing to my side with Clarke in tow. Four middle-aged hikers in lederhosen ran to assist as Mom scrambled up, ignoring her own scrapes to attend to mine. My front wheel and both left-side packs had come off.

"Daisy! Are you all right?" Fred asked as Clarke and the hikers asked the same of Susan.

"Yes," we said together, embarrassed at our clumsiness.

"I'm sorry, Daisy," Mom said, fastening my wheel and reattaching my packs. No, no, Mom, it was all my fault—I wasn't concentrating. Thanking everyone, Mom hopped aboard and pedaled off, then both of us started to shake at the close call. If a car had been passing when we fell . . . "Look for another radweg," Susan called ahead to Clarke.

Radwegs—bicycle paths—took longer but were safe and quiet. We turned onto a tiny path that wound up through plush green meadows at the base of jagged peaks as the light softened to gray and the thin air turned cold. Maybe we needed to turn south after all—summer seemed to have ended at the German-Austrian border.

A young woman stuck her head out of a farmhouse window as we stopped to consider where to stay for the night. Why not here? After going inside to meet the family and their dinner guests, Mom and Clarke put up their tent in the field and cooked their own dinner crouched around their little stove for warmth, then joined the family for wine on the back porch, protected from the wind by the house. Fred and I, on the lee side of the tent, lay in the grass, and after gently attending to my abrasions, Fred wished me sweet dreams and fell asleep.

I lay awake a little while longer, thinking about the fragility and brevity of life, then drifted off myself after Mom and Clarke were safely tucked inside their little tent. It rained during the night, and freight trains passed one after the other next to our camping spot, waking us all, brakes screeching as they rounded the corner above the farm.

We emerged from a deserted mountain trail into the resort village of Kirchberg like a slap in the face. Although the village was beautiful, it was crowded and noisy, too bustling for us. Where did all the people come from? Our tiny road to the village had been deserted. Buying as little food as possible, Susan and Clarke ate yogurt and bread and hustled us out of town after a brief walk through a fancy store to get out of a thunderstorm.

Near Kitzbühel, we stopped for lunch under the roof of a train shelter and then rolled into the beautiful town. When Mom saw a sign for McDonald's hamburgers, she needed only a quick ride through. "Don't you want to stop?" Clarke asked.

"Nope."

Groaning up another pass in a cold wind, we found ourselves in the middle of a bicycle race complete with police escorts and television cameras. "Wouldn't it be cool," Fred asked, grinning, "if our littermates spotted us on 'Wide World of Sports'?"

I looked down at my scarred frame covered with fat packs and pretty decals. "I don't think they'd recognize us," I remarked, nevertheless proud that I'd carried Mom 8500 kilometers through nine countries in six months.

"Shall we try a campground, Clarke?" Susan asked late in the afternoon. "I could use a hot shower." Near Steinpass, where we would cross into a finger of Germany before going back into Austria near Salzburg, we found a campground for seven dollars. "That's an awfully expensive shower," Mom said sadly. "Let's see if we can find a barn for the bikes instead."

"As soon as you cross the border," the campground owner told us in English, "cut off the road to the right. There's a small road that will lead to a bike path."

Soon the tiny forest road opened onto thick meadows edged with deep woods. The rain had stopped, and everything was clean and fresh and smelled of pine and sunlight. Two farms shared the meadow. We stopped at one and the farmer's wife and her adorable puppy showed us where to camp. Early the next morning, the farmer arrived at the tent door on his tractor to deliver homemade cake on a blue china plate.

Following forest and river bike paths all the way to Salzburg, we jumped back to the highway only long enough to cross back into Austria. Rain again threatened. The trees dripped and Fred and I discussed what a wonderful route this would be on a hot summer day. As it was, we rolled fast to keep warm. In Salzburg, we spent most of our time next to the river eating lunch and greeting passersby who weren't as friendly as folks from the villages. Maybe we were all too dirty.

We'd been watching clouds crowd the sky. "Maybe we'd better not sightsee," Clarke said. "This storm's starting to look nasty."

Mom looked up at the sky above the cold, jagged mountains. "Which way, south or east?"

Clarke thought only a moment. "South. Why go to Vienna when we enjoy the countryside more?"

The wind rose as we hurried out of town. "Yuck, Susan," Clarke said from behind me, "you ran over a slug and now it's squished all over your clothes pack!"

Oh, ick. I hopped around, trying to unstick it. "Get it off, Clarke," Mom and I pleaded. Clarke cleaned up my pack with a twig, then we hightailed it down the path as large raindrops ticked loudly on our waterproofing and the soft rush of heavy rain swept up behind us. The sky was suddenly black.

"Head for shelter!" Clarke shouted as the thunderstorm overtook us, drenching us as lightning and thunder cracked and boomed on all sides. We crowded inside a bus stop enclosure but the wind shifted to leave us standing in a cold shower. "Across the road!" Clarke pointed to another bus shelter and the four of us scrambled inside.

Usually, when it rained, we kept going. But this storm was too big—too much lightning, too much wind, too much cold, too much rain. After an hour, the storm hadn't abated but Clarke decided to wait only thirty minutes more before continuing. Why, do we have an appointment somewhere, I wondered, unwilling to leave the shelter until the storm was over, no matter what.

Boom! Thunder crashed as the sky lit up like an explosion. As the lights of the house across the road went out, we took perverse pleasure in seeing the television go dark through the window after counting our own fingers and spokes. "Maybe when that guy can't watch TV," Clarke said shakily, "he'll let us into his garage." The wishful thinking grew to include the man's warm house for all of us and an oven-baked meal for our riders, but it only made us feel worse; and when the half-hour was up, Mom and Clarke forced us into the finally-diminishing storm, splashing through puddles, dodging the leftover showers only in our imaginations.

Somehow, we managed seventy kilometers, but between Kuchl and Golling, our frozen bodies called a halt at a little farm where a young woman milked cows inside the barn. Nodding assent to Mom's teeth-chattering request to camp, she went back to her work as we sloshed through the slimy cow pasture to find a flat place to roll out the tent, cold and tired and wet.

It was stormy all night and Fred and I slept little. Scrunched up, trying to cover my nose with my handlebars to keep warm, I worried about whether Mom and Clarke's tent would hold in the wind. After draping the wet tent over a tractor to dry early the next morning, Mom and Clarke packed and ate bread, then folded the damp tent in a driveway full of cow dung. "Are we having fun yet?" I asked Fred, as we stood dripping in the driveway.

"Not that I'm aware of," he replied, skittering away as the manure-covered tent was slung on his back.

Black clouds bundled together in big blobs overhead, crowding each other until they filled the sky to overflowing. Knowing that they would burst sooner or later, we hurried to the nearest village, where our riders took turns going into the market for warmth, their clothes still wet and cold from the day before. "Why won't they let *us* inside?" Fred groused. "Dogs can go in restaurants all over Europe."

"We're not dogs, Fred," I answered, shivering. "Come stand closer." We snuggled, but it wasn't enough.

From Golling, it was uphill and cold and rainy. Fancy little tourist towns were strung together by silken meadows and tiny ski slopes, but as the afternoon grew older, the rain increased and the temperature decreased as we climbed. Our frames frozen clear through, we found a home for the night in between splotches of cow manure in a muddy yard hung over a cliff, too tired to stay awake for the storm.

By the time Mom woke up the next morning, the rest of us were looking over the map. "We have tunnels today," Clarke announced.

"Fine," Susan responded. "We may get run over, but we won't get wet."

They packed their soggy tent after scraping off as much manure as possible, then tied it and their sleeping bags around our smelly flanks. Our hosts had already left for work by the time we were packed, so we said goodbye to their rabbits and followed the road down to the river in a heart-stopping fall that numbed every single one of our body parts. The road ended at an aluminum plant. "Now what?" Mom asked. The last thing that she and I wanted to do was grind back up the hill.

Clarke pointed to a group of workers who gestured to a steep flight of stairs leading up to a railroad track, then pulled while Mom pushed Fred up the stairs, their frozen hands slipping on his wet packs. "Be careful!" Fred yelled as Susan's feet slipped on the icy metal stairs.

"Nosiree, not me," I insisted when it was my turn, digging in my wheels at the bottom of the stairs. "I'm afraid of heights."

Fred looked over the top as Mom and Clarke came to get me. "Then you'll have to spend the rest of your life here alone," he said uncharitably.

"Gee, thanks, Fred," I growled as Mom stroked me reassuringly and gently pushed my behind up the first stair as Clarke tugged from the front. Okay, okay, I said to myself, shutting my eyes while they maneuvered me up the steep, icy stairs to the tracks. If I'm dead, I reasoned, at least I won't be cold and wet anymore.

A little road connected the plant to the main highway, and we climbed 500 feet on a fifteen-percent grade in less than two kilometers. Mom and Clarke got off and pushed us two-thirds of the way. "At least this is warming me up," Clarke panted. Mom wheezed, unable to answer.

Once on the highway, a long tunnel gave us a break from the wind and rain, but inside it was dark and clammy and full of fumes. Our eyes burned and passing cars sounded like freight trains. I followed Fred closely, breathing hard, frightened, unable to see the potholes and curbs in the darkness. Mid-tunnel, the road turned slightly downward and we shot out as fast as we could, gasping for clean air, thankful for daylight and even the rain mixed with snow.

At Badgastein, while Clarke fixed another flat, Mom bought Fred and me tiny bells for our handlebars, then fixed tomato and cheese sandwiches on a bus stop bench. Snow was on the mountains and I was so numb from the cold that my spokes felt brittle. Then a young man stopped to visit, explaining that we would have to go by train through the next tunnel, over the top of the Alps. "If you hurry, you can make the two-thirty train; it's only five kilometers from here."

But the five kilometers were straight uphill. The wind pushed us up, though, chasing us with another storm. At the top, we found the station. "Go around back and wait," the ticket seller told us. "You must get on the end of the train."

Already at the station, the train was a series of open flatcars onto which motorists would drive their autos like a ferryboat. "Fred, we can't manage that! There's nothing to hold onto! We'll be pitched off into the dark and mashed like slugs!"

"If we don't freeze to death first," he added. Then we spotted the boxcar, and a passenger car at the end. Inside the boxcar, six little stalls with gates would keep Fred and me warm and snug, and we chuckled at our foolishness as Mom and Clarke tied us into adjacent stalls next to a motorcycle, patting our rears before leaving for their own cozy ride the last ten kilometers across the Alps.

As we pulled into the station at Mallnitz, it was snowing lightly and strong winds tousled the trees into a frenzy. Thank you, no, I said to Mom when she came to get us. It's cold out there. Let's spend the night on the train.

She didn't listen, and off we came, kicking and pulling, unwilling to leave our toasty-roasty stalls. "Come on, guys," she coaxed, "it's downhill."

And downhill it was, eight kilometers of twelve-percent grades with a strong tailwind. Shrieking, Fred and I hurtled down the switchbacks too fast, gravity and the weight of our packs pushing us faster and faster, out of control. It had taken four hours to climb thirty kilometers in the morning and only two to fall down fifty in the afternoon. And with a little help from a train, we were over the Alps.

Chapter 27

"Boy, Daisy, Italy doesn't look at all like Austria," Fred exclaimed almost as soon as we crossed the border, shielding the bright sun from his eyes with a handlebar. "It even feels different, Fred, like the whole country's on fast-forward." Everything hurried—the traffic, the language, the gestures—and the countryside seemed jumbled, out of place, too busy with fun to keep itself orderly. Mom was ecstatic—this was the country she'd most wanted to see.

We were more than dirty. After days of rain and cold and cow manure and steep alpine passes, the sun felt like a miracle. When Mom and Clarke spotted an icy stream churning under an ancient granite bridge, they plunged everything into the river—themselves, Fred and me, clothes, sleeping bags, tent—and spread dripping fabrics and bodies among the warm rocks to dry while they drank cool Italian wine. "This is heaven on wheels," Fred sighed, stretched out on the warm rocks, shiny and clean, spokes flashing in the sun as they slowed to a stop.

Back on the road, we rolled downhill next to the river between farms strewn across the hillsides like dried leaves. "What a wonderful country, Fred!" I exclaimed, caught up in Mom's joy.

Italy was ragtag, disheveled, scruffy—but full of life and exuberance. And the Italians! Whenever Mom and Clarke asked for permission to camp in someone's garden, it was granted, served up with an invitation—no, a command—to join the family for a meal. While Fred and I guarded the tent, sprawled in the long Italian grass—Italy didn't allow for decorum—Mom and

Clarke spent glorious hours drinking wine and eating—and eating—with their new Italian friends. Mom was in heaven; actually, we all were, embraced in the open arms of these wild, happy, lively people.

I was proud of Mom's Italian after just a semester's study in college. She seemed to be breathing it in with the Italian air. Anyone into body language, of course, could carry on an hour's conversation with any Italian by just watching his or her arms and legs. Nevertheless, Mom was applying herself to this language and these people with an enthusiasm that I hadn't seen before. After all her troubles with Clarke, I was delighted to see her so happy. "Could you live in Italy permanently, Fred?" I asked one evening as Fred and I visited with a dog and a white rabbit as Mom and Clarke shared wine and antipasti with their family near Osoppo.

The rabbit twitched her long ears. "You stay with us, *amici*?" she asked in bunny Italian. *"Va bene!"*

"I don't know," I laughed, "I was just thinking out loud."

"I'll live wherever you do, Daisy," Fred announced, his eyes bright. "Italy, America, France, the Gobi Desert—it doesn't matter in the least where I am, as long as I'm with you."

"Don't be silly, Fred," I said, embarrassed but flattered. "You just don't have anyone to flirt with now that Betsy and Zelda are gone."

"Ouch!" he exclaimed, rolling backwards.

And he was right. Our friendship was growing into something much more than our brother-sister relationship at the start of our trip. Technically, of course, we weren't related at all. I'm a Specialized, Fred's a Trek. When I found myself jealous of Betsy and Zelda upon their arrival in England, I should have guessed that my feelings for Fred ran deeper than just buddies; but it wasn't until the young bicycles left Germany that I realized how much he meant to me. I couldn't have taken this trip without him, and the thought of our being separated sometime in the future was unbearable, apparently to us both.

My new feelings weren't totally comfortable to me, however, because I enjoyed my independence; being constantly aware of another bicycle was unnerving. But it had its advantages, like now, when Fred brought me an especially succulent mouthful of grass. Dropping it near my front tire, he pushed it toward me shyly. "Here, Daisy, dessert."

Just before I fell asleep, I asked Nagle to help me sort out my feelings. He smiled. "You don't need my help, little one. Just listen to your heart."

The next morning, Mom and I led, continuing south. Thirty kilometers into the day, she stopped. "Let's cross the river," she suggested.

"Why?" Clarke asked. "That's not what we decided last night."

"I know. It just feels right."

We crossed the river, and at the first intersection a small white car pulled alongside. "Where are you from?" the driver asked in English.

"America. Colorado," Clarke responded.

The extraordinarily tall and handsome Italian unwound himself gracefully from the tiny car. "I lived in New York for two years," he explained. "My name is Alexandro. Please, would you come home with me for a glass of wine? It's only a few kilometers," he added when Clarke hesitated.

Mom chuckled. "I knew there was a reason we changed our route," she said. "Kidnapped again. Sometimes we scare me."

Alexandro pointed out his village on our map. "My family owns a small winery," he explained.

When we arrived in the tiny town thirty minutes later, a villager directed us to an ancient palace up a long road. "What if this is the wrong place?" I said to Fred, a bit awestruck.

"They'll probably shoot us," he responded helpfully.

At the end of the long path, we stopped between the main palazzo and a two-story guest house, unsure where to inquire after Alexandro. Then he rounded a corner, throwing open his arms in welcome. "You found us! Come, meet my family. My brother Marco speaks English, but my parents do not."

"Which building do you live in?" Mom asked.

"The big one," he answered, smiling. "My father bought it a few years ago and we've been restoring it ever since. A short woman with copper hair emerged from a side door. "Ah, Mama," Alexandro moved forward, embracing her. The woman shook hands gravely with Mom and Clarke, then smiled with twinkling eyes. Close behind followed Franco, Alexandro's father, who greeted us and then turned to respond affirmatively to a question from his wife. "My mother wishes you to have lunch with us," Alexandro translated. "Come. While Mother prepares lunch, let me show you the palace."

"I think we have more than enough time for a nap," Fred said, flopping down in the shade, covered in heavy packs.

"I hope we can get up again," I said, grunting as I collapsed next to Fred.

Several hours later, I struggled awake to see Mom and Clarke emerging from the palace with Alexandro. "But Mother insists," Alexandro was saying. "You and your husband have been on the road a long time. Mother has prepared this room for you both to rest." He laughed. "And it never does any good to say no to my mother."

"Nor to any Italian," Mom laughed. "Go back to sleep, Daisy," she said as she passed. "Clarke and I are going to have a siesta in a real bed for a change."

Fred opened one eye. "I wish they'd stopped to take off our packs," he said. "I can't sleep in packs."

"Oh?" I replied, but he'd already fallen back asleep without hearing me.

Blue sky shimmered with sunshine high overhead, embracing the whole countryside, the whole country, the whole world, with its glorious light. A light breeze ruffled the trees into a dance of light and shadow that moved and shifted in the rich, green grass of my own bed. Could one burst from happiness? Touching Fred's front tire with my own, I stretched, adjusting my packs more comfortably, then rested my head in the cool clover and drifted off to sleep once again.

It was almost sunset before Mom and Clarke reappeared, looking clean and refreshed from their long nap and showers. "We're spending the night here," they explained, unpacking us.

You look pretty, Mom, I said, nuzzling her hands as she scratched my handlebars. Naked, Fred and I rolled in the grass to rub off the dry sweat before lying close to each other as Mom and Clarke went back inside the palace for dinner. "Now maybe I'll be able to sleep," Fred said, yawning.

"You've been asleep all afternoon," I pointed out.

"Have not," Fred replied, indignant.

"Then who's been snoring by my side?"

"I don't know, Daisy, probably a rabbit. While you've been sleeping, I've been guarding our packs." Men, I thought briefly, then admired for a moment the fading colors of the riotous Italian sunset before closing my eyes to my own sweet dreams.

In the morning, we left the winery with regrets and five bottles of wine tucked into our panniers. Two replaced Clarke's water bottles on Fred. "Who needs water," Clarke said, "when we have your *vino?*" As everyone hugged, I noticed that Clarke and Mom stood far apart, keeping the family between them.

Not far from the palace, gray clouds bunched overhead and then settled, gathering determination for a storm with the same gusto that everything else happens in Italy. Mom, I sensed, was gathering for a storm of her own. Rolling under the leaden sky, my heart filled with apprehension. Please, not another argument! Fred could feel the tension, too. "Why can't Clarke and Susan get along as well as we do?" he asked as they trudged into a panetteria for crusty, fresh rolls. I had no idea. "After all," Fred observed, "everything that happens to them, happens to us."

"We've had our problems, too, Fred."

"I know, but working them out has made us stronger, and better friends."

All the warmth had gone out of the day by the time we found shelter under a covered picnic area in a public park, and Mom and Clarke ate their bread in silence, shivering with cold as rain burst from the sky, surrounding the shelter with silvery curtains and drumming on the metal roof above our heads, locking us in. "I'm through, Clarke," Mom said finally. "I'm not willing to live my life without an open, honest, intimate relationship with my husband. If we both want it, it will happen; but if you don't, then there's nothing I can do except wish you well and be on my way. The relationship we have now isn't enough, not for me."

"What are you talking about, Susan?"

"After six months on the road, we finally get a whole afternoon with nothing to do, and you sit in an armchair and write poetry. Same for after dinner and this morning. You ignored me completely."

"So?"

"I'm tired of being your buddy. If I don't appeal to you, that's fine. But we both deserve to have some romance in our lives."

"All you think about is sex."

I glanced at Fred, blushing. "Don't be ridiculous, Clarke," Mom continued in a ragged voice. "I'm talking about *communicating* with each other, about sharing our feelings, about falling asleep in each other's arms like married people who are in love." Like Fred and I do, I thought. Poor Mom.

As usual, the argument went nowhere. Fred and I, wanting to stay out of the crossfire and unwilling to take sides, hunched against the picnic enclosure, rocking back and forth between our wheels to keep them from falling asleep under our heavy packs. Fred finally whispered, "I don't understand Clarke. I loved cuddling next to you at the palace."

"I don't understand either one of them, Fred," I said sadly.

Finally, Mom and Clarke slumped next to us, cold and lonely, more apart than ever. "I wonder what would happen if we just pitched our tent under this roof," Clarke said eventually, looking at dry Fred and me and at his own still-dry clothes.

"We don't have permission, and I don't want to get kicked out of here after dark," Mom said miserably, pulling long pants and a sweatshirt for each of them out of my clothes pack. Zipping up tightly, they urged us into the storm. It was five o'clock. For two hours, we pushed ahead, water streaming down our muddy faces to sting our slitted eyes, rain pelting our bodies like tiny pins. It was awful—a perfect reflection, however, of our riders' mental condition.

"Are you all right, Daisy?" Fred called back after yet another car drenched us in a waterfall.

"Head's still above the flood crest," I answered, trying to be cheerful. Mom and Clarke didn't say anything to each other, pedaling in silent misery ten feet apart physically, no doubt miles apart mentally.

Was Fred thinking what I was, about what he and I would do if Mom and Clarke split up? Would Fred come with Mom and me or feel that he had to stay with Clarke? Surely I couldn't leave Mom to go with Fred! But how could I leave him? I started to sob then, at the injustice of even having to consider such a decision. Please, somebody, make it all right between them!

For the first time in Italy, our request to camp was turned down—four times in a row. I wasn't surprised. Mom and Clarke looked horrible, and not just from the rain. "We'd better help out, Fred," I said as we pulled up to the fifth farm. "If we don't, we're liable to drown tonight."

Mom knocked on the door. *"Buona sera, signora,"* she said, dripping, to the woman who answered. *"Mi chiamo Susana e questo é mi marito Clarke. Siamo Americani sopra bicicletti per un' anno."*

"What did she say, Daisy?" Fred asked.

"What she always says—'My name is Susan, and this is my husband

Clarke. We are Americans bicycling for a year.' " The woman stared as all four of us crowded closer under the eaves. "Pretend to look harmless, Fred," I directed, "and wet and cold and hungry."

Fred tipped his handlebars toward the ground. "I don't have to pretend to be wet and cold and hungry," he said as Mom continued in Italian.

"Is it possible, please, to sleep here for one night? We have a small tent and need only water."

The woman looked from Mom to Clarke to Fred to me, then insisted that she didn't have an extra bedroom. Unwilling to let number five get away because she didn't have something that we didn't need, Mom asked if she had a garage or barn where we could get in out of the rain. Finally, the woman understood Mom's request or decided that we wouldn't bring flood or pestilence into her house. *"Ah, si, signor e signora,"* she laughed, and pulling on a sweater, ran through the rain to a wide doorway at the end of her house that opened onto a room full of chickens and rabbits. "Okay?" she asked.

All four of us sagged in gratitude, temporarily of one mind. *"Si, signora,"* Mom said. *"É buono."* Indeed, this was very good. In fact, it was perfect—the woman allowed Fred and me inside, too!

"There is a bicycle god," I said to Fred, flopping down by his side as our riders followed the woman inside for dinner half an hour later. The rabbits and chickens scratched and nestled together also, and I felt welcome and safe, for the moment at least.

"Good night, Daisy," Fred whispered, steam rising from his frame as he dried in the warm room.

"Sweet dreams, Freddy."

Chapter 28

WHILE MOM AND CLARKE took a bus across the lagoon into Venice two days later, Fred and I stayed in an open shed. "Bicycles aren't allowed in the city," Mom explained.

I thought I was more than a bicycle, I grumbled as she walked away. I'd wanted to ride in a gondola with Fred. But now instead of being serenaded by a gondolier with a ribboned hat as we drifted under someone else's power along the glittering canals of the romantic city, sun shining on our new love and hopes, Fred and I spent the day tucked under a construction crane that guarded a dilapidated house but certainly couldn't sing a note. An old German shepherd and a little fuzzy mongrel, plus ten cats and a goose, were our Venetians. "I'm afraid of that crane, Fred," I said, looking up.

The metal giant looked down, twenty times my size. "I wouldn't hurt you, *cara mia*," he said in a rusty voice. "I've been retired, put out to pasture. I guard the house because I've nothing else to do, but who would want it?" He swung his big arm around the littered yard, sounding so sad that I felt horrid. Here Fred and I had daily adventures all over Europe, the trip of our young lives, while this poor thing stayed home every day. Even in his prime, he didn't do much but lift junk at construction sites. Humbled, I rolled to his feet and apologized. "Oh, don't get me wrong," he said, "it's not so bad here. I love my family."

Mom and Clarke returned about five o'clock. "Venice is full of cats," Mom said as she loaded my packs. "No wonder—no cars and lots of fish." She thought for a moment. "But how could anyone five hundred years ago figure out how to build a city on top of water?" I shared my day's discovery with her—this part of the mainland, I announced, is full of cranes. "What?" she asked, not really listening, as Danilo, head of the house, strode toward us with a huge oil can, drenching Fred and my derailleur chains with black, oozy goo before Mom could stop him, then herded her back to the front yard for a family photo while Fred and I said goodbye to the crane and the cats.

"Oh, ick," Fred said as black oil dripped down his legs.

When we rolled away from the house a few minutes later, the sticky stuff splattered everywhere, and from the knees down, all four of us were dipped in black before we got to the corner. "Oh, ick," Clarke said. Out of sight of the farm, he and Mom tried to wipe us off with grass, smearing the gooey oil into black sticky streaks.

"Oh, ick," I said, shaking a pedal.

We stopped at a scruffy little farm west of Dolo. "We fit right in with Italy," Fred said, looking at my body with something less than admiration.

"No," I disagreed. "We fit into a tar pit. Jeepers."

He laughed. "As long as we're tar babies together, Daisy, I don't mind."

"I mind, Fred. First we get left behind in Venice and then we get thrown into an oil can. Really."

The farmer approached, no doubt curious about the oily apparitions in his field. Before Mom could ask permission to camp, however, Giovanni invited us to stay and his wife asked Mom and Clarke for dinner after apologizing for having only two eggs. Fred and I rolled and rolled in the grass, trying unsuccessfully to scrape off dirt and oil. "If those nice people had only two eggs, why did Susan accept their invitation?" Fred asked, wiggling. "Don't they need the eggs more than Clarke and Susan?"

"I'm sure they do, Fred," I said after thinking a moment. "But I'll bet that Giovanni and Maria would have been terribly hurt if Mom had refused. In Europe, it seems to be the giving that matters, not the gift. In America, I think the gift is most important."

"That's sad."

"And it makes me realize, Fred, that all that black oil this afternoon was a very fine gift, too. It was what Danilo had to offer. All that mattered is that he wanted to give us something that would help us on our way; what it turned out to be makes no difference." We both stopped scrubbing our bodies.

Later, as Mom and Clarke crawled into their tent, Mom whispered, "Did you hear Maria say that she'd never been to Venice, Clarke? It's only a fifteen-minute drive from here."

In the morning, Maria and Giovanni insisted that Mom and Clarke join them for coffee and juice and salami sandwiches. Certain that the Americans' breakfast was to have been the Italians' dinner, Mom and Clarke nevertheless seemed to realize that the offer was too important to refuse, and I guessed that we all left the farm proud of our dirty oil streaks.

Near a tiny village late in the day, my saddle fell apart, spreading pieces of bolt and bracket all over the highway. As we looked for its parts, an old man helped us find the sheared bolt, then gestured for us to wait while he bicycled home to find another. "Do you hurt anywhere, Daisy?" Fred asked.

"No, of course not, Fred," I replied. "It was only my saddle."

Although the man returned with a new bolt, it was too short. "Use my seat, Susan," Clarke offered. "I'll ride to the next town standing up."

"What if there's no bike shop?" Mom asked, worried.

"One problem at a time," he answered, transferring Fred's saddle to my back. The mounting was too skinny, however, so the saddle slid right to my back instead of a foot higher; and Mom pedaled through the village, knees pumping high but certainly more comfortable than Clarke, who stood up like a jockey in his stirrups for the eight kilometers to Lúsia.

There, the whole village gathered at the bike shop to hear who we were, ask about our trip, and offer help. The shop owner wouldn't charge for fixing my saddle, and one bystander raced home to get a bottle of prosecco to celebrate my successful repair. *"Grazie, signor, mille grazie,"* Mom said to the man as she tucked the bottle of sparkling wine with a flourish between the tomatoes and onions in the basket on my head. Rolling out of town next to Fred, I held my head high under the champagne hat, delighted with both my shiny new seat post and my still-oily legs.

We continued west into a huge, red setting sun. After an hour, Clarke asked, "How far have we ridden today?"

Mom consulted the odometer behind my right ear. "Seventy kilometers."

"It's been a tough one," Clarke said, no doubt tired from his upstanding ride. "How does that vegetable farm look?"

"Grand," she replied. Everything in Italy looked grand to Mom.

For the first time in this country, Mom and Clarke crawled into their tent and cooked their own dinner, speaking their own language with someone familiar. As Mom washed their dishes in the garden hose half an hour later, however, our host came outside to invite them in for coffee and wine with his family. "You are fluent in my language, *signora*," he insisted.

"No, no," Mom protested in Italian, "but I am very surprised at how much I understand when you speak."

In the morning, Mario and his family were already rinsing their morning vegetable harvest in concrete ponds, lettuce heads bobbing like giant green apples, by the time Mom finished washing clothes and her hair in the hose. As Mom tied the last of the laundry to our panniers, she shouted goodbye to our hosts and we trundled off, bright morning sun at our backs.

As we rolled along, I thought about Mom and Clarke, trying to decide how they were doing together. Although they weren't arguing, they didn't seem close. Diving into this country with her arms and legs flying, Mom seemed to be ignoring Clarke, refusing to let him ruin Italy for her. Clarke appeared not to notice that he'd been put on the fringes, perhaps glad of the distance between them. Fred and I seemed to be the only thing connecting the two of them; if it weren't for our own relationship, I felt, they'd drift apart and not even notice until they couldn't find each other again.

An hour and a half into the morning, we stopped at Lendinara for directions. Somehow it hurt my heart to watch Clarke, standing in front of me—feet planted firmly on each side of Fred next to the church steps, bent over his map, his long brown body growing down like a stem out of a white mushroom helmet—struggling to communicate with a dozen chattering Italians who each wanted to pick the best route to Cinqueterre, near La Spezia on the Ligurian Sea. Somehow he seemed all alone.

Mom and I had our own entourage also, another baker's dozen who were more interested in who we were than in where we were going. As Clarke gestured and tried to speak Italian with his hands, with no help from Mom, who was engaged in her own happy conversation, I was once again filled with pride that these two middle-aged Americans showed up on Europe's doorstep day after day, night after night, and were accepted with huge trust and friendship. Why couldn't they be happy together? Didn't they understand what they were accomplishing here?

Two days earlier, after leaving Giovanni and Maria's west of Venice, Mom had acknowledged for the first time how hard it really was to knock on doors every night. "Take the normal stress of being a houseguest, Clarke, and add permanence, being a houseguest every night for a year; then be a guest of a stranger; arrive with no invitation whatsoever, dirty and smelly and tired, then have to earn permission to stay from someone who has never even heard of you. And if that's not enough, do it in a foreign language!"

Clarke didn't respond for some time. "You're right," he said finally. "But you forgot the part about our being the only Americans many of these people have ever met. The way we act influences how these Europeans may always view our country."

"No wonder this is so emotionally and physically exhausting sometimes," she said.

"I can't imagine traveling any other way, though. If we'd been regular tourists, whatever they are, we wouldn't have learned nearly as much about the people or the languages or the customs."

It was quiet for a time between them. Mom spoke finally. "But I get really frustrated because my ability to communicate is so limited. And because sometimes I'd rather sleep or write or read or talk to you than start from the beginning with strangers every night. We spend so much time repeating ourselves—who we are, where we're from, what we're doing. . . . "

"Maybe it's time to have everything, Susan, our friends and each other." Clarke dragged the words out reluctantly, one by one. "Maybe it's time to slow down enough to talk with each other about more than routes and groceries and where we'll stay for the night. You're right—all of our real conversations are with strangers." Glancing at Fred, I held my breath, delighted. "We still have six months left and we've been through ten of the dozen countries we considered to begin with," Clarke continued. "How far have we traveled?"

Mom consulted her little journal. "Almost nine thousand kilometers, fifty-four hundred miles."

"Well, then, let's slow down."

In spite of their encouraging words to each other and their apparent understanding of what a challenge their life together was, it still felt like they were miles apart, at least compared to Fred and me. But they were trying, I decided, if only with words.

Now, in Lendinara, they allowed themselves to be kidnapped twice—first by a man named Carlo and his daughter Silvia. "My father would like you to have coffee with us," Silvia said to Mom in Italian mixed half-and-half with English. Mom waddled me up to Fred, parting the sea of gesturing Italians to forward the invitation. Without a moment's hesitation, Clarke agreed, and leaning Fred and me outside a tiny ristorante, filed in for espresso and a bilingual language lesson followed by a visit to the village church.

Vito met us on the church steps after the tour—he'd been part of Clarke's crowd. He spoke a little English, he explained, because he'd spent six years as a prisoner of war in Africa and Egypt in World War II. Now, with thumbs in his pants that rode high on his stomach, he tipped back and forth and said in slow English, "Come. You will eat at my house." Clarke and Mom looked at each other, immensely amused. When they'd talked about slowing down, I'm sure they hadn't meant rolling to a halt. "Come," Vito commanded. "My wife, she has prepared a meal already for you." He must have run home after we'd gone to the cafe, issuing orders or requesting permission to have guests, depending on his relationship with Mama.

Vito and several friends escorted the four of us home, tucking Fred and me into a little shed next to Vito's old black utility bike before leading Mom and Clarke with great ceremony into the house. While Fred tried to talk with the Italian bicicletta, mostly in big gestures, I fretted about Mom and Clarke, worrying that Clarke would get mad that they weren't making more progress in spite of his comments two days earlier. Dear Fred read my mind. "Don't worry about it, Daisy," he said gently. "You can't do anything. Let's enjoy our time together while we have it. But for now, my Italian vocabulary has run out and this bicycle wants to know what we think of his country. Can you translate?"

Attempting to be polite, I acted as interpreter for Fred and the dignified old bicycle, but all I could think of was Fred's comment about enjoying our time together 'while we have it.' Obviously, he wouldn't leave Clarke to be with me if our family broke up. I'd have to be the one to choose, between Mom and Fred. I can't, I just can't, I thought, miserable. My only hope was that Italy would work a miracle so that Clarke and Mom would settle their differences and be happy together again.

It was several hours before they came to retrieve us, rubbing their full stomachs. Slowly, Vito climbed aboard his heavy black bicycle and escorted us proudly through town. After posing like a soldier for photos with both Mom and Clarke, he hugged and kissed each of them, shook their hands twice, then said in Italian, through tears, "You will stay with us, in our hearts." Then he pedaled off toward home, turning to wave, his old bicycle wobbling as Vito looked over his shoulder one last time.

Just outside town, a car had hit an elderly woman and her bicycle. She wasn't hurt but her bike was. The motorist and his passengers were already attending the shaken woman, so Fred and I comforted the bicycle suffering by the roadside, her front wheel crumpled. "What will happen to her, Daisy?" Fred asked anxiously.

I shrugged tearfully, cradling the old bicycle gently. "They'll put her down, I suppose." Then, seeing the pain in Fred's eyes, I reconsidered. "Maybe they can replace her front wheel and straighten her frame, Freddy."

Five kilometers down the road, after calling a cheerful hello to a young woman who passed on her bicycle, we stopped to check the map. The woman pedaled back to help, and Mom asked for directions. "Let's go," the Italian said in English, pedaling back the way we'd come, and I wondered if we were being kidnapped by Lendinarians one more time as we followed the bicycle into a driveway leading to a small factory.

The Italian returned after a moment with a stunning young woman dressed stylishly in black. "I am Chiara," the chic woman said in English. "My sister says that you need help. What can I do for you?" After giving us directions and asking about our trip, she said, "My husband is a bicyclist, too. He just got home from Austria, Hungary and Romania—I know he'd love to meet you. Would you have dinner with us?"

It was four o'clock and we'd traveled only fourteen kilometers for the day. "May we put our tent in your garden for the night?" Clarke asked. Maybe he really *was* willing to slow down and be with Mom!

"Of course," Chiara answered. "Follow me."

As we raced after Chiara's little car, Mom groaned, "But I'm still full from lunch."

Clarke laughed. "Remember, never say no to an Italian."

That night, tucked into Chiara and Maurizio's garage, Fred gently nudged my shifter. "Why are you so grumpy, Daisy?" I didn't answer. "I think Clarke and Susan are getting along pretty well," he continued. "Didn't Clarke agree to spend more time with her?"

"I think Mom's given up," I said finally.

"No, she hasn't, Daisy. Susan's not a quitter. Don't be such a pessimist."

I started to cry then, voicing the real reason for my sadness. "You said you were leaving me, Fred."

He rolled backwards. "I did not! When?"

Sobbing uncontrollably now, I couldn't answer. Finally, I blurted, "You said for us to enjoy what time we have together, Freddy. To me, that means you don't intend for us to stay together." I couldn't help it; I broke down completely. "You don't like me anymore, you want to get rid of me, you'd rather be with Clarke. I'm dirty and ugly and you'd rather find a pretty new girlfriend like Betsy!" All my fears poured out of me, along with my tears. I felt like an idiot, but I couldn't stop myself.

"Oh, for heaven's sake, Daisy," Fred had to shout to be heard over my wails. "Of course I like you. I love you. I don't care how dirty or scratched you are. It's you I love, your personality, your liveliness, your wisdom. It's not your spokes or your brake cables or your front wheel. What's the matter with you?"

I sniffled, trying to control myself. "But you said that we might not stay together," I insisted in a small voice.

"We might be killed by a car tomorrow. Why not enjoy each moment as it's given to us without worrying about tomorrow? If something happens between Clarke and Susan, we'll deal with it then."

Fred was right, of course. But I had to say, in spite of myself, "You mean you may not stay with Clarke if he and Mom split up?"

"I don't know what I'd do, Daisy." My heart fell. He looked at me sternly. "Would you leave Susan?"

And of course I couldn't. Could I?

Chapter 29

ONLY ONE MORE MOUNTAIN pass stood between us and the west coast of Italy. Only a week had passed since we left Venice on the east coast, and only ten days since we had entered the country, but it seemed like forever for some reason. It was the beginning of week thirty, and we were well over the 9000-kilometer mark.

From Réggio Nell'Emilia, the road climbed 4000 feet over the next seventy kilometers, over forty miles. The first afternoon, we traveled only twenty-five kilometers because of rain and killer grades, stopping about six o'clock to buy groceries. Cold wind and fading daylight convinced us to stop at the next town, but there wasn't one. An old brick building was deserted, and we clambered on, up and up, frozen inside and out, all four of us, until a tiny group of houses and a cafe stuck to the hillside gave us someone to ask for permission to camp.

In the morning, we continued to climb in cold drizzle. "How are your knees, Susan?" Clarke asked when Mom signaled a break by collapsing on a stone wall.

She held out her legs, knees fat as muffins. "They hurt."

"How are *your* knees, Daisy?" Fred asked.

"Do I have knees?"

Fred chuckled. "I never know what you have. Sometimes you're a bicycle, sometimes a horse, and sometimes I think you're human."

"Oh, well. Yes, I suppose that's true, Fred. What does it matter, anyway?"

"It doesn't, I guess. I was just wondering who you are today. You don't seem very here, you know?"

"I'm here all right. I wish I weren't. This is some hill, huh?" In truth, my mind wasn't on the mountain, or on the rain and cold. It was on Mom, and on what might happen to Fred and me and to Mom and Clarke if their tentative commitment didn't last. At each turn, however, a spectacular new view took my mind off my worries, at least for a moment.

Hoping to snatch another quick break near a solitary house hanging over the road, the cold wind changed our minds just as a woman hailed us from the balcony of the cliff house. *"Buon giorno, signora,"* Mom called back.

"Caffe?" the woman offered.

"We can't let our muscles cool off, Susan," Clarke decided. "Sorry. Coffee sounds good to me, too."

Mom shouted back up the hill. *"No, grazie, signora. É impossibile,"* then explained in Italian that she couldn't let her knees get cold. Two seconds later, the woman bounded out of her house holding a pair of striped woolen legwarmers from her daughter's dance class. Delighted, Mom slipped them over her knees and followed the woman inside, grinning. "Remember, Clarke," she admonished, "one does not say no to an Italian!"

Fred and I stood in the wind, huddled together. "Where are *my* legwarmers?" I asked. "What if we freeze solid while those two drink steaming hot coffee?"

"Here, Daisy, let me keep you warm," Fred offered, leaning toward me.

I panicked. Already afraid that I'd lose Fred if something happened to Mom and Clarke, I found myself unwilling to let him get closer, physically or emotionally—if I cared about him any more than I did already, I'd never survive if we parted. "Stop it, Fred!" I said, pulling away.

"What's the matter with you, Daisy?" he replied, offended. "What do you think I could do with our packs between us?"

"I don't know, Fred. Please." I pushed him aside. "Just leave me alone, okay?" I knew that I'd hurt his feelings but I couldn't help it. Why make it worse for us both?

"Well, sorry," he said sarcastically. "I lost my head. Excuuuuse me!" We turned our back wheels to each other, colder than ever without each other's warmth.

Finally, Clarke and Mom returned, full of hot espresso, and headed us back through the damp mist up the mountain. "What was that?" Mom shouted up to Clarke a few minutes later as I veered to miss a smashed fuzzy something-or-other.

"I have no idea," he called back.

Mom shrugged. "I'll file him under 'miscellaneous,' " she decided, mentally scooping the dead animal onto our spirit ark. Business was brisk again in Italy.

Near the top of the pass, we ran out of energy. It was six o'clock and the temperature was dropping too fast to keep warm, no matter how hard the four of us pedaled, with and without legwarmers. "The nearest town is another twenty-five kilometers," Clarke said after studying the map while Mom rubbed her knees and jumped up and down to keep from freezing.

"I can't make it."

"We'll have to look for shelter in the trees somewhere, then. How's your water?"

"Almost empty, Clarke, but I'd rather go without than ride fifteen more miles today."

Slowly we pulled ourselves up the mountain, pushing and pulling with every muscle we had or could invent until a narrow road cut off the highway to the left. Two young girls walked arm-in-arm near the intersection. "Does this road lead to a village?" Mom asked in Italian.

"Si, signora," they replied. *"Due chilometri."*

Mom and I looked dubiously at the road hunching up the mountain like an inchworm. Two kilometers maybe, but straight up. "If you can't make it, Susan," Clarke said, "we'll camp somewhere along the way." Fred didn't say anything, apparently still upset with me.

The road wasn't as bad as it looked, but the houses in town hung like starfish on a coral cliff above the river. "There's no place to put a tent," Mom complained.

At the very top of the village, however, a house across the street from the church had a tiny flat patio where we were given permission to camp. "Be careful where you walk, you two," Mom said to Fred and me as we stepped over the flowers that framed the patio like ruffles.

As soon as Clarke and Mom had filled their tent with packs against the gusty wind, our host suggested that they move the tent closer to his garden shed for shelter. Too tired to move anything heavier than their own legs, they asked instead if Fred and I might lean against the shed. "Si, signora, si," the man said, then bustled us both inside the warm, dry enclosure.

We spent the night listening to the rain and to the church bells across the street. They rang the hour; and on the half-hour, they rang the hour plus a different note. We always knew what time it was, because we were always awake. And as much as I wanted to apologize to Fred for my cold shoulder, I didn't know how, because I still felt the same way. He ignored me all night.

At seven the next morning, as the church bells played "Santa Maria," all four verses no less, Mom and Clarke were invited inside for coffee and bread and French brandy. "You two are spoiled," Mom said when they finally pushed us outside into the wet morning two hours later. "How do you manage to sleep all snuggled inside your own house while Clarke and I sleep outside in a wet tent?" I hung my handlebars. If only she knew how unsnuggled we'd really slept!

It started to rain as we reached the main highway, and the gorgeous mountaintops toward which we'd labored for three days were lost in clouds. In fact, everything was lost in clouds, including Fred, who was only a few feet ahead. "I hope there aren't any cars close behind," I called up to him, my voice echoing.

"Stay close to the edge of the road."

"I can't see the edge of the road."

We knew we'd reached the top only when the road flattened under our wheels, then we picked up speed and raced the wind and the rain and the clouds down the mountain's back, dropping almost 3000 feet in eighteen kilometers. I thought I might freeze to death; if so, I wouldn't have to worry about who stayed with whom when our lives fell apart.

In Fivizzano, Mom and Clarke shopped for groceries while Fred and I stood in another downpour, too miserable to talk, then we waded along the highways until we found the port city of La Spezia. Turning north toward Cinqueterre, where I'd assumed we'd be treading flat coastal highways, the road spiraled up above the harbor like a tightly coiled spring.

After eighty kilometers, every one of them steep and wet, we found a house clinging to the edge of the mountain whose owners let the four of us sleep in their garage. Fred and I flopped down on either side of Mom and Clarke, as far apart from each other as we could get, bone tired.

The morning air above La Spezia was thin and watery, washed clean and pale by the rain. As we climbed, villages clung to the mountainsides like stone masks to an ancient wall and vineyards marched up the hills in dusty brown rows, holding onto each other and the rocks, defying gravity. We were looking for the five coastal villages of the Cinqueterre. After several long tunnels, a sign directed us to a narrow shelf road crossing the mountain cliffs by the sea. Up we went, ridden and pushed, hot and tired, not understanding the logic of a high road without attachment to anything—every few kilometers, a road plunged off down the side of the mountain to a hamlet on the rocky coast.

Under a blistering sun, we climbed higher and higher. When a clunkety old truck bounced past, billowing exhaust fumes, Mom gagged. "I'm not sure I can go on without a rest, Clarke. I'm about to pass out."

"How are we for food?"

"Don't even mention the word. But to answer your question, we're out." While Mom rested, Clarke rummaged through my food pack to find chocolate, cherry preserves and mayonnaise. "If I can't make it to Monterosso, Clarke, you're going to have a horrible dinner," she said weakly.

"If you can't make it to Monterosso, you're going to have a horrible time getting help if you need it."

The road narrowed and became dirt, and we bumped along between potholes filled with rainwater. The weather was brutally hot and humid and there was no shade along the mountaintop, just dusty vineyards and occasional farms strewn uphill like discarded trash. The road continued to climb, then we came to an intersection—with the road we thought we'd been on. Down and down it went, falling from the sky to the resort town of Monterosso in an exuberant rush. The village crowded against the sea in a puzzle of pale colors: ocher, salmon, slate, red and brown. Terraces and balconies wedged between bright apartments and hotels, reaching for the sun. It was another world.

The one campground didn't allow tents. After six exhausting hours of travel, we couldn't stay, and all the houses that might have garden space were high above us. "I can't go back up, Clarke, not today. There's nothing left in me."

As we rolled for the umpteenth time down the main street along the beach while Mom and Clarke tried to decide what to do, a loud voice erupted from the open door of a bar. "Hey, you two! Stop! There's an American bicyclist in here!"

The California woman was en route to a ten-day bike trip through France, complete with assist vehicles to carry her luggage. Eyeing our packs, she shook her head in disbelief, and after hearing about our habit of staying in private gardens and fields, shook her head again. "I'm going from here to Florence," she told us. "You're welcome to stay at the house I've rented if you can get there in three days."

Mom looked at Clarke, who was studying the map. "We can just make it if we pedal eighty-five kilometers a day through terrain just like this," he told her. Fred and I looked at each other with big eyes, forgetting our fuss for a moment.

"We only managed thirty in six hours today," Mom reminded him.

Andy, the bar owner who'd hailed us from his doorway, came out on the steps. "It is illegal to camp anywhere but in the campground," he explained in English, "but I will help you find a place to stay. Come back at five-thirty. If you're not fussy, I'll sort you out."

Two hours later, we returned. "Put your bicycles in the garden behind the restaurant and eat dinner," Andy commanded. "Then I'll find you something."

"He just wants our money," Mom groused as she pushed me into a corner by the fence.

"Oh, be quiet, Susan," Clarke snapped. "At least he said he'll find us a place tonight, which is more than we did on our own."

Mom sighed. "I know, Clarke. I just want today to be over."

Fred and I were all alone. For awhile, we watched the garden's dinner guests without a word, their vacation laughter a sharp contrast to our own silence. Soon, the tension that stretched between us became unbearable. "Fred," I said. "I adore you. I truly do, more than anything. But I'm afraid that I'll lose you, afraid that Mom and Clarke will lose each other, that we'll all lose each other." My voice cracked. "I don't know what to do."

Fred rolled a tiny bit closer, no doubt afraid that I'd hit him. "It won't do any good to build a wall between us, Daisy. Then we'll lose each other for sure. We don't know what will happen between Clarke and Susan. I know that they love each other—they have to, or they wouldn't be here together. Please, don't cut me out of your life. I love you with all my heart. If for some horrible reason, our days together are numbered, let's live each one as much as we can, okay? Please?"

Unable to respond, I crept closer, and we spent the night with our handlebars wrapped around each other.

Chapter 30

MOM AND CLARKE ENDED up at the vacation flat of a Scotsman and his wife after buying them beer until midnight. The next morning, Mom pulled me from the fence, sighing. "I'm sorry, Daisy," she said wearily, "but we have to climb back up that cliff again." I balked. "I know, friend, I feel the same way. I'd rather die than pedal you back up this mountain and go through what we did yesterday to find the next village."

"I'll help you, Daisy," Fred offered, eyes soft with kindness. "I'll push both you and Susan if you need it."

Clarke was silent as he straightened Fred's packs. He looked tired, too. And once we'd started climbing up the mountain, nobody had enough energy to help anyone else. It was all each of us could do to keep moving, rolling each foot forward on the hot asphalt.

While Mom and Clarke discussed politics to take their minds off their physical pain, Fred and I, attending to the business at hand, had no energy for talking; it was all we could do to climb the steep cliff, scratching and clawing up the fifteen percent grade as sun poured down in molten streams of humidity, burning our frames. Once, however, as we folded around another hairpin curve, Fred turned his handlebars and winked, bless his heart, sweat pouring down his front fork, giving me the mental strength to drag myself a little farther. Did somebody say we were on vacation?

After days and months and years of grueling, hot, torpid labor, we topped the ridge and then streaked into Levanto in time to get a campsite and spend the afternoon at the beach. "I can't believe we've been on the road only half a day," Fred said, exhausted.

"Half a life is more like it," I groaned, sinking down on the hot sand next to a stone wall after getting a big drink from the village fountain.

"Will they let us swim?" Fred asked, yawning.

"Maybe. But right now, I need a nap."

I didn't wake up until late afternoon. As the sun dipped behind a gray haze, the sea flattened to slate, its glitter disappearing into bumpiness, its light flat and unshadowed. The brightly-colored beach people were leaving in couples and small bunches, trailing cold seawater over the sand, their laughter fading, disappearing into the village to return the sand and ocean to its monochrome of gray and white.

Fred hadn't stirred, asleep at my side, twitching tires perhaps still grinding up the morning mountain in his dreams. How lucky I am, I thought, touching his front wheel. Then I looked for Mom and Clarke, a hundred feet down the beach, at the edge of the water. For half an hour, they sat apart in silence. Then Clarke lay on his stomach on their only towel, feet toward the ocean, arms cradling his head. Perhaps he'd fallen asleep. Mom, in a raggedy t-shirt over her swimsuit, sat on the sand, back rounded, knees up, muscular legs crossed at the ankles, brown arms wrapped around her swollen knees. She didn't move. She just stared at the ocean, detached from everything, I sensed, even herself.

When Fred woke up, I pointed her out to him. She hadn't moved. "Is she all right, Daisy?" Fred asked, concern in his voice. "She looks so unhappy!"

"I know, Fred. And I don't think Clarke's even noticed. I haven't seen them talk, even once." Sure enough, when Clarke stirred and stood up, pulling the damp, sandy towel after him, he walked toward Fred and me without even glancing toward his wife. "Uh-oh," I said softly.

Fred nudged me reassuringly. "Susan can take care of herself, Daisy," he whispered.

I looked at him sharply. "Can she?"

He didn't flinch from my gaze. "Yes, she can. We all can."

After dinner in the tent, it began to rain, and Mom and Clarke got into another rip-roaring fight about their relationship, and it went on forever, getting nastier and louder. "Shut up, Susan, everyone can hear you. This is a campground, not some forest in the middle of nowhere."

"I don't care who hears me, Clarke. I'm sick of worrying about every stranger in the world instead of us. I'm sick of everything, including you." I cringed, pulling at my tether. "Get out of the tent, Clarke. I wish I never had to see you again. I hate you!"

Here it comes, I decided, grabbing for Fred with my handlebars, terrified, tears running down my frame. Here on the east coast of Italy, in Levanto, on the Ligurian Sea, in a happy place called the Cinqueterre, the Italian Riviera, my world would dissolve, my family split open like a rotten egg for all of the world to see and smell. I was humiliated, ripped to shreds, aching for Mom, aching for myself who would now have to choose, aching for my Fred. Whatever had happened to the joy of Italy?

Fred held onto me, hugging me for dear life, just as scared as I. Wrapped around each other, we were awake all night, listening to the storm inside the tent and to the one outside that drenched us with rain and washed away my tears.

Pale morning sun enveloped the campground in watery gray light. Everything dripped. In silence, Mom and Clarke emerged from the tent with their wet packs, haggard and pale, then emptied their muddy nylon shelter of leftover rainwater without a word. Bundling the dripping tent in her arms, Mom headed for a wash basin, shoulders slumped in defeat, while Clarke wrung out clothes and draped them in the trees, his eyes hollow and dark. Fred and I watched silently, holding handlebars, then followed timidly as Mom and Clarke straggled back to the beach, ten feet and light years apart, to be alone with their despair and perhaps to decide what to do next.

"If this is what love comes to, Fred," I whispered, "I want no part of it." I pulled my handlebar away, but Fred grabbed it back, gripping it tightly.

"No, Daisy, it isn't. They're not us. We need each other now, more than ever. They need us, too. No matter what happens, they can't get out of here without us."

We stayed at the beach all day. I watched over Mom, who huddled on the sand, looking broken, like a seashell after a storm. Gazing out to sea, she seemed blind to everything but her own turmoil, which I felt as if it were my own.

The long horizon surrounded us like the rim of a cereal bowl, flat and unending, glittering sunshine that filled our eyes with too much light. Motionless, I watched Mom, and when I thought I saw her heart fly beyond the cereal bowl rim like leftover milk, obliterated in the sun, I jerked back into my own skin, frightened.

Fred hadn't moved, and we stayed close together, each with our own thoughts and worries about Clarke and Mom but tied together with a bond that, I now knew, could never be broken, wherever we ended up, together or apart.

The spirit dog Nagle stood on the sea wall, staring toward the ocean and Mom, his shaggy white hair ruffling in the breeze. "What can I do to help her?" I asked him.

"Nothing, little one, except love both her and Clarke. That's all any of us can do."

The next morning, and the next, neither Mom nor Clarke mentioned leaving Levanto. Each day, they walked to the beach and sat on the sand a few feet apart. Each afternoon, they stopped for ice cream on the way back to their tent for a silent dinner. Fred and I followed them like rolling shadows, watching, worrying, invoking the bicycle gods, afraid. Nagle stayed at Mom's side every minute.

The third night, Mom and Clarke prepared a pasta salad and took it to the beach for dinner. As the sky and the sand blended into darkness, Clarke made a life-sized sand sculpture of a reclining female and Mom molded the face of a man. And then in the morning, they washed their tent and clothes and bodies and pedaled us out of the village, back up the mountain, just before one o'clock. When had they decided? When would they tell us?

As we neared La Spezia again, Fred and I rolled slower and slower. What would happen to our family when we reached the city? Would either Mom or Clarke take a train for Rome, then fly to America? Would this be the moment of choosing? "I won't ask you to take sides, Fred," I said finally.

"I couldn't anyway. I see too much wrong in both their hearts."

"Wrong?"

"Maybe broken is a better word, Daisy."

Two kilometers later, I continued. "This isn't about right and wrong."

"What is it about? I don't understand."

"I'm not sure, Fred. These two people are in agony, make no mistake, but I don't think it has to do with whether or not they love each other." We stood above La Spezia, ready to topple down the last steep hill into the city, then I had a horrible thought. "Fred! Freddy," I whispered urgently. "I just realized that we won't have a chance to choose what happens to us if one of them leaves Europe. Even if we decide to stay together, and I want to, who would ride the second bicycle?"

"Oh, blast, Daisy!"

And instead of flinging ourselves down the last mountain, whooping and hollering as we always did on downhill grades, Fred and I rolled as slowly as we could, dragging our wheels. Fred was in front. "Hurry up, Clarke," Mom fussed.

"I can't, Susan. My brake pads must be rubbing the rims. You lead if you're in such a big rush."

"Fine. Let me pass." Then when I wouldn't go any faster, "Cripes, Daisy's stuck, too." Boy, you don't know the half of it, lady. What did all of us do to get into this mess?

The train station loomed ahead, larger than life. The closer we got, the slower Fred and I rolled, until we almost rolled backward. "What's the matter with these bikes?" Clarke said once, and I thought he might hit us. If he did, I'd bite him. He'd needed it for a long time, as far as I was concerned.

And then the train station was behind us half a block. Then a full block. Then we turned the corner and threaded out of town, toward Pisa. "Is there an international airport nearby?" Fred asked, unable to see the map strapped to the top of his head.

"I don't think so, Fred. Could Mom and Clarke have decided not to split up after all?"

"Maybe they're waiting for Pisa."

At an ancient farm a few miles northwest of Pisa that evening, an old woman allowed Mom and Clarke to put their tent next to her stone barn. As they filled their water bottles from the hand pump above the stone laundry tub in the garden, she told them in Italian that she couldn't believe that they were riding bicycles all over Europe. "I am ready to die," she said. "I am eighty."

Late that night, Mom and Clarke had another argument: bitter, desperate, without hope, resolving nothing. Fred held me while I ached for all of us. Nobody slept.

In the morning, the old woman told us that if we returned in two months, she would already be *"mort, dormire,"* dead, sleeping. As we started down the little road, Clarke turned to Mom, eyes bright with tears. "Life is so short,

Susie." He hadn't called her "Susie" in a long time, and my head popped up to listen. "Why do we spend it fighting?"

"I don't know."

In Pisa, the traffic was horrible—ancient narrow streets only wide enough for horses and carts now had to accommodate cars, parking, and fat us. They didn't. But the miracle of Pisa, to me and Fred anyway, wasn't found at the Piazza di Miracoli, where the leaning tower leaned, but rather that four of us went into the city and four of us left it a few hours later, our little group still intact. Thrilled, I followed Fred, who raced out of town, singing at the top of his lungs. "Whatever was wrong with my bike yesterday," Clarke commented, "seems to have corrected itself."

"Daisy seems fine, too. In fact, I hardly need to pedal; we must have a tailwind."

Oh yes, oh yes, life is good. At least today, I reminded myself. One step at a time, Daisy, one day at a time, one moment. Mom and Clarke were talking again. At the moment, that was enough. I poked at Fred's rear tire, pushing him along toward Florence, and he kicked up his wheels and skipped ahead of me, laughing. For the moment, even a truce was like heaven.

"I feel really weird today, Clarke," Mom said after awhile. "Like there's a message I'm supposed to be getting."

"Like in France, the day we met Gilles and Régine at the farmer's market?" Clarke asked.

"No. The message won't come from someone else." An hour later, she spotted a small park in a tiny village. "Let's stop for awhile. Maybe eat an early lunch."

Fred and I rolled around the little park, then settled under the trees in the shade to await further developments, spokes crossed. As Mom sliced off a chunk of bread for sandwiches, Clarke poured her a black plastic cupful of wine from their almost-empty bottle of Italian red. "I feel like I'm slowing down, Susie. I've felt that since Cinqueterre."

Fred and I glanced at each other, uneasy. "Maybe our intuition is just reminding us to take more time for ourselves, like we promised," Mom said. She took a deep breath. "I still want this to work, Clarke. I'm sorry about Cinqueterre. I don't hate you."

"I know you don't."

They sat for a long time, mostly in silence, then Mom wrote while Clarke strolled through the woody park. Immensely relieved, Fred and I leaned against a big tree, head to tail, wishing we could switch flies off each other's backs. The spirit ark slept except for an Italian butterfly that flitted around my head, enjoying the sun, and Nagle, who kept his eyes on Mom.

"How about going back to Spain after Italy or Greece?" Clarke asked after another turn around the park. "It was a beautiful country, but we missed something there."

"People?"

"Yes. We didn't really start getting to know families until France."

"I've thought about that, Clarke." Then, after a very long moment, "What about Morocco?"

Much to Fred's and my delight, Mom and Clarke talked all afternoon about what might be next in their lives together. Even though they never seemed to receive any more messages, from themselves or others, well into a second bottle of wine, they discussed going to a monastery in Nepal or Tibet. "Would they let us go with them, Daisy?" Fred asked.

"I don't know, but if not, at least we'd be together wherever they left us. I can't really picture us in hooded monk's robes." Well, actually, I kind of could and it was very funny.

Chapter 31

IN FLORENCE, WE FOUND an old and bustling tourist center full of
Americans. As we crossed the river Arno, the Ponte Vecchio off to the
right looked like a dollhouse bridge full of tiny shops balanced on the
span like child's blocks. Trotting slowly through tiny, crowded streets in the
old part of the picturesque city, we stopped at the steps of a beautiful cathedral
while Mom poured water into her wine cup for a hot black dog that drooped
down the stairs like a charred rag. He wouldn't drink until his mistress returned
to give him permission. "I'd like to spend some time in Florence without the
bikes," Clarke said as the dog delicately lapped the water and carefully kept an
eye on Fred and me.

Thanks a lot, Clarke, I thought, but knew that Mom would never leave me,
not even for a minute, not after all we'd been through lately. After all, I was
her only real friend. "Let's find a place to stay on the outskirts, then," she said,
however, "and take a train back tomorrow." Mom!

"For heaven's sake, Daisy," Fred said as I stomped down the street.
"Wouldn't you like some peaceful time together, just you and me?"

"Yes, of course, Fred. But what if we miss something fun?"

"Since when is being with Clarke and Susan fun?"

Mentally, I sifted back through recent days like postcards until I could find
a pretty picture, surprised to find so many, all through northern Italy, from the
east coast to the west; but the beautiful memories were interspersed with really
awful ones tucked into my mental album like black flags of undeveloped film.
"Good point, Fred."

It was rush hour when we left Florence, swimming like guppies through the fast car sharks, darting in and out of near misses, getting lost. Frustrated, Mom and Clarke went inside a sleazy cafe for cold drinks and directions while Fred and I fretted nervously around the light pole outside, guarding each other and our belongings. "Is there Mafia in Florence?" Fred asked.

"If the Italian Mafia has been in New York for seventy years, it's probably in Florence. Watch your backside, Freddy."

"I'd rather watch yours."

"Fred!"

After following the railroad tracks through scary industrial areas of scrappy junk and old warehouses with broken windows, we finally found a large stone house off the road near a suburban train station. "What if the Godfather lives here?" I asked, still jumpy.

He didn't. Instead, two nice young couples were renovating the house, two sisters and their husbands who spoke excellent English, and they invited Mom and Clarke for dinner and gave them permission to leave Fred and me in the yard the next day. "It sure will be nice," Mom remarked when she and Clarke came outside for bed about midnight, "to get up in the morning and leave our 'house' just like everyone else in the world."

"You shouldn't have asked if we could camp here a second night," Clarke said, snarly. "It seems imposition enough to ask to store the bikes while we take a train into Florence tomorrow."

Mom sighed. "So we'll pack up in the morning and leave after our day in the city." So much for leaving in the morning and returning home at night like everyone else in the world, Mom.

Fred and I spent the next whole day saddled with 200 pounds of gear. Instead of running around and rolling in the grass as planned, we just stood, fat and grumpy, nibbling Italian grass salad dressed with soot and cinders from the trains. So much for *our* day off!

Mom and Clarke returned to the house about six o'clock. "Boy," Mom was saying as they hobbled up the driveway, "it sure takes different muscles to walk than to bicycle. I'm not sure I have it in me to ride around looking for another place to stay tonight."

"I don't think I do either, Susan. I guess maybe we should stay here after all."

"Should I bite them, Daisy?" Fred asked bitterly.

"Be my guest."

Mom knocked at the door of the old house. "We planned to leave this evening," she explained in Italian. "We felt that we were imposing by asking to stay a second night. But we're very tired. Would it be all right to put up our tent again?"

The Italian smiled. "We wondered why your bikes were all packed this morning. Of course you may stay."

Mom approached Fred and me. "I'm sorry, you guys. Here, let me help you get these packs off." Oh, gee, don't you want us to sleep with them on, I groused, then felt guilty and nudged her hand. Difficult as I thought my life was at the moment, it was nothing compared to Mom's, and I vowed to spend more time with her at the end of each day. Lately, Fred and I had gone off together as soon as we were unpacked, partly because we enjoyed each other's company and partly because we wanted to stay away from the tension between Mom and Clarke. Now, I decided, it was time for all four of us to become a family again, and that night, Fred and I slept close by the tent.

In the morning, we retraced our circuitous route to Florence, stopping at a small shop to buy underwear for Mom. She returned empty-handed, unwilling to squander a day's allowance on a pair of panties. "I'll just continue in rattiness," she announced. "Besides, I'd just ruin anything I bought anyway, scrubbing it on river rocks."

A boy of seven or eight stepped up behind us as Mom pulled me away from the wall. Spreading a newspaper over my handlebars, he turned his grimy face up to Mom's. "Buy a newspaper!" he demanded in Italian.

"*Grazie, no,*" she said, smiling.

"*Per favore, signora,*" the child pleaded. The paper wasn't even current.

Suddenly, a man burst out of the store and yelled at the boy, who darted into a small crowd crossing the street. "Be careful, *signora,*" he said to Mom, gesturing wildly with his arms. "That boy," he indicated with a flourish where the boy had disappeared, "he was trying to get into your packs while he covered his hands with the newspaper."

I pictured the little urchin running down the street with a handful of Mom's tattered underwear. "We don't have much to steal," Mom said to the shopkeeper, "but thank you."

We climbed into the hills of Chianti on a small road that wound around and around through ancient Tuscan stone houses set high up into the mountains. Villages were few; some had been discovered by tourists and some hadn't. We liked the ones that hadn't, of course.

At the top of a steep pass, we looked down into the valley but saw no houses or farms or villages—the road wound down the mountain like a discarded ribbon with nothing at the end. It was six o'clock, and I began to worry about finding a place to stay before dark. Finally, we spotted an old church next to an ancient house, and Mom and Clarke tucked Fred and me into a small storage shed full of hay, then zipped themselves inside their tent just outside the doorway.

"Help, Daisy!" Fred screeched in the middle of the night. "A giant praying mantis is attacking me!"

"Easy, Fred, don't hurt him," I said. "Hello, aren't you cute?" I said to the praying mantis, which perched like a little green stick atop Fred's front tire. Then a scorpion wandered over to investigate the commotion, and Fred and I spent hours listening to the bugs tell stories and to the hourly church bells.

As always, we awakened to the birds and the breezes and the weather, whatever it was. We were part of nature and lived it, not just as observers but as participants. This morning, the air was crispy, like crackers, until the pale sun baked its edges to soft gold.

The road to Siena was full of the sounds of nature—the wind in the trees, tittering birds, the tiny rustling of animals hidden in the dry leaves. Fred and I lumbered happily along the small Italian road, fat with packs, tires softly rubbing along the pavement like quiet breath, our black panniers faded to tie-dyed gray. As the morning sun touched the treetops, I was filled with respect for the sanctity of the earth and its inhabitants, including, of course, praying mantises and scorpions.

"Stop," Clarke said from in front. "Listen." Together, the four of us listened to the silence of man, the noises of nature—the rustles and the tremblings and the scratches, the flappings of wings, the skitterings of insects, the passage of air—all the racket that most people would consider silence but that we considered a symphony. I was proud of Mom and Clarke for being able to hear it. "It would be wonderful if man hadn't come along to ruin all this," Clarke announced finally.

I disagreed. As far as I could tell, anyway, man had a place also, even if just to observe and record, like Mom was doing with her writing. Surely man's ability to reason had a purpose. "Maybe if we could be more accepting of our fellow man . . . ," Mom began.

"Why do you have to disagree with everything I say?" Clarke flared like a struck match. "Can't you ever agree or just keep quiet?" Fred and I looked at each other, sighing.

"Why can't I say what I think, Clarke?" Mom asked, clearly hurt. "You always do."

"I said one sentence. I just want to be quiet."

"I said just one sentence, too. Who says that we talk only when you want? Cripes, Clarke, it's such a pain to be with you."

The serenity of the morning fell next to the dead grass along the edge of the road, and we rolled the rest of the way to Siena in silence. There, Clarke got into an argument with some teachers at a private school who wouldn't allow us to eat lunch on the grounds, then after finding a picnic bench in a park downtown, he and Mom spent so much time discussing a route to Rome that they left the ancient city without seeing anything, steering us southwest toward the front laces of Italy's boot.

From Siena, the national highway shot straight toward Grosetto, bypassing the villages instead of wandering from one to the next like the secondary roads that we usually picked. Hour after hour we rolled through dark tunnels, up and down steep passes. No one lives in this part of Italy, I decided, wondering where Mom and Clarke would find food for the night.

Clarke signaled a halt at the entrance to a tunnel near dusk. "This one's long, then there are two more short ones before a town called Civitella. Hopefully, we can get there before the markets close."

"We've already ridden sixty horrid kilometers," Mom complained.

"I don't think we have a choice unless you see a village somewhere." Clarke gestured toward arid hills and scrubby brush as he attached his tiny flashlight to Fred's front. Fred's headlight had burned out long ago. Earlier in the day, Clarke had scavenged a broken taillight from the side of the road and now fastened it to Fred's rear while Mom made sure that the leftover orange fluorescent bunny tail covered as much of my hind end as possible. Then off we went into the black hole.

I could see absolutely nothing after the first few feet of uphill grade and followed Fred by sound, breathing fast and shallow in the stale exhaust fumes. Suddenly, a truck entered from one end or the other, its engine reverberating from both walls to fill the entire space around us. I panicked. Which way was it coming? "Fred!" I screamed, but of course he couldn't hear me. Holding my breath, I finally saw headlights with relief; the truck was in the other lane and passed us unscathed except for blinding us for an instant.

Then Clarke pointed to the right, his arm a black shadow in the reflected headlights; rats ran alongside, jumping down into storm drains along the curbs. Keeping my eyes on the faint glow of the tiny reflector stripes on the back of Fred's pedals and breathing through my mouth, I hurried as fast as I dared, clattering, trying to keep up, unwilling to think of what would happen if I hit the curb or a pothole.

As the truck echoed out of the tunnel behind us, we were engulfed again by total blackness; clouds of diesel fume choked our lungs and burned our eyes. Tears streamed down my face and I wished I had hands to wipe my eyes.

Engines again! This time, a car and truck entered from either side of the tunnel and the car veered around us just in time to get back into our lane as the oncoming truck passed, its horn screeching. "Hurry!" I screamed, but even I couldn't hear me.

"Are you all right?" Fred hollered when the tunnel finally emptied.

"I can't see, Fred! Slow down!" Hoping for another vehicle to illuminate our way but terrified of falling into an occupied traffic lane, I tried to follow the noise of Fred's tires but the sound was obliterated by the roar of the next truck, and the next car and the next, paralyzing me with panic until they'd careened safely past with a deafening roar and a blast of exhaust fumes and horns.

Panting, my heart beating as fast as hummingbird wings, I finally spotted a glimmer of light up ahead that illuminated a dim outline of Fred. The end of the tunnel! Flinging myself forward with all of my strength, we burst out of the end drinking great gulps of air and dusk. "I wasn't sure whether I'd get run over or die of asphyxiation," Mom gasped when she could, "but I knew it would be one or the other. How long was that thing?"

"About two kilometers," Clarke said between deep breaths. Fred's frame was trembling.

"And we have two more?" Mom asked in a small voice.

"They're shorter."

"Leave my body to the rats, Fred," I said.

After eighty kilometers of mountains, we found the turnoff to Civitella, a small village at the top of a long, steep road. It was almost dark. "Do you want to wait here while I ride up to get food?" Clarke offered.

Why, yes, thank you, Clarke, I thought, I'd be happy to wait for you and Fred to climb that mountain. "No, thanks," Mom said instead although her legs were shaking with fatigue. "We're in this together." So the four of us crept to the top of the village in the dimming light to find only a jar of antipasto and some noodles at a tiny market.

At the only house in the village with a flat space big enough for a small tent, a man stood in the yard. Mom's hurried request to camp was answered with the suggestion that we would be fine in the public park, that in fact the park would be much better. Much better, indeed. He made me nervous. What if he sent someone to rob us? "Did that guy back there seem weird to you, Clarke?" Mom asked as we hurried toward the park, looking back over our shoulders as the man watched our progress with interest. I imagined him rubbing his hands together in anticipation.

"Yes. But maybe I'm just imagining things."

"No, he's not, Daisy," Fred whispered. "We'd better take turns guarding the tent tonight."

After hiding under a little party shelter at the back of the square, Mom and Clarke locked Fred and me to the enclosure. "They may get us, Clarke," Mom said, "but they're not getting our bicycles."

"How can we protect Clarke and Susan if they're protecting us?" Fred asked, pulling at the lock.

I kicked at the cable, uncomfortable. "Maybe if we bark loud enough, it will scare any robbers away."

"Do we know how to bark, Daisy?"

"I don't know, Fred, but we'd have to do something! Growl, then, or whinny, or clank your derailleur chain. Just stay awake for a change, okay?"

"Well, I certainly won't fall asleep from a full stomach," he grumbled. "There's no grass here."

Mom and Clarke fared no better from what I could hear inside the tent. "What a perfect ending to a horrible day," Mom said, writing in her journal. " 'After a terrible dinner cooked by waning flashlight,' " she read out loud, " 'we struggle through a cold water sponge bath only to shuck ourselves into smelly sleeping bags to wait for burglars.' For once, Clarke, I wish that Daisy and Fred were watchdogs instead of bicycles."

Since none of us slept much, except maybe Fred, there was no reason not to get up early the next morning to put as much distance as possible between us and the strange little village, and we raced sixty kilometers down out of the mountains before noon.

At a deserted little beach on the coast just north of Orbetello, we stopped for lunch and an hour's sunbath. Fred sprawled on the sand at my feet and fell asleep instantly. I puttered about for a bit looking for something to eat, but all the seagrass was too salty so I gave it up and plopped down next to Fred, my packs bulky outriggers.

"I keep thinking about the book, Clarke," Mom said, sitting cross-legged on the ground, her legs sticky with sand and sweat.

"What about it?"

"This is an incredible story, whether or not I'm talented enough to write it. But where does it end? Every night seems to be the same—knock, explain, camp, become friends, leave. My Italian is good enough now that it's not even a challenge to communicate. I almost feel like we're getting lazy—the bicycling, although it's still hard on my knees, is just another part of my life, like sleeping in a tent on the ground every night. It's like breathing. I don't even think about it any more. Bathing and washing clothes in rivers, the same."

Clarke sat silently for a time. "Maybe it's time to make a change."

"Yes, but what? We don't seem to have direction anymore; we're just wandering aimlessly, biding our time without learning anything new. It's gotten too easy—and too hard."

"The hellos and goodbyes?"

"Yes."

"How about taking a break?" Clarke pulled the map off Fred's head, waking him, then pointed out to sea toward at a hazy bump on the horizon after studying the map's tattered, damp folds. "There's an island out there called Monte Argentario. Maybe we could camp in the woods or on the beach for a few days of quiet, then decide what to do." Smoothing out a crease that split Monte Argentario in two, he added, "There seems to be a convent on the top of the mountain. What about asking permission to stay there?"

"Let's try the beach, Clarke."

"Oh, boy," Fred said, fully awake now. "Vacation at the beach! I can work on my suntan!"

"Only if somebody remembers to take off your packs," I reminded him.

Chapter 32

I F A SEAGULL WERE flying off the west coast of Italy north of Rome, Monte Argentario would look as if a little mountain had slipped into the sea and was holding onto Italy for dear life with two arms, really causeways, with a little town at the elbow of one. There are two roads on the island, one around its circumference to the fishing village of Porto San Stefano and the other up the mountain to the monastery. That's it, except for a radio tower above the convent.

After traveling around the north half of the island on the curvy road cut above the sea, we found Porto San Stefano bundled at the foot of the mountain like a rockslide that stopped just short of the sea in a clutter of faded colors— pale yellows and creams and ochers, everything roofed in red tile. Its harbor was full of yachts and fishing boats.

We spotted a Gucci store. "There's no way we could ask here to stay in someone's garden for a few days," Clarke decided. "I wonder if any of these yacht owners needs crew."

"Ugh. I might have to chop heads off fish," Mom replied.

She inquired at a small grocery store about the road up the mountain. "It is allowed to visit the *convento*," the owner explained in Italian, "but the road is extremely difficult. It is very steep. It would not be impossible to ride up on bicycles," he continued, eyeing our packs with a shake of his head, "but it would be very, very hard, *signora*."

It took an hour to ride the seven kilometers to the monastery under gathering black clouds. "We're not Catholic, Daisy," Fred puffed and panted up the mountain. "What if they won't let us in?"

I could see it now: a flock of ancient black-frocked monks, ropes around their middles and hands devoutly folded below white heads bent in prayer—the picture of serenity in somber light and shadow—interrupted in their morning meditations by two chattering bicyclists in flagrant shades of yellow and blue who descend on the holy walls with their scruffy pack bicycles, offending everyone.

But no one was about when we arrived. As thunder rumbled in the distance, Mom and Clarke strolled through the empty chapel like tourists, apparently too uncertain to knock on the door even after all these months, then sat on a wall outside in the deserted courtyard hoping to be rescued from their dilemma. Finally, a monk dressed in a black robe and blue tennis shoes ambled down the hill after spotting the 'U.S.A.' sign on Fred's rump. "Thank God I've someone to talk to!" he exclaimed. "No one inside speaks English," the monk said sadly, "and I speak no Italian."

Father Brendan was a seventy-five-year-old Irish monk on his way to Rome for a beatification ceremony as a reward for fifty years of service to his church. The monastery was the founding convent for his order, the Passionists, he explained, but his visit wasn't very satisfying, poor fellow, because he couldn't communicate with his fellow monks. "Why can't they talk to each other in Latin?" Fred asked me.

Mom told Father Brendan that we were looking for a place to stay for a few days. "Your Italian must be much better than mine," the blue-footed monk replied, "so I don't think I can ask for you. But it might be possible to have your request granted if you can find a way to ask. There's another convent house farther up the mountain; maybe you could find help there."

The storm broke then, all of a sudden, cracking open the sky to send sheets of rain in rivers over the ground as we huddled next to the wall and coveted the weather inside the convent's front door. When it opened, however, it was only for another monk to come outside to kick a small shivering kitten with runny eyes away from the entrance. I lunged for the mean monk as Clarke retrieved the dripping animal and deposited him into Mom's arms, where he fell asleep, purring, keeping both of them warm. "That cat should be killed,"

Father Brendan said with disdain, edging under the roof. "Its eye infection might be catching."

Mom bundled the kitten closer in her arms, turning away to shield her new friend from the man's words. "This cat should be healed," she retorted. "It has as much right to life as any human."

"What kind of a place *is* this, Fred?" I asked.

Father Brendan hammered on the door to get inside, leaving the rest of us in the downpour to hope that the Irish monk would at least reappear with the person in charge. He didn't. Clarke and Mom split a roll and an orange for lunch, with yogurt and a cup of bitter local wine. The kitten ate some bread as Fred and I found some decent grass by a stone wall under some dripping trees.

Rain continued to wash across the courtyard, and lightning and thunder were the only commentary to our misery. Thoroughly drenched and cold and feeling as unwelcome as the cat, we came to the conclusion that it was time to at least resurrect Father Brendan. After pounding on the door, we were told that he was sleeping and that the man in charge was away. "What about the other convent up the mountain?" Mom asked in Italian as she stood in a deluge.

"The Superior's name is Padre Vittorio," the old monk said, then shut the door in her face. The wet kitten jumped from her arms and ran around the chapel.

"This place certainly doesn't feel like a sanctuary," Clarke said. "Let's try this other convent."

Wondering what steep, muddy field we'd sleep in if we were again turned away, we scrabbled up an even steeper half mile to another very old building and asked for Father Vittorio. "He is sleeping until four," a young woman explained in Italian. "You will not be able to talk to him then either, but I will relay a message if you wish."

At that moment, two young men appeared with their hands full of wild mushrooms. Like the woman, they were dressed in work clothes instead of monks' robes. "My name is Paul," one said in English. "May I help?"

Clarke stepped forward eagerly. "We have been sleeping on the ground for eight months," he said. "We are tired and confused, unsure of what to do next. Would it be possible to find shelter here for one or two nights?"

"I will ask Padre Vittorio at four," Paul said. "You will have your answer in an hour." Then he went inside the warm monastery, leaving us outside in the rain. Mom slid to the mud next to my feet, her back against the gray stone wall. As the rain picked up momentum again, she pulled the collar of her dirty blue jacket tighter around her neck and tilted her face to the sky for another bath or perhaps to wash away her tears of frustration. I tried to comfort her as Fred and I huddled close together, stomping our tires to keep warm.

A few minutes later, Paul came to the door to invite Mom and Clarke into the kitchen for tea. "They're probably afraid they'll have two drownings on their hands if they don't," chuckled Fred, trying to keep his sense of humor as water poured from the roof onto the top of his head. Then he looked at me, eyes soft. "You know, Daisy, one of the things I love about you most is your resilience. You make the best of whatever happens."

I smiled. "I don't feel very resilient, Fred. I feel wet. But I guess I just enjoy life too much to fight it. Most of the time." Thinking back over the last thirty-two weeks, however, I could think of lots of times that I'd complained and argued and tried to change things, particularly when Betsy and Zelda were with us. But it had never done any good, so maybe I'd stopped, or slowed down my sniveling a bit. I hoped so. "Anyway, Fred, thanks for the kind words. I always know I can go on because you're beside me."

Fred put his drippy handlebars around my neck and we stood together in the rain, leaning against each other.

An hour later, after the rain finally stopped, Mom and Clarke emerged from the convent with Paul. "Nothing will be required of you," the young man was explaining. "You may take whatever you wish from the garden and are welcome to join us for meals or not, as you wish. Let me show you around." Fred and I trailed at a discrete distance as Paul escorted Mom and Clarke through the gardens. "This building was the original prayer house for the larger convent below. It had been abandoned for ten years before we turned it into a place for healing—no one wears robes here, even the monks; the people are young and everyone works." He chuckled. "You don't have to worry about burglars—they're all on the inside. The monastery down the hill, however, is very traditional and doesn't understand what we do here. It's full of old monks who want only to give the sacraments."

"They certainly didn't seem to know what to do with us," Clarke commented.

"No, I would guess that they didn't," Paul smiled as he studied Clarke and Mom's wet clothes and faces streaked with dirt. "If you like, put your bicycles in this storage room." He opened a first-floor door in a crumbly building across the courtyard from the main convent. "Sometimes we use it as a nursery, but there are no children here at the moment."

Enormously grateful, Fred and I rolled inside, trailing water. Ragged toys were scattered about the floor and dusty cobwebs lay in a thin brown sheet over the sparse furniture. Fred sneezed. I looked at my feet, now standing in a puddle of my own doing. Mixed with the dirt on the floor, it was turning to mud. "I don't care where we stay, Fred, as long as it's out of the rain."

Mom leaned me against the wall by the streaky windows. "Here, Daisy, let me get those wet packs off," she offered, pulling sleeping bags and dirty laundry from my rump. Thank you, Mom, I thought, relieved, leaning away from the wall so she could unhook her clothes pannier from my right side.

As she started up the stairs behind Clarke, he called over his shoulder, "I'll bring up the rest of our stuff, Susie. Why don't you take a nap?"

"Great idea," Fred said, and soon he and I were curled together in a muddy corner of the nursery, fast asleep, while rain again pelted the windows and streamed down the walls unnoticed.

I woke up in the middle of the night as lightning filled the room with eerie blue light. As the black trees of the mountaintop were silhouetted by the jagged waves of light, one after the other, I wished that Fred were awake or that Mom weren't so far away upstairs. This didn't feel right. Suddenly a storm exploded across the mountain and thunder echoed and re-echoed as it traveled around and around the tiny island. Fred scrambled upright. "Holy cow, what was that?"

In frightened silence, we watched rain pour out of the flashing sky in great curtains, drenching the earth all over again as if the day's storm hadn't been enough, while thunder crashed and roared and vibrated with a life of its own.

When morning came, we tiptired outside into the thin, still mist, afraid to talk out loud for fear of bringing down more wrath upon our heads. Clarke was already in the garden, picking grapes. We slipped past as he turned toward their second-floor room with a double fistful of big purple grapes dripping with rainwater. "What's going to happen to them, Daisy?" Fred asked. "What do you think they'll decide here?"

"I don't know," I answered, wondering if last night's storm were a bad omen, "but at this point I don't care as long as it includes both of us."

"Would you go back to Morocco, then?"

"At least we're in much better shape now, Fred, and could run away faster. I'd prefer Greece or Yugoslavia, of course, and Spain was nice."

"What if they decide to go home?"

I remembered the year I'd spent in the garage with the snow shovel before Fred and Clarke entered my life. How lonely I'd been! Although it seemed a lifetime away, only nine months had passed since we left for the desert to practice for Europe. Now, after 10,000 kilometers of living my bicycle life abroad, I'd acquired strength, stamina, and a terrific suntan. And numerous scratches and scrapes, a garden of decals and some new parts: back tire in France, front wheel in England, headset in Germany, numerous inner tubes and brake pads and cables. Somewhere along the way, I'd discovered Spanish, French, German, Italian, and smatterings of Flemish and Dutch.

Much more important, I'd developed a warm and loving relationship with my mother, who treated me with as much respect as if I were human. I adored her—she'd turned out to be an incredible companion, a faithful friend who was willing each day to take me with her wherever she went: pedaling me up steep mountain passes in the blistering sun; plowing through long, black tunnels filled with haze and exhaust fumes, potholes and rats; darting between cars and curbs in big cities; hugging the tiniest line of the highways' edges as thousands of cars and trucks brushed past. On rainy days, she pedaled down the road, drenched by each passing car, bracing against the winds the best she could so that I wouldn't fall. When I did, she always helped me up again, ready to continue. She didn't seem to mind that we were always dirty, and wet from rain or sweat.

Mom and I danced together in the sunlight in bike path mazes through fields of ripening grains. We flew down from mountain peaks, almost afraid, the wind and sun freshening our spirits together. We saw herds of sheep and goats and cattle, oceans and rivers and fields and mountains and canyons. We toured the great cities of Europe: Madrid, Paris and London—soon, we'd see Rome. We'd been to Seville and Valencia and Barcelona, Nîmes and Calais, York, Edinburgh, Antwerp and Brugge, Frankfurt and Munich, Salzburg and Innsbruck, Venice and Pisa and Florence and . . . .

"Daisy! Are you all right?"

I shook myself free of memories. "I'm fine, Fred. I'm just not ready to leave Europe, I guess."

"I'm not ready to leave you, Daisy, ever. I'll go back home with you, or to Morocco. If you want to climb the Himalayas, I'm game for that, too." Fred cleared his throat. "Please say you'll never leave me."

If there's a bicycle god, I said to the monastery, don't make me choose between Fred and Mom. I don't think I can. And if I can't choose, I can't ask Fred to choose, no matter what he says. To Fred I said, "Let's take a walk."

Slowly, handlebars touching, we rolled to a little spot above the flower garden that overlooked the bay 1200 feet below, watching rain drip from the branches of the trees surrounding the convent. Behind the thin, cool air, the ocean merged with the mainland in mist, and the tiny houses of Orbetello strewn at the water's edge looked like miniature golden sugar cubes, each with a red hat. A ferry boat cut a thin white wake into the gray water as sea breezes ruffled the trees below. Neither of us spoke.

Turning from the gardens, we rolled deep into the woods and found a clearing where we rested quietly in thick grass, pedals together. After a time, the sky brightened and the sun dappled the ground around us like a golden nest of bright coins. Ten or twenty white butterflies, perhaps on a visit to the spirit ark, raced through the sunshine every which way, like flying flowers. "Butterflies always look happy, don't they?" I said as they flittered around my ears.

"They make you a pretty halo, Daisy," he replied.

After a shy, small lunch of thick, rich Italian grass drenched with the sweetest of rainwater dressings, Fred turned to me. "Daisy?"

"Yes, Fred." I lowered my eyes.

"Do you realize how much things have changed between us since the beginning of this trip?"

I smiled. "I used to consider you my little brother."

"I know," he laughed, "and it drove me nuts."

"But then I realized how strong you were, Fred, and I started looking up to you instead. I never could have survived Morocco without your courage. By the time Betsy and Zelda arrived, I realized that you were more to me than a brother. You were my best friend. Maybe more than that already, or I wouldn't have been so jealous when you fussed over the twins."

"I was stupid. Betsy and Zelda are darling and bright and full of potential, Daisy, but they don't have your beauty, your inner strength, your love of life and all things in it. You're quite an inspiration, you know."

"Really?"

We looked at each other in silence, our eyes full of admiration and respect and deep friendship. And love. "Why don't Clarke and Susan feel about each other the way we do?" Fred asked suddenly.

"There's something going on between them that I don't understand, Fred, something that has nothing to do with whether they care for each other, like we said after Cinqueterre. Maybe there's something they need to work out in themselves that's reflected only in each other."

"Then they won't split up right now, Daisy, no matter what they say." Fred's intense gaze was making me nervous, so I rolled to the edge of the meadow to look for Mom. She was sitting in the garden, her back against a shrine to Jesus, writing on blue airmail stationery, her curly hair shiny and clean. Nagle lay at her feet. "Don't run off, Daisy," Fred said gently. "I want to ask you something."

Fidgeting, I came back. What was the matter with me? Framed by the deep green woods of the mountaintop, Fred looked wonderful: strong and blue and handsome, wheels planted firmly in the deep meadowgrass, eyes bright and shining. I gave myself a shake to straighten out my brake cables and chain; dust from our dirty nursery hotel flew up around me and I wished I'd had a rainbath.

"You're the most beautiful bicycle in the world, Daisy," Fred said, reading my mind as usual. "Even dusty and scratched and loaded with a hundred pounds, you look like a million bucks because of who you are inside. I'd be honored to be at your side forever." He gently touched my handlebars. "Can bicycles get married, Daisy?"

Oh, my. "Bicycles can't even talk, Fred." Then tears filled my eyes and I couldn't continue, overwhelmed by emotions all rich and glorious and joyful except one that reminded me that choosing Fred might mean losing my mother. Thinking of the terrifying rain storm, I tried to guess its message.

"Clarke and Susan aren't breaking up, Daisy," Fred said, feeling my fear. "But if they do, I'll happily go with you and Susan if you'll have me." He shrugged. "Clarke is, well, he's Clarke. I love bicycling with him—he's strong and fast and challenges me to do my very best. That's good for me. He's a great person to take on a bicycle trip, and after all, that's my purpose in life. Until you arrived on the scene, of course. He and I are great friends, but we're not inseparable like you and Susan. He wouldn't mind buying a new bicycle. Susan would. I'd be proud to be with both of you. Daisy, you don't need to worry about my choosing. I already have."

Chapter 33

HE NEXT AFTERNOON, FRED and I rolled slowly toward the little overlook above the sea after bathing separately in a little stream in the woods. Chittering birds in soft blue- and gray-feathered coats fluttered in the trees above us, swooping from limb to limb in a merry dance, their various songs harmonizing in an intricate melody like an acappella choir.

Yellow and white butterflies flittered about the flower garden, twinkling in the sunshine. When Fred stopped to pick a big bouquet of pale peach and lemon and lavender flowers, the little butterflies exploded upward, filling the sky with a frenzy of light. Without a word, Fred tucked the flowers around my handlebars, then touched my nose with his. I felt like a princess.

Already standing at the overlook above the sea was the spirit ark: the dogs and cats and hedgehogs and birds and rats and weasels and foxes that had all found a way to go with us on this trip. Our wise little Nagle gestured us forward, his white coat clean and fluffy like a cloud. "Don't be afraid," he said gently. "You two have done things these past months that most could never do. Declaring your love to the world will be easy. You've already proved your strength together, your commitment, your ability to meet life's challenges head on, hearts open, wheels first. Now we're ready to hear what you have to say to each other."

I looked at Fred, seeing my own life reflected in his shining frame as he began to speak. "Daisy," he said softly, then hesitated. Clearing his throat, he began again, a tiny bit louder. "Daisy. You are my best friend and my teacher.

You're the bicycle I respect most in the world, and you're beautiful. If you will marry me today, I'll spend the rest of my life at your side, protecting you, challenging you, and loving you. Together, we'll raise little tricycles if you want, or if you'd rather travel, I'll follow you to the ends of the earth."

"I don't know about tricycles, Fred," I smiled, "but I do know that I want to spend the rest of my life with you. You are my life now. Yes, dear friend, I accept marriage to you, with joy, with honor, with respect for your own life and desires. There's nothing I want more."

Nagle stepped forward again, and the other spirit animals pressed close around us. "Susan and Clarke have decided to return to America," Nagle said softly. I gasped, hurt that they hadn't consulted us, wanting this beautiful trip to continue forever. Nagle held up a paw. "It doesn't matter where you travel in life, children," he said. "It matters only how you live. Life is not about where you go, anyway—it's about how you go. It's the ride that counts. Right now, it is time to leave Italy, time to help Susan and Clarke work out their differences, time to go home. All of us," Nagle gestured to the spirit animals crowded near, "will go with you."

I couldn't speak. Taking a small white flower from my own frame, I tucked it behind Fred's left brake lever, then kissed him gently on the nose. "I love you, Fred."

"I love you, too, Daisy," he whispered.

Together, we hugged each of our spirit friends, then rolled slowly through the garden, led by birds and butterflies, the path scattered with sunshine and flowers. As we passed the shrine of Jesus, we spotted Mom and Clarke, holding hands, deep in conversation. Mom looked up, curious, and I wondered if she'd seen the little ceremony. I'd explain later—I knew she'd be happy for me. For now, it was time to be with Fred. I blew her a kiss in my mind, then followed Fred along the path, trailing flowers.

Afterword

Not long after returning home, Daisy and Fred took a dive off the back of Clarke and Susan's van when their bike rack collapsed. By the time Clarke could turn the van around on the divided highway, both bikes were gone. After Susan wrote an article about the bicycles and their trip in their small-town newspaper, pleading for help or information, the man who picked them up off the highway returned them safely.

Not that many months later, both bikes were stolen off the front porch of Susan and Clarke's house. More than a year later, after Susan and Clarke divorced, Susan received an early morning call from the local bike shop owner. "Are you sitting down?" Steve asked.

"What's up?"

"I have Daisy. You'd better get down here."

Five minutes later, Susan was at the bike shop, where the owner waited on the curb in front. He put his arm around her. "There's not much left," he explained, escorting her inside.

Hanging on the ceiling of the shop was Daisy's frame – no wheels, no pedals, no seat, no gears or brakes – just the metal frame with the country stickers and the handlebars with the pale blue ribbon that had attached the bell that Susan had bought for her in Austria.

Steve explained that someone had found her in a ditch and brought her in to be fixed up. "I told him no, that the bike was stolen and I knew the owner would want it back."

"Did he find Fred, too?" Susan asked.

"I'm afraid not. Clarke's bike was most likely sold at a bike swap. Whoever stole the bikes probably didn't want to chance someone recognizing the stickers on your bike, so they stripped off her components and threw her frame off the road a few miles north of town."

Daisy has all new components now, and still lives with Susan in the Colorado mountains. Although Susan has a second bike named Moose, Fred is Daisy's first and only love, wherever he is.

Here's to you, Fred.

About the Authors

A third generation Colorado native, Susan Musgrove was raised in Denver and majored in creative writing at the University of Redlands, California. After a number of years as a stockbroker in Dallas, she moved to the Colorado mountains, where she met and married Clarke. Soon afterward, they and their mountain bikes Daisy and Fred left for the year-long bicycle trip that is the subject of this book.

After returning to Colorado, Susan and Clarke divorced, then Susan moved to Denver and became a partner in a wealth management team at a major brokerage firm. After 23 years of giving investment advice, she retired in 2010 and now lives in a little house in the forest above Evergreen, Colorado, with her two shelties, Katy and Ditto, and her two bicycles, Daisy and Moose.

To find out more about Susan and her writing and photography, log on to her website, www.foresthousepress.com.

Daisy is a multi-lingual 1985 Specialized Rockhopper who traveled to Spain, Morocco, France, England, Scotland, Belgium, Holland, Germany, Austria and Italy with Susan and Clarke and his Trek mountain bike, Fred.

Upon her return to America, after being stolen, stripped and thrown into a ditch for a year, she found her way back to Susan and then helped write this memoir as a companion book to Shifting Gears, which was published in 2008.

Daisy doesn't have a website, but maybe she should.

www.ingramcontent.com/pod-product-compliance
Lightning Source LLC
Chambersburg PA
CBHW022120080426
42734CB00006B/202